MY LIFETIME
IN LETTERS

UPTON SINCLAIR WITH PORTRAIT OF MARY CRAIG SINCLAIR

MY LIFETIME
IN LETTERS

Upton ^{Beall} Sinclair

UNIVERSITY OF MISSOURI PRESS

COLUMBIA

36809
Copyright 1960 by
THE CURATORS OF THE
UNIVERSITY OF MISSOURI

*Library of Congress Catalog
Card Number 59-14141*

*Printed and Bound in the United States of America
by* VON HOFFMANN PRESS, INC.

Introduction

In the course of sixty-five years as a professional writer, beginning at the age of fifteen, I accumulated a mass of papers. For the past forty-five of these years my wife mounted guard over this treasure, building four storerooms to protect it from fire and earthquake, silverfish moths, flying termites, and predatory friends. There were some two hundred and fifty cardboard cartons of files; the original manuscripts of some sixty books and as many pamphlets; and eight hundred volumes of foreign translations, from fifty-five countries and in sixty languages — each volume representing a separate edition, no duplicates.

Looking this collection over, I realized what a treasure it contained: letters from most of the great minds of our half century; and such oddly contrasted personalities—George Brandes and M. K. Gandhi, Jack London and Bernard Shaw, Edith Wharton and Thomas Mann, William Dean Howells and Maxim Gorky, Julia Ward Howe and Lincoln Steffens, Luther Burbank and Romain Rolland, Bertrand Russell and Vachel Lindsay, Conan Doyle and Sherwood Anderson, Peter Kropotkin and Arnold Bennett, Alfred Russel Wallace and William Jennings Bryan, Frank Harris and Leon Trotsky, Henry James and Bartolomeo Vanzetti, H. G. Wells and Senator Borah, Karl Kautsky and William McDougall, Gertrude Atherton and Eugene V. Debs, H. L. Mencken and George Santayana, Albert Einstein and King C. Gillette, Maurice Maeterlinck and Rabindranath Tagore, John Masefield and Eugene O'Neill, Frederik van Eeden and Theodore Dreiser, Sinclair Lewis and Theodore Roosevelt.

When I undertook to select from the many thousands of letters those to be included in this volume, I found it difficult because the letters and personalities were all interesting to me. Most of my life I have stayed at home, writing a book, and have kept my friendships by mail. Experts have estimated that my collection contains 250,000 letters; there were eight tons of paper carried away to the Indiana University library. My wife, in the course of the years, had set aside seven thousand letters as being of special importance; and as this book contains some three-hundred, you can imagine the arguments we had—I putting in and she taking out, or vice versa. The criterion has been general interest, both of the person, and what he or she had to say. We had thirty-two letters from Einstein and 178 from Mencken—and who could possibly agree that we chose the best? Often I recalled a poem that was in one of my childhood's books, about two parents who, because of poverty, had to part with one of their little ones, and went from crib to crib in the night, asking, "Which shall it be? Which shall it be?"

I decided to limit most of the book to the two early decades of my career. They were decades in which world history was made, and world literature also. It was during this period that my novel, *The Jungle*, published early in 1906, produced considerable public excitement. The *New York Evening World* wrote: "Not since Byron awoke one morning to find himself famous has there been such an example of world-wide fame won in a day by a book as has come to Upton Sinclair." I had always been very poor, and now I had some money; also I had a cherished faith that in co-operation lay the remedy for most of our social ills. An ardent utopian, I published, on June 14, 1906, in a weekly magazine, the *Independent*, my program to establish a co-operative home, a small community of writers who with their families would share the burdens of housekeeping and child care.

So came into existence the "Helicon Home Colony." I bought, mostly on mortgage, what seemed to me a dream place, a large and beautiful building which had been been a fashionable boys' school, close to the Palisades of the Hudson River and not far from New York City. Soon this luxurious co-operative home was filled with "intellectuals," all pleased with its informality and congenial atmosphere. Among those who came at the outset, in November, 1906, were two students who had left

Yale in their senior year, preferring my brand of education—or so they said. Both of them aspired to be writers; they had no money, but were willing to do work of any sort. The sort available was tending our large furnace, sweeping floors and stairways, and other household chores. So it was that I came to know a novelist-to-be who was destined to be the first American awarded the Nobel Prize for Literature—and who in the presence of the King of Sweden would tell the world that Upton Sinclair was "internationally better known than any other American artist whatsoever."

His name was Harry Sinclair Lewis, and we called him "Hal." Later on, in New York, he was known as "Red," and allowed only his oldest friends to use the name he had dropped. He was tall and lanky, with red hair and complexion. Very soon he and his friend, Allen Updegraff, had discovered another writer-to-be, my young secretary at the colony, Edith Summers. These three asked the privilege of a table to themselves in our dining room; we called it amiably "the literary table." Edith was shy, small, and blonde, wearing spectacles—having ruined her eyesight by working for several years on the small print of the Funk and Wagnalls dictionary. She was as quiet as a little mouse, and had lived in our Princeton farmhouse for a year or two without our having any idea of her literary aspirations.

I am not by nature personal, and it never occurred to me that something other than literature was being discussed at that table in Helicon Hall; that Edie and Hal were falling in love and getting engaged.

It was more than half a century later, when I was in my eightieth year and Hal had been in his grave for six, that there came into my hands evidence of what had been going on: a love-letter and some poems from Hal to Edie, written not long after the burning of Helicon Hall in March, 1907. He had gone to New York and got a job, to earn money so that he could marry his girl.

The Lewis letter occupies five pages, single-spaced—too long for this book. It is a learned letter; the writer was only twenty-two, but on the very first page he mentions many literary works, from *King Lear* to *Ghosts;* later he discusses my first wife, and the idea of getting a house in the woods at Point Pleasant, New Jersey, where we were spending the summer, with Edith still as my secretary. He discusses the financial details of married life; he thanks God that he left Yale, and devotes a page to the futility of life there; he tells about a walk on Staten Island, and getting a glass of beer with a "Raines law sandwich" (the law ordered that beer could be served only with a "meal," so you ordered beer and a sandwich and paid only for the beer; the sandwich served for all customers all day).

There is a lot in the letter about "Up," who is Updegraff, not Upton. "Up" is having success, and Hal is pleased; "Up" has wandered all the way to Wyoming, and there will be a story in that. There are "sweethearts" and "dearhearts" all through the letter, and the pair are evidently very much in love. Incidentally, there is mention of a "dear little cabin" into which they "broke" in the woods near Helicon Hall one night.

But the marriage did not come off. Hal went back to the despised Yale and got his degree. Edith soon afterwards married Updegraff, and bore him one son; later she divorced him and married C. F. Kelley, an artist. They went to raising tobacco, and out of this came a fine novel, *Weeds*. Letters from Edith referring to this novel, and Hal's praise of it, will be found later in the present volume. To round out the story, I mention that "Up" went to live in Paris, and published much poetry and fiction. So it would appear that literary colonies *do* produce literature. What other group ever raised a janitor to win the Nobel Prize?

Except for a few silent corrections of unintentional errors in spelling and punctuation, or occasional deletions, the original texts of these letters have been maintained throughout. Brief identifying or explanatory items appear in the text in square brackets [ ]; my own comments on the individual letters are italicized.

I wish to thank the individual correspondents or their heirs or estates for permission to publish all of the letters appearing in this book. I wish also to thank the Indiana University Libraries for cooperation in many ways.

UPTON SINCLAIR

Buckeye, Arizona
June, 1959

xii

Contents

xvi

MY LIFETIME
IN LETTERS

The Letters

HARRY SINCLAIR LEWIS [1885-1951]

On Board S.S. Antilles
Monday, January 5 [1917]

Dear Upton:

I finished *Sylvia's Marriage* at 5 this morning while we drove, rolling, through a roaring snow-storm, with waves smashing on the forward deck, every few minutes! I had begun yesterday, and when I could not sleep this morning, with the damned berth pretending it was a fiery untamed bronco of the Western plains, I got up and finished *Sylvia*. The contrast of the reeling boat and shriek-ing wind with the hot calm of Sylvia's bungalow on a Florida key and the drama of the baby's eyes—!

1

I liked the book through and through; it was convincing and held me—made me forget the ship and the mess with Germany, of which the wireless has been telling us here on board.

In a few hours, N.Y. for the first time in 14 months!

Our best to both of you!

As ever,

SINCLAIR LEWIS

Harry Sinclair Lewis, American novelist, is the author of Main Street, Babbitt, Arrowsmith, *and many other works of fiction.*

Sylvia's Marriage *is my novel, published in 1914, dealing with the subject of venereal disease, taboo in those days.*

About this letter, Grace Hegger Lewis, his wife at that time, writes me:

"At first I was bewildered by the letter of January 5th. The date should have been February 5th. After leaving you in Pasadena, we went to the Grand Canyon, New Mexico, New Orleans, and there took a small boat to New York. The prospectus promised us 'five golden days at sea,' but we ran into a blizzard and it was a hideous journey. On February 4th, 1917, the Southern Pacific steamer 'Antilles' received the following Marconi wireless and printed it in its daily news bulletin: 'Washington: Diplomatic relations between the United States and Germany have been broken . . . If an American ship is sunk by a German submarine it will be followed immediately by a declaration of war!'"

HARRY SINCLAIR LEWIS

St. Paul, Minnesota
November 12 [1917]

Dear Mrs. Sinclair:

I hope that long before this you will have received my telegram advising you to accept Brett's offer.

We spent eight months in New York City, and there was born one son, Wells Lewis—most healthy and husky, as is Grace. Now we've come out for the winter and spring—possibly next summer, too—in this middlewestern environment, watching the solid, stolid Real America in its faults and virtues, its stability and reluctances. And there is an easy friendliness here rather pleasant . . . . Also lower rent!

Our warmest greetings to both of you, and our regret that your letters came so tardily.

As ever,

SINCLAIR LEWIS

Did you read my *The Job?* I *think* it's a real book.

"Brett" is George P. Brett, president of the Macmillan Company, who published King Coal, *my novel about life in the Colorado coal camps. My wife had asked Lewis's advice about the offer. The book was published in 1917. At this time Lewis was getting the local color for* Main Street, *and that was indeed a "real book."*

3

HARRY SINCLAIR LEWIS

> Chatham, Massachusetts
> May 28 [1919]

Dear Upton:

Please note, for your mailing list, the new address above. We've just come, and will be here till fall.

Your quiet, unanswerable, conviction-carrying rebuke to Mike Williams re *The Prophet for Profits* is a *masterpiece*—far better than Stevenson's *Father Damien*. I wonder if Mike will ever dare to answer it?

> SINCLAIR LEWIS

Early in 1919 I published a book, The Profits of Religion: A Study of Supernaturalism as a Source of Income and a Shield to Privilege. *The book was an attack, not upon religion, but upon the abuse of religion throughout the ages. It gave offense to many of the partisans of privilege, among them a one-time friend, Michael Williams. Mike and I had met at the Battle Creek Sanitarium, and had collaborated on a book called* Good Health: And How We Won It. *To write the book I had taken Mike, his wife, two children, a nurse and a secretary, to Bermuda, paying all the expenses for the winter. When the book was finished, Mike took the manuscript and his family to New York, the agreement being that he would find a publisher and send me half the proceeds. He had received an advance of $2500 and put it all into his pocket, leaving me*

4

stranded in Bermuda. That was in 1908; and in 1919, when The Profits of Religion *appeared, Mike had become editor of* Commonweal, *a weekly magazine in New York, and also a member of the board of directors of the Pontifical Institute of Sacred Music; but he had never refunded the money. He now wrote and published in his magazine a bitter attack upon my book, entitled "A Prophet for Profits." At this time I had a small monthly called* Upton Sinclair's, *and I told there the story of my dealings with my faithless friend. The unhappy man later died an alcoholic.*

HARRY SINCLAIR LEWIS

Washington, D.C.
January 15, 1921

Dear Upton:

I'm mighty glad you like *Main Street.* No, I haven't yet read *100%* but I shall. I came somewhat late to *Brass Check,* and was enormously impressed by it, enormously interested in it—and as always astounded by your ability to get so much done with only twenty-four hours a day to do it in!

My very best regards to your wife.

As ever,

Sinclair Lewis

References are to my novel 100%: The Story of a Patriot, *published 1920, and* The Brass Check, *my study of American journalism, published 1919.*

5

Forest Hills Inn
Forest Hills Gardens,
Long Island, N.Y.
June 16, 1922

Dear Upton:

I received the proofs from Mr. Floyd. Though, hang it, I shan't be able to read them for some time; what with finishing my work on my new novel, *Babbitt.*

As to the danger of the incoming shekels turning me from radicalism—see *Babbitt*!

It was bully to see you, and I hope that next time there won't be so long an interim.

Luck!
Ever!

Sinclair Lewis

c/o Harcourt Brace & Co.
New York, N.Y.
August 19, 1922

Dear Upton:

I've asked Harcourt Co. to shoot you out a copy of *Babbitt* just as soon as possible. Many thanks for your interest in it.

Yes, I tremendously want to see your education book; but I'm unreachable just now—I'm wandering with no fixed address. Lord, I bet it will be a tremendous book!

I called on Mrs. Debs yesterday. What a lovely woman she is!

Ever,

HAL

The reference is to The Goose-Step, *my book about the financial control of American colleges and universities, published 1923.*

I was indeed interested in Babbitt. *I sent the publishers a quote which they advertised extensively:*

"I am now ready to get out in the street and shout hurrah, for America's most popular novelist has sent me a copy of his new book, Babbitt. *I am here to enter my prediction that it will be the most talked-about and the most-read novel published in this country in my life-time."*

HARRY SINCLAIR LEWIS

Georgian House
St. James, London S.W.
April 19, 1923

Dear Upton:

London now, after two months in the West Indies and the Spanish Main. Yes, I'm doing a novel not exactly of a small-town doc but of a medical scien-

7

tist. I tried to get started with the Labor novel but found I wasn't quite ready for it.

No, I haven't yet received the *Goose-step*, but I'll get one somehow here in London.

Ever—

SINCLAIR LEWIS

Lewis of course is referring to Arrowsmith. *The "Labor novel" was a project that he talked about for many years. He did a lot of interviewing and note-taking, but never wrote the book.*

HARRY SINCLAIR LEWIS

Georgian House
St. James, London, S.W. 1
May 19th, 1925

Dear Upton:

Thank you very much indeed for your letter about *Arrowsmith*. I know exactly what you mean about the necessity of understanding the purely mental part of healing as well as the material, scientific side. But you must remember that in dealing with Dr. Gottlieb I must concentrate on his point of view. And after all, I do, I think, give credit to Dr. Silva, who is the "artist healer," and who would quite agree with you on the need of the purely human side of healing. I wish that I knew enough about Abrams to be able to fight that out with you, but I must wait until summer when it may be possible

8

to bring De Kruif and you together, and let the two of you fight it out, while I hold the sponge—and possibly a revolver in case of necessity.

I hope to get hold of *Mammonart* here in London before I sail—which will be in 5 days—so that I may read it on the steamer. If I do not, I shall get hold of it in New York.

No, the Labor novel is not forgotten—anything but! Only the time has not even yet come for it. After all, I was planning *Main Street* for 15 years before I wrote it, and I have always been glad that I did not write it until I really felt ready for it.

My profound regards to Madame, and our hope that we shall see the two of you before very long, now that we are returning.

Ever,

SINCLAIR LEWIS

I stood a lot of teasing because of my efforts to get a really scientific investigation of the "electronic reactions" of old Dr. Albert Abrams of San Francisco. All I can say now is that he anticipated more of the discoveries of modern physics than any person I know of. Again and again in after years I would come upon items in the news that would cause me to turn to my wife and say, "Abrams!" And if his reactions were a fraud he succeeded in fooling a committee in England headed by Sir Thomas Horder, Physican to the King and now Lord Horder. Their published verdict was: "Something does happen." What I had tried in vain was to get such a committee in the U.S.

9

HARRY SINCLAIR LEWIS

New York
October 19, 1925

Dear Upton:

Hell's bells, I know, of course, that you don't regard the "Psalm of Life" as a great poem. But I
did want you to come in on this article because
Mammonart is (although I disagree, naturally, with
many of your contentions, as one would have to do
with any living book) so important in making people get rid of their shibboleths about the art.

I have already received a copy of *Bill Porter* and
read it with interest.

I think that I shall be in California before the
winter is over and if so I shall certainly see you and
have a talk.

Ever,

SINCLAIR LEWIS

*References are to my study of economic and class
forces that controlled the world's literature through
the ages, published in 1925; and my three-act play
based on the life of O. Henry, 1925.*

10

HARRY SINCLAIR LEWIS

Kansas City, Missouri
May 14, 1926

Dear Upton:

Thank you for the very amusing clipping.

I had hoped very much to be able to come and have a good long while with you on my way back through Los Angeles but I had to hustle through without stopping and so couldn't even call you up.

I am at length starting the novel on preachers [*Elmer Gantry*] which I have planned for years and I have just reread *The Profits of Religion* with vast pleasure.

Ever yours,

HAL

THEODORE ROOSEVELT [1858-1919]

Washington, March 15, 1906

My dear Mr. Sinclair:

I have your letter of the 13th instant. I have now read, if not all, yet a good deal of your book, and if you can come down here during the first week in April I shall be particularly glad to see you.

I do not think much of your ecclesiastical correspondent. A quarter of a century's hard work over what I may call politico-sociological problems has made me distrust men of hysterical temperament. I think the preacher furnishes his measure when he compares you to Tolstoy, Zola and Gorki, intending thereby to praise you. The abortiveness of the

11

late revolution in Russia sprang precisely from the
fact that too much of the leadership was of the
Gorki type and therefore the kind of leadership
which can never lead anybody anywhere save into
a Serbonian bog. Of course the net result of Zola's
writings has been evil. Where one man has gained
from them a shuddering horror at existing wrong
which has impelled him to try to right the wrong,
a hundred have simply had the lascivious, the beast
side of their natures strengthened and intensified
by them. Oliver Wendell Holmes has an excellent
paragraph on this in his *Over the Teacups*. As for
Tolstoy, his novels are good, but his so-called religious and reformatory writings constitute one of
the age-forces which tell seriously for bad. His
Kreutzer Sonata could only have been written by a
man of diseased moral nature, a man in whose person the devotee and debauchee alternately sway, as
they sometimes do in successive generations of de-
cadent families or in whole communities of un-
healthy social conditions. In the end of your book,
among the various characters who preach socialism,
almost all betray the pathetic belief that the individual capacity which is unable to raise itself even
in the comparatively simple work of directing the individual how to earn his own livelihood, will, when
it becomes the banded incapacity of all the people,
succeed in doing admirably a form of government
work infinitely more complex, infinitely more difficult than any which the most intelligent and highly
developed people has ever yet successfully tried.
Personally I think that one of the chief early effects

12

of such attempt to put socialism of the kind there preached into practice, would be the elimination by starvation, and the diseases, moral and physical, attendant upon starvation, of that same portion of the community on whose behalf socialism would be invoked. Of course you have read Wyckoff's account of his experiences as an unskilled laborer of the lowest class [*The Workers*]. Probably you know him. He was a Princeton man wholly without the physique to do manual labor as well as the ordinary manual laborer can do it, yet in going across the continent his experience was that in every place, sooner or later, and in most places very soon indeed, a man not very strong physically and working at trades that did not need intelligence, could raise himself to a position where he had steady work and where he could save and lead a self-respecting life. There are doubtless communities where such self-raising is very hard for the time being; there are unquestionably men who are crippled by accident (as by being old and having large families dependent on them); there are many, many men who lack any intelligence or character and who therefore cannot thus raise themselves. But while I agree with you that energetic, and, as I believe, in the long run, radical action must be taken to do away with the effects of arrogant and selfish greed on the part of the capitalist, yet I am more than ever convinced that the real factor in the elevation of any man or any mass of men must be the development within his or their hearts and heads of the qualities which can alone make either the individual, the class or

13

the nation permanently useful to themselves and to others.

Sincerely yours,

THEODORE ROOSEVELT

P.S. But all this has nothing to do with the fact that the specific evils you point out shall, if their existence be proved, and if I have power, be eradicated.

Roosevelt's reference is to The Jungle *and the campaign it had started for meat-inspection reform. The President of the United States, at that time in his fifth year in office and busy with the overwhelming affairs of the nation, including the atrocious conditions in the Chicago stockyards, here cannot resist pausing to debate the value of the great literary men of the world.*

THEODORE ROOSEVELT

Washington, April 11, 1906

My dear Mr. Sinclair:

I have received your letter and also your telegram. From the latter you seemed to be a great deal more agitated than the facts warrant. Your Chicago correspondent showed a distinctly untrustworthy habit of mind in his telegram about "columns of official whitewash from Washington." There has been no official whitewash or official anything else sent out from Washington. The information to which he refers came from a Chicago newspaper to their Washington correspondent. Your correspondent shows his caliber when he states that further action will be of no effect and that you had better fight in the papers. This is enough to prove his utter untrustworthiness. As for Commissioner Neill and Mr. Reynolds, surely you cannot imagine that men as well known as they are could go to Chicago and have their presence remain entirely unknown. All that they can investigate are matters concerning which it would be impossible suddenly to make changes. For example, if there is a big false tank anywhere it cannot be gotten at at once. The investigation by a special man to be put inside to find out the exact facts will be something that will doubtless take months, and to have it known that such was our plan would of course hurt our efforts. So far I have not seen even a hint of it develop. If it gets out it will be only through your own friends.

As for attacking *The Jungle* in my speech next Saturday, I have no more idea of doing so than I have of attacking in that same speech the packers on what *The Jungle* contains. I shall of course do nothing until I have data on which to base action.

Let me repeat that both you and your correspondents must keep your heads if you expect to make your work of value. You say you "cannot believe" that I will "allow falsehoods to be telegraphed to the *Chicago Tribune* in my name," and that you feel you are "entitled to a vindication." Most certainly you need not believe that I will permit such conduct, for I have not permitted it and should not dream of permitting it. Nothing has been telegraphed to Chicago in my name so far as I am aware, and so I do not know what you would expect to be "vindicated" about. I am really at a loss to understand what it is to which you refer.

Sincerely yours,

THEODORE ROOSEVELT

P.S. Since writing the above I have received your letter. In it you take exactly the right position. I have not spoken to the *Chicago Tribune* correspondent on the matter and have not the least idea what the *Tribune* has said, but it cannot be any quotation from me because I have said nothing. Keep quiet, just as I shall keep quiet, and let the investigation go on. I have been trying to find out from the Department of Agriculture if anybody gave out from there any information as to the alleged report of the Department. I was not satisfied with this report, as it did not seem to me full and specific enough, and have notified the Department that I shall consider it merely as a preliminary report and that it is not to be given out in any way or shape and that I wish it verified. Neill and Reynolds will help verify it. All I can say, my dear Mr. Sinclair, is that I intend before I get through to be able to have authoritative reasons for saying "proved," or "unproved," or "not susceptible of proof," or "probably true," or "probably untrue," of each specific charge advanced against the packers. I cannot afford to be hurried any more than I can afford to be stopped from making the investigation. It may take months before we can get a really satisfactory statement. P.S. No. 2. Your second telegram has just come;

16

really, Mr. Sinclair, you must keep your head. It is absurd to become so nervous over such an article. Hundreds such appear about me all the time, with quite as little foundation.

Mr. Roosevelt's reference is to a two-column article which had appeared on the front page of the Chicago Tribune, *signed by the* Tribune's *editor who had come to Washington in the emergency. It gave a detailed account of President Roosevelt's intention to make a speech denouncing* The Jungle *on the basis of an investigation he had conducted for that purpose. On the day that story appeared I received seventeen telegrams from friends in Chicago. Knowing that the editor was a personal friend of Roosevelt, I was greatly distressed.*

The last sentence of this letter is an extraordinary comment on the American press. I am sorry that I was not free to quote it in The Brass Check. *Now it appears in the eight stately volumes of the Roosevelt correspondence. For permission to publish this and the previous letter I am indebted to the courtesy of the Harvard University Press.*

THEODORE ROOSEVELT

Oyster Bay, Long Island, N.Y.
June 1st, 1915

My dear Sinclair:

I thank you for your letter and appreciate it.
Let me see you when I am with Parker at Pass

17

Christian without fail. I would particularly like to meet Mrs. Sinclair, as she is a cousin of my friend Clive Metcalf; but my tennis days are over. Don't ask me to sign any documents at this time.

Faithfully yours,

T. ROOSEVELT

How well he knew me!

THEODORE ROOSEVELT

Oyster Bay, Long Island, N.Y.
July 2nd, 1915

My dear Mr. Sinclair:

I thank you for your letter and the enclosure. But, my dear sir, George Creel has made such utterly untruthful statements about me and about Governor Johnson that it is idle for me to pay any heed to anything he says on any matter.

Sincerely yours,

THEODORE ROOSEVELT

George Creel was a political journalist; during my "Epic" campaign for the governorship of California in 1934 he justified completely T.R.'s comment.

18

THEODORE ROOSEVELT

Oyster Bay, Long Island, N.Y.
July 7th, 1915

My dear Mr. Sinclair:

Just what do you mean by asking me to "look over" the book? If it is simply to read it for my own satisfaction and interest, you may be sure I shall do so in any event. But if you mean you would like me to write something about it, I should doubt whether I should be able to do it, because my own view is that we suffer particularly from cheap sketchy half-truths and three-quarter falsehoods about serious works of this kind and that in order to write anything serious I should have to write a volume; and for that I have not time.

Faithfully yours,

THEODORE ROOSEVELT

The book to which the President refers is my The Cry for Justice: An Anthology of the Literature of Social Protest, *1915.*

19

New York Office
247 Madison Avenue
January 1, 1919

Dear Sinclair:

Perhaps I shall be less shocked by your book
[*The Profits of Religion*] than you imagine — although I will not guarantee this! I have an idea that
I often used dogma or theology or ecclesiasticism
where you would use religion, which to my mind is
entirely different.

Faithfully yours,

T. ROOSEVELT

*This letter reached me on the day after my morn-
ing paper reported his death.*

JACK LONDON [1876-1917]

[1905]

Here it is at last! The book we have been waiting
for these many years! The *Uncle Tom's Cabin* of
wage slavery! Comrade Sinclair's book *The Jungle*!
And what *Uncle Tom's Cabin* did for black slaves,
The Jungle has a large chance to do for the white
slaves of today.

It is essentially a book of today. The beautiful
theoretics of Bellamy's *Looking Backward* are all
very good. They served a purpose and served it
well. *Looking Backward* was a great book. But I

20

dare say that *The Jungle*, which has no beautiful theoretics, is even a greater book.

It is alive and warm. It is brutal with life. It is written with sweat and blood and groans and tears. It depicts not what man ought to be, but what man is compelled to be in this our world, in the Twentieth Century. It depicts not what our country ought to be, or what it seems to be in the fancies of Fourth of July spell-binders, the home of liberty and equality of opportunity; but it depicts what our country really is, the home of oppression and injustice, a nightmare of misery, an inferno of suffering, a human hell, a jungle of wild beasts.

I quote above the first three paragraphs of a letter written by a man to whom I attribute a considerable part of the success of The Jungle. *Jack London wrote this letter after the book had been declined by five publishers as "too shocking." When it appeared in the* Appeal to Reason, *a Socialist weekly paper with close to a million circulation, a publisher was soon found and the success of* The Jungle *began. And not long after the letter was printed, Winston Churchill, later Prime Minister of Great Britain, published a two-part account of my book in a London weekly magazine.*

In calling me "Comrade," London meant Socialist. There were no Communists in those days.

Jack London—oysterman, sailor, laundry-worker, adventurer—grew up in the tough school of sailors and poverty. A wharf-rat of the Oakland, San Francisco Bay area, he managed to get through high school, then went through hell in the Klondike. London came back with something better than gold: the material for several novels and uncounted short stories. The author of The Sea Wolf, Martin Eden, John Barleycorn, *and* The People of the. Abyss, *he became one of the most widely read and beloved literary heroes of his time—certainly one of mine.*

JACK LONDON

Tasmania
January 18, 1909

Dear Sinclair:

Have been sick a weary, weary time. Am down here in Tasmania. Am arriving home soon. Am writing letter.

JACK LONDON

Such was the sad outcome of his venture to explore the South Seas in a small sailing vessel, the Snark, *with only his wife and one man to help him. In a similar post card, which I do not have at hand, he wrote me that he had got "seven tropical diseases."*

22

JACK LONDON

Hobart, Tasmania
January 21, 1909

Dear Sinclair:

During the last three months I have received an accumulated year's mail—several brief letters of yours in the bunch. During the last six months I have been too sick to write letters to anybody. I bought a copy of *Metropolis* [my novel dealing with fashionable society in New York, published in 1908] yesterday in Hobart. Haven't read it. Was in luck to get it. Am down here trying cool weather for what ails me. Have just pulled through two fresh attacks of fever.

JACK LONDON

JACK LONDON

Glen Ellen
California
August 24, 1909

Dear Sinclair:

(All ink—pencils out of commission)
In reply to yours of Florida origin.
Back at last.
Good Health to hand. Oh, you fakir! I heard that after publishing said book you had been sojourning and fasting at Battle Creek!
I want to send you a copy of my *Martin Eden* when it comes out.

23

When are you coming out this way again? When you do, come to me. We're great on vegetables, and we've a better climate (1,000 times) than Carmel.

Sincerely yours,

JACK LONDON

I was never a vegetarian on principle. Most of my life I was looking for a diet that would permit me to overwork with impunity. In my old age I have found it, and am a vegetarian again—but not "on principle."

JACK LONDON

Glen Ellen
California
Nov. 23, 1909

Dear Sinclair:

One of my motifs, in this book, was an attack on individualism (in the person of the hero). I must have bungled, for not a single reviewer has discovered it.

Sincerely yours,

JACK LONDON

The above is an inscription in a copy of Martin Eden, *one of London's best novels.*

24

JACK LONDON

Glen Ellen, California
February, 1, 1910

Dear Sinclair:

Just got back to the ranch, and am getting off to you today your opening chapters of "Love's Pilgrimage." It's certainly going to be a hummer, and I cannot begin to tell you how anxious I am to see the rest of it. You've just got me all keyed up over the development of this boy. Just the same, I want to tell you that your book is going to be the rawest, reddest meat that has been slammed at any American publisher in the last five decades. All I'm afraid of is that you won't find a publisher with guts enough to bring the book out.

Wishing you all the luck in the world,

Sincerely yours,

JACK LONDON

For heaven's sake let me see the rest of the MS when you get it along.

A publisher was found, and the novel was published in New York (1911) and London (1912).

JACK LONDON

Glen Ellen, California
March 26, 1910

Dear Sinclair:

I have forwarded the MS of "Love's Pilgrimage" a couple of days ago to Mrs. [Dell] Munger, having added that postscript you sent me, to the scenario. All I can say is that it is an amazing book—absolutely by itself. There is no other book like it.

Of course, great difficulty will be to find a publisher.

Samuel the Seeker [my recently published novel] has just come to hand this mail. I sent off to you this morning a copy of my last book, just out—*Lost Face.*

Ernest Untermann is here with me just now, and he is translating some of my books into German. And he and I are both curious to learn what sort of royalties we may expect from German publishers of translations. Can you help us out with anything from your experience?

When are you coming out to the Coast again?

With love to you,

JACK LONDON

Untermann, American Socialist editor, lived to old age, retired, became a sheepherder, and painted the mountains while the sheep grazed. He sent me two fine paintings, which went with my collection to the Indiana University Library.

26

JACK LONDON

Glen Ellen, California
July 17, '10

Dear Sinclair:

In reply to yours of July 10. Charmian [his wife]
has pulled through and is now on the mend. Will
be out of the hospital in a couple of weeks more.

Yes, I've been reading your *Physical Culture*
articles. But, I have theories of my own. I'll expound 'em to you some day.

You bet I want to see more of the book [the manuscript of "Love's Pilgrimage"]. I was dreadfully
rushed with the last installment. Give me a little
more time, this time. How long is it going to be?

With love,

JACK LONDON

JACK LONDON

Glen Ellen, California
November 2, 1913

Dear Sinclair:

In reply to yours of October 18, and thanking
you for your good words about *John Barleycorn.*

No, you have misunderstood me when you
thought my distrust of you was due to your being a
non-drinker. I cannot say that I ever distrusted you
at all. My feeling was one of alienness. It was your

27

sex-poise, or, sex-attitude, or whatever it can be called, that bothered me, and that still bothers me. I do not get this from personal contact with you, I get it only from reading your books. It is so foreign to me that it keeps me out of touch with you. In short, it is a temperamental lack of touch.

Sincerely yours,

JACK LONDON

I had met Jack only twice, when he visited New York in 1905, and both meetings were spoiled for me by the sight of his drinking. He entertained me by boasting of his alcoholic exploits—stories which he, told later in John Barleycorn. *In that book he declared that he was the master of his liquor—but it was not so. I have told this tragic story in* The Cup of Fury, *1956. A curious fact, that Jack voted for Prohibition, but could not enforce it upon himself.*

JACK LONDON

Glen Ellen, California
February 18, 1915

Dear Sinclair:

My telegrams have already carried to you the more important part of the situation. I shall most likely in the next several days be able to get out the introduction to you before I sail for Hawaii.

I heartily agree with you that George Sterling's "The Coming Singer" is the thing with which to end the book. That is big poetry. Any man who fails to recognize the beauty and the height and power of "The Coming Singer" does not know what poetry is. I stand for that where you have placed it and almost I would demand that it should appear as a foresheet at the beginning of the entire book, giving a cue to the content and spirit and beauty of the book.

At any rate, no matter what happens, please see that the publishers give me a few copies of the book [*The Cry for Justice*] at cost price when it is published.

Sincerely yours,

JACK LONDON

He wrote the introduction, calling the work "this humanist Holy Book." It is a noble piece of writing, and a monument to his memory. When he wrote it, he had less than two years to live.

JACK LONDON

Glen Ellen, California
August 18, 1916

My dear Sinclair:

In reply to yours of July 19, 1916—

I have just returned home from Hawaii, and after a few days at Bohemian Grove am on the ranch again. Will be at home now, off and on, until September 20th. Why not plan for you and your wife to run up and visit us at this time? It is a dandy place to work; if you wish to you can stay in your own room and have your meals sent in to you and work twenty-four hours out of the twenty-four.

We make no demands in this way upon our guests, and on the other hand, insist on doing our own work. Sometimes we do get to-gether, when our guests are willing to get to-gether with us.

You and I ought to have some "straight from the shoulder" talk with each other. It is coming to you, it may be coming to me. I may illuminate one or the other or both of us.

Sincerely yours,

JACK LONDON

P.S. The first two weeks in September shall be at Sacramento State Fair.

J.L.

Three months after writing this letter he took his own life, at the age of forty. It was John Barleycorn's doing.

CHARMIAN K. LONDON [1871?-1955]

Glen Ellen, California
December 2, 1916

Dear Upton Sinclair:

I am not going to let any more time go by, despite the waves and billows of correspondence that are sweeping over me at this time, before letting you know how profoundly grateful I am to you for your generous tribute to our Jack. This is the sort of thing that gives me the most personal help—for the big men of the world to come through and appreciate the man—the man himself. We all know he was a great artist, and a great thinker; but that he was a great man in himself is the greatest of all. And Jack was that great man. This appreciation is making itself manifest all the time, and fills me with a sense of the fitness of some things.

Do not ever make any mistake in this: that although Jack disagreed with you in some ways, he believed in you and your true genius. If I could believe anything, I'd like to believe that right now he is smiling his great smile down upon you for your true and splendid evaluation of him.

With the best wishes in the world,

Sincerely yours,

CHARMIAN K. LONDON

Shortly after this letter was written, Charmian, Jack's widow, visited us and commented to my wife: "I now sleep soundly for the first time in many years."

HENRY JAMES [1843-1916]

Lamb House
Rye, Sussex
March 5th, 1908

Dear Mr. Upton Sinclair:

I am signing with pleasure and enclosing herewith the new form of Appeal on behalf of the testi-

31

monial to dear Horace Fletcher; my gladness to participate in this remains just what I wrote you of it. I appreciate the grounds for the new form, and hope it may all now go on straight and easily. May this also reach you straight in your oh so-to-be-envied isle of Eden.

Believe me yours very truly,

HENRY JAMES

As early as 1900 I had been deeply impressed by James' novels and had written a study of them, calling him "the leisure-class historian." In 1912, in the New Reform Club in London, H. G. Wells pointed him out in the dining room, saying, "A rear view of the Grand Cham eating a mutton chop."

"Isle of Eden" was Bermuda. Horace Fletcher, 1849-1919, was a sweet and kind old gentleman who set out to propagate the idea that the way to assure perfect health was to masticate your food thoroughly. I met him, and fell under his spell. Throughout my life, whenever I experimented with diet, I was laughed at and called a "health crank." But today the whole world, under the leadership of medical men, is experimenting with diet, and learning about cholesterol, vitamin deficiency, and that villain, table salt.

GEORGE STERLING [1869-1926]

Carmel, California
October 28th, 1908

Dear Sinclair:

Of course I'll meet the noon train on Saturday— it will be a pleasure. You'll be able to find me by hunting for a dissipated-looking person in a grey cap.

After your train leaves San Jose, look up into the mountains to the East and you'll see the Lick Observatory. It always gives me a thrill to see that "watch-tower on infinity," as I called it once.

I wish I could be at the Dreamland Rink [an auditorium where I was to speak] tomorrow night, but I'm *anchored* here till at least the 15th.

Select a seat on the right hand side of the train, from San Francisco to San Jose. Then change to the left from San Jose to Morgan Hill (to see the observatory), and then back to the right for the rest of the trip.

Sincerely,

GEORGE STERLING

In 1903 Jack London sent me a copy of The Testimony of the Suns *by the California poet George Sterling, and wrote in it: "I have a friend, the dearest in the world." So you will find Jack frequently mentioned in the following letters.*

This poet laureate of California and darling of the literati, was tall, erect and athletic; his profile bore a striking resemblance to Dante's. He was

33

tender-hearted and generous to a fault. He was educated in a monastery, intending to be a monk. He was influenced by Father Tabb's poetry and later by Ambrose Bierce; during his lifetime hundreds of his poems and articles were published in magazines, in addition to thirteen volumes of poems.

My wife has told in her memoirs, Southern Belle, *how Sterling met her before she married me. He fell in love with her, vowed to write her a sonnet a day for a hundred days, and did so (*Sonnets to Craig *was the published title). These, and an even greater number of love letters, are now owned by the Indiana University Library. Those addressed to me are many and I have selected a few, divided into two lots, the earlier before I married Craig, and the second written after that.*

GEORGE STERLING

Carmel, California
July 2, 1909

Dear Boy:

I was glad to hear from you, though sorry about Belasco and Gerson [David Belasco had accepted my play, "The Millenium," and kept me waiting in vain for a year or two]. The stage seems to taint, and usually *rots,* about everything that touches it, especially those who are responsible for the stage—partial payment, it may be, for the insincerity of the

34

pseudo-art of acting. But you already know my intolerance for it.

I hope you're having good times at Cutchogue, which is not far from Sag Harbor, my birthplace, and home till I was nearly twenty-one. I've sailed scores of times to "Rose's Grove," opposite you across Little Peconic Bay.

Before I forget it, let me ask you to assure me that you've destroyed that "Leopold" diatribe—the more I learn of the Congo matter the more it seems evident that I was at least partially unjust [reference is to Sterling's poem on King Leopold of Belgium, and his rule of the Congo].

And about that back-exercise I taught you. Time increases my admiration for it, and the strength it imparts. *But don't overdo it*, or you'll become what the trainers call "stale," which is hell.

I had a letter from Jack, written off Pitcairn Island on May 2nd. By then he had recovered his health, and had out-boxed the three mates of the "Tymeric." And a few days ago his aunt wrote me that he'd cabled her from Panama on June 25th to send his mail to New Orleans. So doubtless he'll keep his promise to me to be back in July, in time for the Bohemian Club Jinks.

They've shown me how to make Yogurt, which I'm excessively fond of. My garden wasn't much of a success—the gophers are too numerous; but with Yogurt I can defy the wolf.

My uncle crowded a hundred dollar bill on each of us when we were last in Oakland (Monday) and took us to dinner and to "The Merry Widow"—a bestial affair. I don't care for this "rich relation" business, but don't see how I'm to sidestep it as affairs are at present. They'd not, and never could, savvy. I'm fairly industrious, but my stuff is slow to sell. I seem fated to care to write only on "impossible" subjects. My latest poem, 150 lines long, is on *orchids*! Influence of Coryell's hothouse. But even my more "human" stuff doesn't seem to go. I don't see why the enclosed shouldn't sell; perhaps it will if I'm patient!

We've had about twenty straight days of warmth and sunshine, and there's nothing left to rent in all the town. Peet's home is now half-completed, and he bunks there o'nights to guard his household goods. I expect a big crowd here "over the 4th" to get me to fix mussel-bakes for them, and Barkis is willin'—they to furnish all transportation.

Well, write when you feel like it. And love to you and yours, from

GEORGE STERLING

GEORGE STERLING

Carmel, California
August 25, 1909

Dear Upton:

Your letter reached me while I was at Jack's where Carrie, Blanche and I spent five or six days; so I was able easily to give B your message. Jack is all right now—weighs 8 lbs. more than he ever did. He smokes just as terribly as ever, but drinks

36

less. To *me*, booze is scarcely even an *attraction* any more, and I feel better than ever before in my life.

That fasting scheme is all right. I believe it will cure *anything*. I've tried it myself, but as nothing was amiss with me, I got, naturally, no particular results. Am drinking yogurt daily, now, and find it a great food.

London has *nine* books ready for publication—the industry of the man! If I can get out one every two years I'll think I'm doing very well. He will soon visit us in Carmel . . . .

As to the "Leopold" poem, I'll be content if you promise to destroy it when you come across it. It may take me years to make up my mind about the truth of that matter. I dread being unjust.

The summer weather has been wonderfully good, and keeps improving. A young woman was drowned off the main beach, nine days ago, and they're still seeking the body—with divers, now. It should come to the surface in a day or so more . . .

I'm fairly busy, but this climate seems to take all the mental energy out of me. When it gets a little colder I imagine I'll get more work done. Mrs. Atherton came over from Del Monte to see me, and gave the climate a black eye—said she wondered that anyone could write a line.

But nothing I can write seems salable, and I suppose I'd better try to write some sort of a play. Damned if I'll write about skyscrapers and airships . . . .

London hadn't done any original work since last

December, but had begun on a new novel, in which he takes a great delight, when I was there. He calls it "Burnt Daylight." I didn't ask him what it was all about.

I've not attended a Ruskin Club meeting since the tragedy. What? Jack gives two lectures for the party this month. Wish I could.

We both send you love and best wishes.

GEORGE

Mrs. Atherton was Gertrude. Carrie was George's wife. Jack London's book was published as Burning Daylight. *The "tragedy" was that George was supposed to introduce me at a banquet, but couldn't because he drank too much on the way to the place.*

GEORGE STERLING

Carmel, California
December 8, 1909

Dear Upton:

I'm ashamed of the crudity and (as I've said) *shrillness* of that Leopold "poem", and am also ashamed to see it in print, especially since William Watson had done the work so much better. So I let it die.

Of course I've seen the Asquith poem [by poet-laureate William Watson denouncing Lady Asquith], and don't doubt that it was richly deserved. [Richard] Le Gallienne is being delivered of a mess of wretched doggerel on the subject. It's needless for me to say that I don't subscribe, as he and the Public Pig seem to do, to the tradition that a woman can say what she will and go unpunished *merely because of her sex.*

I've not heard from Jack for over a week. Hear he is coming to Del Monte in a friend's automobile, soon. If he comes I'll be kept busy getting mussels for a few days.

Yes—send on the love-poems. They'll have to be wonders to beat Updegraff's. I've just finished a 15 stanza poem I call "Moonlight in the Pines," and will tackle a dramatic poem tomorrow.

I'm so poor that it keeps me energetic. I put in four or five hours every morning, out in the cabin, which I keep warm by a fire in the cook-stove there. At present the rain is falling fast and steadily, so I'm just as well-off in-doors . . . .

Be sure that *Physical Culture,* in printing that photograph, doesn't mention my name, nor even Carmel. Otherwise some busy-body will smell me out, and the S.F. weeklies re-print or comment for the public midriff.

A 200 ft. steam-schooner (for lumber) has gone ashore down the coast, near Lafler's, and is going to pieces. No lives lost. Wish I were there. Lafler has probably become a wrecker.

Guess I would better bring this aimless scrawl to an end.

Talofa!

GEORGE

39

GEORGE STERLING

Carmel, California
February 21, 1910

Dear Upton:

The last two times you wrote they were mere notes, no answer to my letter. Hence my silence.

Have just wasted 40 days in the bay cities. Gee! But it's good to be back! You picked a poor winter for coming to Carmel: it's been sweet and mild here, with many days as warm as June.

Say, you'll kill yourself if you write at such an incredible rate, and *fast*. Don't go too much on Carrington, or you'll find yourself in the bat-factory [Hereward Carrington's books on psychic research]. London will tell me about the novel, I hope. He and his wife are to visit us in a few days, to remain two or three weeks. Wish you were here.

About the poems [some poems of Harry Kemp whose letters appear later]: there's *awful* good stuff in them *in spots*. But along with that are crudities and banalities. It would take me a whole morning to criticise the poems in writing, and I cannot afford the time. If you wish, I'll return them with brief marginal comments.

I just had a long letter from Mary Austin. She is doing well in London, and gives no intimation as to when she'll return to Carmel . . . .

I sold a couple of poems to the Century, and a long one to the *Pacific Monthly*. At present am doing nothing but answer letters—they've been piling up on me.

We both send love to you and yours, and hope to
hear from you soon.

As ever,

George

GEORGE STERLING

Carmel, California
August 29, 1910

Dear Upton:

Whenever I look at the pile of unanswered letters
on my desk, I'm tempted to groan and flee—as usually I do. It's not quite sloth nor indifference—more
a deep-rooted distaste for that wretched compromise, correspondence.

I've meant to write you a score of times, and probably would have done so had I had anything in particular to say. I didn't reply to your pamphlet about
endowing writers [a reference to my magazine article in the *Independent*, July 28, 1910, later a
pamphlet, calling for endowments for poets. This
is one subject on which the world has taken my
advice], because the proposition seemed to me a
hopeless one, yet one I was unwilling to cast cold
water on. Here is *my* notion of it—not for publication. I speak only of the poet, as he's the only one
who seems to show qualities of endurance, except in
rare instances.

Now, it *would* be a fine thing could we save the
occasional "Chatterton or Keats." But who on earth

41

is going to tell him when he bobs up? Were anyone to have eyes of discernment, it would seem to be the great poets themselves; but it would make you sick to read, in Clutton-Brock's *Life of Shelley*, how he and Byron underestimated and patronized Keats, a greater poet than either of them. Had Byron had a vote, it would have gone to men who are now utterly forgotten. It's true that Shelley gave Keats a final panegyric in "Adonais," but that was merely for the purpose of writing "Adonais." He had to have some sort of skeleton to robe in that glorious flesh.

If the editors of our magazines can't discern genius when they see it (and they can't), it's not likely that minor poets (and we've no others) are going to do so. And if they could they're so pitifully jealous a crowd that no one of them could be trusted in such a matter had he a friend of letters whom he could advance. It's a case of the old question, What is Poetry? And what poetry is is a thing that damned few persons, to my notion, ever know. If it's one thing it's not stuff of "a forward-looking tendency," nor of "a new and path-breaking nature." We turn to science and economics for such stuff. Your own absurd (to me) estimate of "Breshkovskaya" [a poem by Elsa Barker which I later included in *The Cry for Justice*] is excellent proof at hand. It's one line approaching poetry is "the red halls of spiritual death." As a poem it hasn't the vitality of a canary with the pip. And so I can see that were you one of the judges (and you'd be as likely to be one as anybody else) that only verse that had an "uplift", that would serve as a sort of sociologi-

42

cal tract, would have much chance. At the best, your judges would pick out such rot as treats of skyscrapers and airships; and the small folk who "write of their day," such as Kemp and [James] Oppenheim, would land the prizes, while Wm. Vaughn Moody, Cale Young Rice and my humble self would receive the advice to become more utilitarian in our work—were we noticed at all.

In the meanwhile, the equivalent of Keats would probably have done his work, despised by editors and unknown to the public, and gone his destined way to senility or death.

And yet—and yet—sometimes it seems to me that could one Poe be saved in a thousand years by your plan, it's more than worth while, even though one may question the wisdom of the scheme for keeping alive a great poet in the interests of a world not 1% of whom understand great poetry. And to me and a few others whom I can't help admiring, poetry seems great in just about such ratio as it eliminates "purpose, end or care." Of course you've a legal right to call anything you choose "poetry," and if all you really care for (and I reverence you for it) is human progress, well and good. And yet you have equally a right not to be surprised if a few of us poets, or even near-poets, don't agree with you.

By the way, of the imposing list in your pamphlet I choose only a dozen names of whom I can say that they'll be famous two hundred years from now, and they are practically all poets! But gaze backward, and see if that hasn't been the trend.

There was nothing "vital" about the work of Poe and Keats (like most of the others), and they had no propaganda to adduce. What they had to give (and it was all for which they cared) was beauty, sheer beauty. But giving that, how mighty was their gift! How enduring! How unpayable! I shall enclose here an "essaylet" by Bierce that puts my case as no other writer could. Please return it after perusal. To me it is like the sound of a great trumpet under a lovely sky.

But enough of this, though it is the merest outline of *part* of what I have to say on the subject. Indeed, did the spirit so move, I could write on the subject a book of hundreds of pages, and prove my points by "abundant precept and example." But I spare an undeserving world! If you care to hear from me any more, after this "destructive criticism" of your plan (which may, of course, work out all right, after *all* I've said), I'll promise to answer your letterlets more promptly, in the days to be, even though I have, as now, no particular news.

This summer found and leaves me a host: God knows how many visitors and guests I've had! But most of them were worth while, and I'm not so remorseful as I might be about having done so little work since May. I've sold four or five poems to the *Century* and *Harpers*, and plenty of them to western magazines. In the September *Pacific Monthly* is a six-page poem of mine I wish you'd read. It seems to me a fair compromise, if such can be, between life and beauty; at least, there's a theme, tho' most men of my age will not like it, seeing themselves as

44

"Duandon." So saw Hopper [a California novelist] and others.

Don't you bother to send me *Samuel the Seeker*. I've meant to order it for months, and shall do so today. I found your article on fasting most interesting, and have often heard it referred to. *I* manage to keep in a state of more health than is absolutely comfortable by eating only 1½ meals a day, by leaving booze alone, and by keeping my dorsal and abdominal muscles in training; I once showed you how; my admiration of the scheme increases with the experience that time brings.

Carrie is very well too, and sends regards. We were in Yosemite in June, with Bierce [Ambrose Bierce, journalist and fiction writer], his brother and other of his relatives. Early this month B and I went up to the grove-play of the Bohemian Club, where he and London became good friends, to my delight —and surprise, for B. had been objecting to some of Jack's views.

Well, the autumn is about here, glory be! and visitors are now becoming rarities. When this pile of letters has melted, I'll be able to buckle down and write some verses. I've a score of things in mind, including a play for our forest-theatre here.

I'd be glad to have you get Miss French's book. You can get it for $1.00 by ordering through me. The edition of 500 will soon be gone. *I* have sold about 100 of it.

This letter has been so long that you'll have to give me a little more time on those poems.

45

We've had a cool summer, and welcome warm days once more.

With best wishes to you and yours,

As ever, faithfully,

GEORGE STERLING

Miss French is Nora May French, a young poet who later took her own life.

GEORGE STERLING

Carmel, California
November 14, 1910

Dear Upton:

I think I owe you a letter, so here goes. I received the Bierce "essaylet" all right, and rather agree with the exception you make, though not so sure that he intended to be taken that way. It seems to me too that a poet writes of what he must, rather than what he will; extort his interest or admiration, and he must sing you. What I so admired in the article was B's insistence on the value of enduring poetry—"an unchanging and unchangeable current of eternal good." Just stop to think of the pleasure that John Keats has already given mankind, and he's been read for less than a century! Think of the sum of that pleasure, after a few score of centuries! Why, it seems to me that he was of much more value to mankind than all the other dwellers in great London of his days.

Mr. Bierce has left for Washington, in such haste that I found no chance to say farewell to him. I

46

fear he didn't greatly approve of me. At least he objected to most of my friends, an objection in which I did not sustain him. Perhaps he has a right to be implacable, but it doesn't make his society an unmixed delight.

London has just finished a cruise on the bays and rivers. We may visit him in a couple of weeks . . . .

Carmel showed up with eleven socialist votes this year. Don't you think California did itself proud? One thing that helps, out here, is the fact that it's the 2nd automobile-using state in the Union.

Carrie is very well, as usual. Of course, *I* am. Have been very busy of late, and have finished several longish poems, all unsalable, on account of length. Also I've written an imitation of the Book of Job, just a chapter. I think it'll attract attention when it appears in my book next spring. But I'll not send it to a magazine, for they'd not dare to print it. Not that there's anything inherently objectionable in it; but one isn't "supposed" to imitate Holy Writ, and most folks believe it impossible to do so—wait till they see my 43rd chapter!

I've been reading Chatterton, and am amazed to find how comically overrated he is, as a *poet*. Now I see why one so seldom sees him quoted: there's no especial poetry to be quoted!

I've been doing lots of hunting, but my shoulder got so sore from gun-recoil that I had to give it a rest and the butcher his innings.

As ever, sincerely,

GEORGE

47

Carmel, California
February 28, 1911

Dear Upton:

I've been meaning to write to you these two weeks, but have had a host of things to distract me. For one, I'm planting the three acres of cleared land near me to potatoes. We have a Jap "potato-king" in California, and it pleases me to keep out of his clutches. We have enough of the indigenous variety.

I'm awfully anxious to see your novel [*Love's Pilgrimage*]. If it's half as good as van E[eden]'s praise would indicate, it must be a stunner. You've the knack of being very interesting, and I read your *Metropolis* and *Moneychangers* [my novel dealing with the Wall Street panic of 1907] every few months, for the sheer pleasure their plots give me. As to their veridicity I sometimes incur doubts.

If I'd thought Kemp needed any praise he'd have got more. I'd a notion he thought very well of himself, like most writers who have no great trouble in getting into periodicals. Darn it! He's done some great work! A man can't always be giving birth to masterpieces.

My fool-book won't be out before April 1st—an auspicious date. I'll send you a copy, though God knows it's mere art-froth; which is all I intend it to be. When I get ready to do the other kind of work, I'll do it with a vengeance.

Bierce suggests that *I* answer his "Town Topics"

article: says it is hard on poets. But I've no time; and it's a late day for *me* to be scrapping with the old gentleman. By the way, you're welcome to that phrase, "the melancholy rich," as it's not mine. *I* first heard it used by an army-officer who frequented the Del Monte.

It's as well for you you're not here this winter, which has been exceptionally rainy. It's pouring now, and yesterday we had rain, hail, snow, thunder and lightning. The hills south of us are white with snow — a strange and beautiful sight· If it would stop raining I'd go up and roll in it. We're going up to Jack's on a two-week visit as soon as we receive some fruit-trees I was crazy enough to order at this time of the year. They've delayed us 10 days already....

I've not had a drink this year.

As ever,

GEORGE

More of George Sterling's letters appear later.

LINCOLN STEFFENS [1866-1939]

Boston, October 16, 1908

My dear Sinclair:

So that's where you are! Bishop, California. But where's that? If it's anywhere near San Francisco, go and see Heney. Cheer him up. And let him tell you how Law failed in California and how Politics will win. He doesn't believe it, consciously, but

49

that's because he's a fighter. He'll fight better when he knows. And he's the salt of the earth.

It's no use asking the President to help Lindsey. The President is always for one thing at a time and it's Taft now. Besides, I haven't been in communication with the President since—well, for a long time.

Yours,

LINCOLN STEFFENS

P.S. Tell me your plans when you write again.

Stef, as his friends called him, began as a Wall Street reporter and editor. He cultivated the "big fellows" and always knew what was going on. For McClure's Magazine *he wrote a series of articles,* The Shame of the Cities, *which made him the first of the "muckrakers." He exposed "The System," whereby big business controlled our politics. In 1902 I wrote him an "open letter" pointing out the consequences of this "System" and he told me it was the best criticism of his work he had seen. He urged* McClure's *to publish it, but in vain.*

Steffens was a short, square-built man, wearing a little pointed beard. He was an eager talker, and a devoted friend.

Heney was the District Attorney of San Francisco, fighting the grafters who ran that city for the big interests. Heney licked them—but not until they had him shot and almost killed.

Ben Lindsey was the Judge of the pioneer Children's Court in Denver. He, too, was fighting the grafters—what Stef called "The System."

50

LINCOLN STEFFENS

Boston, Mass.
November 8, 1908

My dear Sinclair:

I was glad to hear from you, very; I always am. You seem to speak in your little brief notes.

But I can't tell you what I'm doing in Boston. It would take too long. It's an experiment that would interest you and when we meet I'll go into it in detail. I don't expect it to succeed; that is to say, I can't let myself think it can. And I'm not worrying much over it, because it will be all the more significant if it fails.

Lindsey won because, for the first time, he hunted up and got at the people, the real people. And half the problem is to reach them. The other half is to make the issue plain.

Heney wrote me that he had heard from you and that he was going to see you, but he's in a hot fight; he's absorbed in it and he forgets. Go and call.

You are in my state, you know. California, the most beautiful kept lady in the Union, and you are in a beautiful place in that beautiful state. I don't know, of course, who all are there, but usually Carmel has some truly enlightened people in it. James Hopper is of it, but he is in New York. Give my warmest regards to the others who are there.

If you go to Sacramento, call on my good old father and mother; Tories, but my sister, Laura, will understand you.

Yours sincerely,
LINCOLN STEFFENS

51

I did not visit Sacramento until a quarter of a century later, when I was the Democratic Party's candidate for Governor. The Steffens' mansion had become the official residence of the Governor. I climbed, as I remember, four tall flights of stairs, and I said: "God save me from having to live here." My request was kindly granted.

LINCOLN STEFFENS

The Players, New York
October 15, 1915

Dear Sinclair:

I know I should have written before, but I'm sailing for Mexico next week, and that makes it necessary to finish up a lot of little things here, be free to stay in Mexico till that beautiful revolution with its wonderful hopes is over and busted. For I have no doubt that American and British capital will buy it up and out and set up civilized law and order.

Your book is good to and for me [*The Cry for Justice*]. I keep it by, and read it a little at a time; and over and over. I guess it will last forever. It is so always new, and so always inspiring. A Bible— for the Faith-full.

Thank you for it, Upton.

Affectionately,

LINCOLN STEFFENS

The Players
Sixteen Grammercy Park
New York, June 29, 1917

Dear Upton Sinclair:

Just back, I find too much mail to answer at length, but it is due you to know that I didn't get your letters to me and to Kerensky in time. I was gone before they arrived. And I don't believe I could get your letter to Kerensky now, by mail. The revolution is very inconvenient.

But also it is very, very beautiful.

I'll tell you about it soon; I'll be out there. I've written some of it for the August *Everybody's*.

My love to the Lady.

Sincerely,

L. STEFFENS

He came, and told us about the revolution that was so beautiful—very few people had been hurt. But then, a year later, he came again, after the second, the Bolshevik, revolution; and that was not so beautiful. The substance of it was this: The Bolsheviks were not grafters; they did not steal; they had the power, and if you had the power, you did not need the money. So it has been ever since.

Kerensky was the Socialist premier of Russia, later overthrown by the Bolsheviks.

53

BERTRAND RUSSELL [1872-   ]

Woolnough, Hennepen Co., Minn.
July 14, 1910

My dear Sinclair:

Very likely you are right. You see I never wrote any fiction and couldn't and don't know how, and hence my experience and view are limited. But if you can include in your scheme something that will enable young writers to disregard totally the remarks, particularly those that are called "Worth while," and never read any of them and estimate their stuff at its true value which is nothing at all, you will do well.

With best wishes.

Yours fraternally,
RUSSELL

Bertrand Russell, English philosopher, mathematician, and now an earl in spite of himself, is referring to my pamphlet proposing endowments for young creative writers.

BERTRAND RUSSELL

Carn Voel
Treen, Penzance
June 2, 1923

Dear Upton Sinclair:

Thank you very much for your play *Hell,* which I read with the greatest pleasure. It is delightful—so full of gusto. I read it aloud with Miles Malleson [actor and playwright—author of *Black 'Ell*], and

54

we were discussing all the time whether the I.L.P. could perform it—for members only, to avoid the censor. The movie part is the difficulty. Have you any ideas about how it could be performed, or do you regard a performance as impossible?

Is it true you have got into trouble with the authorities because they take the same view of the Declaration of Independence as George III took? If so, you have my warmest sympathy and good wishes.

Your sincerely,

BERTRAND RUSSELL

The play Hell *has never been produced. Its story is painfully apposite to the present world situation. An imp from hell steals the key to heaven and locks the occupants inside. The chiefs of hell then amuse themselves by creating a pool of oil on earth and watch the great nations of the earth go to war for possession of it.*

The mention of the "authorities" is a reference to an incident at the harbor of Los Angeles during a dockworkers' strike in which six or seven hundred men had been packed into a jail under especially shocking conditions. I was arrested and held "incommunicado" for twenty-two hours for attempting to read aloud the Bill of Rights of the U.S. Constitution while standing on private property with the written permission of the owner. These events led to the founding of a branch of the American Civil Liberties Union in Los Angeles, and such outrages have not since occurred.

55

Royal Station Hotel, York.
23? April 1912.

Questions (Yes or No.)

Do you care to join the League as here outlined? *No*

Do you care to join in case its plans and program are modified? (If yes, kindly specify modifications.) *Certainly not*

Will you send the names and addresses of other men and women of letters who should be invited to sign the preliminary call? *By no means.*

Will you send the names and addresses of possible members, supporters and sympathizers? *Not one.*

Will you receive a representative of the League, to give information and suggestions which may be of service in extending the work? *Not on any account.*

Will you agree to contribute or collect funds in case of special emergencies? *Most emphatically No.*

Do you care to receive the future publications and plans of the League? *On the contrary.*

Would you care to contribute to its publications. *Not in the least*

Would you care to serve upon its Executive Committee if elected? *It leaves me cold.*

Would you be able to attend a gathering of its General Council to be held in Holland next July or August? *Able, but steadfastly resolved not to.*

Address replies to DR. FREDERIK VAN EEDEN, „Walden", Bussum, Holland. *Walden is presumably an Irrenanstalt.*

Good Gracious, Upton, have you any sense of proportion? What means have you or I of organizing such a thing? Havn't you grown out of this baby stage of making world wide organizations out of three cranks (including President, Secretary, & Treasurer) and the use of a shop parlor in the Old Kent Road once a week? I'm surprised at you.

G. B. S.

56

I had come upon Shaw's writings in 1901 and become a disciple; his letters of that time, alas, went up in the Helicon Hall fire of 1907. I visited him in London in 1912. I was prepared for a sharp tongue, but found him one of the sweetest and kindest of humans. The most abiding impression was of cleanness, both of person and of soul. Also, of course, that wonderful golden beard!

The questionnaire reproduced here was an abortive attempt of Frederik van Eeden and myself to rally the world's intellectuals to prevent the world war which we saw on the horizon. "Irrenanstalt" is German for madhouse; Walden was van Eeden's home in Holland.

GEORGE BERNARD SHAW

10 Adelphi Terrace
London W. C.
3rd May 1917

My dear Upton Sinclair:

I see that the letter to which this is a reply is dated 11th January. That is the sort of thing that happens to my correspondents. When it came I was just starting for the west front; and the experience was so exciting and involved so much writing afterwards that I have never got level with my correspondence since.

57

Since then there has been the Russian Revolu-
and Wilson justifying all the fine things I said of
him when everyone here was abusing him. The
Daily Chronicle said, when his reply to the German
note appeared, "President Wilson seems to think
that the word of the Germans is as good as ours.
What have we done to deserve this?"

I hear all sorts of interesting people being at
Pasadena, which I suppose is due to your having settled there (for six months as usual, eh?) If I ever go
to the States I will try to find where Pasadena is.
They offer me huge sums to go and lecture, apparently believing that I am another Bryan or Billy
Sunday; but I have waited too long.

Always glad to hear from you. Is it true that Mrs.
Upton Sinclair has gone freudig?

Ever

G. BERNARD SHAW

*Shaw is punning here in German. Mrs. Upton
Sinclair was and is anti-Freud. We lived in Pasadena just a quarter-century and were only driven
out by the smog.*

[THE NOBEL PRIZE FOR LITERATURE]

*In the autumn of 1931 there was formed a com-
mittee of nineteen "holders or former holders of aca-
demic positions" to recommend to the Swedish
Academy of Letters the name of Upton Sinclair
as candidate for the award of the Nobel prize for
literature. This committee consisted of Harry Elmer*

Barnes of the New School for Social Research, John Dewey of Columbia University, Paul H. Douglas of the University of Chicago, Albert Einstein of the University of Berlin, Paul S. Epstein of The California Institute of Technology, Robert Herrick of the University of Chicago, Harold J. Laski of the University of London, William Ellery Leonard of the University of Wisconsin, Robert Morss Lovett of the University of Chicago, Edwin Markham of the American Academy of Art and Letters, William McDougall of the University of Oxford, Regis Michaud of the University of Illinois, Franz Oppenheimer of the University of Berlin, Edward A. Ross of the University of Wisconsin, Bertrand Russell of Cambridge University, Frederick C. S. Schiller of Oxford University, J. G. Sleeswijk of the University of The Hague, Harry F. Ward of the Union Theological Seminary, and Fritz Wittels of the New School for Social Research.

The document signed by these scholars was as follows:

"The terms of the Nobel bequest provide that the award shall be made 'to one who has produced in the field of literature the most distinguished work of an idealistic tendency.' For thirty years Upton Sinclair has been making contributions to American literature which seem to us to come under this classification. He is the author of some forty volumes of fiction, drama, economics, and social and literary criticism, and is unquestionably the most widely read of writers living today; his books have been translated into more than thirty languages, and have

59

profoundly affected the thinking of both the masses and the more alert portion of the cultured world. We consider his greatest novels, as *The Jungle, Love's Pilgrimage, Oil, Boston,* an outstanding achievement in the contemporary fiction of all lands, for their mastery of fact, for their social vision, for consistent, honest and courageous thinking, for humanitarian passion, and for vitality and sweep of creative art."

According to the rules laid down by the Swedish Academy of Letters, the committee proceeded to circulate this document among academically qualified persons; and a Professor Quinn of the University of Pennsylvania took offense, and served notice on the committee that if they did not cease their activities, he would circulate a counter-petition and submit it to the Swedish Academy. I have before me a large envelope full of the responses to this challenge. Bernard Shaw, himself a Nobel Prize winner, spoke for the men of letters. The communications were addressed to the secretary of the committee.

GEORGE BERNARD SHAW

> Whitehall Court (130)
> London, S.W. 1
> November 13th, 1931

Dear Mr. Greene:

Nobody has ever challenged the propriety of the award of this prize to me six years ago; but I am

60

quite sure that the twenty-five professors cited by Mr. Quinn were convinced that it was a most unwise selection. The Academy's business is to find out the writers whose positions are so far outstanding that it will be recognized internationally; and such positions are not attained by pleasing the professors. They are never purely literary positions: writers who are great pets in literary circles, and perhaps do exquisite literary work, may have no influence on the thought of their time; whilst rougher talents, exercised forcibly by writers to whom literary graces are not ends in themselves but only bait to catch readers for their ideas, may have just the sort of importance that maintains the Nobel prestige. It is because Mr. Upton Sinclair's talent is of this order that I joined in his nomination as eligible for the prize, and that the professors shrieked with horror at the suggestion.

I put it to the professors as to men who know the history of their own hobby that to award the Nobel prize to an American *belletrist* pure and simple would be a very backhanded compliment to a nation which has rightly placed the militant author with a social conscience, whose pen is a weapon with which to cast down the mighty from their seats, above the idle singer of an empty day (a happy phrase which we owe, by the way, to a man who abandoned the position of the greatest poet of his time to preach Socialism at the street corner). Mr. Upton Sinclair is not a Henry James: he is rather a Daniel Defoe; and though Daniel still lives in his works after two hundred years, his contemporaries

61

put him where several respectable Americans would like to put Mr. Sinclair: in the pillory. The truth is that anything like unanimity as to the merits of an author is, or ought to be, fatal to his chances of winning the Nobel Prize. Thus Mr. Quinn's letter is all that was needed to complete Mr. Upton Sinclair's qualification. It should accompany any recommendation that is made in his favor.

Faithfully,

G. BERNARD SHAW

The 808 signed documents, a bulky package, were duly shipped to the Swedish Academy by registered mail and receipt was acknowledged; and that was the end of the matter so far as this deponent knows. Professor Quinn departed some years ago to that heaven which is reserved for qualified academicians, and I can imagine him sitting on a billowy cloud, twanging a golden harp and reciting a ballad about how he prevented a "muckrake man" from receiving the Nobel Prize for Literature.

GEORGE BERNARD SHAW

Whitehall Court (130)
London, S.W. 1
[date uncertain]

Dear Upton Sinclair,

The Glendale-Busick affair [an American Legion raid upon a meeting in a private home in Glendale,

California] is not one in which a foreigner can interfere without doing more harm than good. I have (at 75) a long experience of cases of the kind. They occur in every country; and they will continue to occur as incidents in what is called the class war—and which unfortunately is not a class war: If it were it would be over in a week; and those who are attacking the existing order of society must be cured by bitter experience of the notion that by repeating constitutional shibboleths they can obtain the protection of the forces of the established government. Whenever the American Legion calls the police the police will help it, because they are allies fighting in the same cause. In the Glendale case the police seem to have called the Legion, with the quite natural result that Mr. Busick was thrashed and his followers routed. What did he expect? And what on earth is the use of his complaining to the thrashers, or of your trying to persuade rich American visitors that Glendale is not a safe place to live in because Socialists are treated there as vermin? You could not give the place a better advertisement.

No: unless the Socialists can protect themselves they must suffer the worst the legionaries and the police can do to them. When they come to you indignantly demanding money and time to waste on lawyers to defend them in court and on protest meetings that only give the legionaries a fresh chance, you must tell them that you have something better to do, and that they must learn how to spread their ideas without knocking their heads against stone walls. The thing can be done, even while the legionaries enjoy a monopoly of their methods, and is being done by yourself and others without breaking of heads.

But in any case, I repeat, the Americans must decide for themselves whether they will beat up Mr. Busick or slaughter their Saccos and Vanzettis and Mooneys; for the moment a foreigner interferes, to yield to him would be an unbearable humiliation: perish a thousand Saccos first.

I enclose a copy of a letter which I am sending by this mail about the Nobel prize, which clearly could not be awarded at all without some guidance from the professors throughout Europe to the Swedish Academy and from former recipients of the prizes.

My wife reads your books with great devotion, which is your guarantee that when you next visit these islands you will be received cordially at our house. We are still at Ayot St Lawrence, but, as you see, have left Adelphi Terrace for a neighboring and much more comfortable flat.

Faithfully,

G. Bernard Shaw

GEORGE BERNARD SHAW

Ayot St Lawrence,
Welwyn, Herts
12th December, 1941

Dear Upton Sinclair,

I am up against the paper shortage in all directions. I am finishing a volume of senile ramblings to be called *Everybody's Political What's What, or Machiavelli Up To Date,* as I find myself in a world in which everyone knows the XYZ of politics, philosophy, religion, science and art, and nobody knows the ABC of them. A Child's Guide to politics is what is needed; and I, being now in my second childhood, and rather deaf and dotty, but still able to write a bit, had better write for non-adults: that is, for 100% Americans and English.

I want to have this book sold for ten cents or so, and printed in editions of 100,000; but I cannot get even the perishable stuff on which such editions are now printed.

The Webbs have had the remaining stock of their great book on Russia bombed and burnt by Hitler & Co.; and my unbound stocks have shared its fate; so the Webb book and most of mine are out of print and not able to get back into it.

Wells has written a letter to the *Times* about it; and I am inciting the publishers to follow this up with an agitation for either or both of two policies: (1) To make room in the ships for imports of paper (and here I cite your offer to send paper), and (2) To place paper making on the same footing as coal mining, munition work, and agriculture as a prime national necessity.

I think that is all that can be done at present.

I have been contemplating your extraordinary career and intending to write to you for thirty years, but have never found the needed leisure at the right moment. I have regarded you, not as a novelist, but

65

as a historian; for it is my considered opinion, unshaken at 85, that records of fact are not history. They are only annals, which cannot become historical until the artist-poet-philosopher rescues them from the unintelligible chaos of their actual occurrence and arranges them in works of art in novels, gospels, dramas, operas, pictures, etc., etc. Until this is done, history does not exist: that is why history is always late; so that the statesmen find themselves with a vivid notion of what happened up to, say, the civil war of 1860, and with no notion at all of what has happened since or what is happening today. When people ask me what has happened in my long lifetime I do not refer them to the newspaper files and to the authorities, but to your novels. They object that the people in your books never existed; that their deeds were never done and their sayings never uttered. I assure them that they were, except that Upton Sinclair individualized and expressed them better than they could have done, and arranged their experiences, which as they actually occurred were as unintelligible as pied type, in significant and intelligible order. I refer them to a play of my own, in which, by bringing Charles II into the same room with Newton and George Fox, and being joined presently by his mistresses, his brother James, and Godfrey Kneller, a collocation which never occurred, I have taught the spectator more of the history of the year 1680 than Macaulay at his best taught in a thousand pages. [*In Good King Charles's Golden Days*, 1939]

Lanny [the protagonist of the Lanny Budd novels], by the way, is just the right choice for a peg to hang your history on.

But dealing as you must with types, bear in mind that they have no individual counter parts. When you lately substituted for Waldorf Astor, Nancy Astor, and myself, a typical London political peer complete with fashionable hostess wife and literary celebrity promoted to the rank of diner-out and society clown, the type pictured was perfect; but it was no more like the three of us than you are like a Tammany candidate for the governorship of New York. I spent three weeks with the Astors at Cliveden last August. I had not been there for eleven years! Waldorf, though like myself he is an absentee landlord, is by temperament a Communist who offended his father by introducing a Bill in the House of Lords to enable people like himself to get rid of their peerages. Nancy is a unique and amusing phenomenon. It would take me a whole chapter to describe her. Her hospitability is utterly indiscriminate as far as class and party are concerned; only you must be "good" or you shan't darken her doors. She won't give you a strong drink, as she is a bigoted teetotaller. She is a Christian Scientist, and, though she is as fiercely Protestant as if she was a Belfast lady instead of a Virginian aborigine, she eschews the Church of England. A Speaker of the House of Commons told me that she was more trouble than ten Maxtons and Gallachers (both Left extremes). Her philosophy begins and ends with her being a good sort; and her being a Conservative means no more than that she lies where she was dropped, as the scope of her mind is not Marxian. I refused all her invitations until I happened to meet her in person at a London party. In ten minutes we were as thick as thieves; and that is what will happen to you if you come to England and make her acquaintance.

However, all this is only to reassure you that the cleverness with which the British aristocracy nurses Labor Leaders and such like into apostacy is lost on me. No London social patronage can impose on an Irish Shaw. I am not proletarian by origin, but super snob.

My wife reads your books to such an extent that I can seldom get at them. As they are too heavy for her to handle easily she has them cut up into sections and rebound for her.

I have a lot more to say to you, but this letter is too long already. It will at least convince you that I have not forgotten you and that you must not reckon our regard for you by the fewness of our meetings.

Faithfully,

G. Bernard Shaw

Lady Astor very kindly gave her consent to the publishing of the paragraph about herself.

GEORGE BERNARD SHAW

September 24, 1943

I note the new address.

I have read the article. It is sound in its wide scope, as it was sure to be coming from you; but how far our present available statesmanship can get with the job, and how far the Nazis have really carried it is another matter.

Here in England we are up to the waist in State-financed Capitalism (Fabian Fascism); and simple Waterloo Restoration, which is what our Diehards want, is impossible. We shall land somewhere between Fascism and Communism.

Government by Anybody elected by Everybody is death to democracy. We must have panels of the qualified. Lincoln's "of" and "for" are all right, but "by" will ruin us unless the people's choice is guided and restricted to capable rulers.

My wife died on the 12th of this month. During her long illness she read the Lanny Budd saga over and over and over again.

G. BERNARD SHAW

Shaw is referring to my article published in the New York Times, *Aug. 15, 1943, calling for internationalization of disputed territories in Central Europe.*

69

GEORGE BERNARD SHAW

Ayot St Lawrence,
Welwyn, Herts
6th January 1949

Dear U. S.

The story about my having written *A Giant's Strength* [my unproduced play] means only that the action of the last two plays I have written takes place in the post-war future. There is no other resemblance. The first of them is called *Buoyant Billions,* and described as a comedy. The other is entitled *Farfetched Fables.* The notion that they continue the biography of Lanny Budd is as baseless as most paragraphs are.

I receive L.[anny] B.[udd] regularly from Werner Laurie; but what can you and I say to one another about our books? We are in the same boat on the same tack. What we have to say has been said again and again for at least 8000 years, apparently without producing the slightest effect: still, there are little groups of Shavians and Sinclairites everywhere, whose influence, though imperceptible, counts for something.

Hardly a week passes but I get letters instructing me how to live forever or how to achieve the millenium in an afternoon. My first necessity is a waste paper basket.

I am half way through my 93rd year, and still regard you as a very special friend, though it is so many years since we met that I still see you as a young man.

70

That is all I can tell you that you can possibly want to know. Take it as a very appreciative wave of the hand.

I enclose a picture of what is left of me.

G. Bernard Shaw

A sad farewell letter and picture, which my wife and I received with tears.

IRVING FISHER [1867-1947]

New Haven, Conn.
1909

People on protein fasts have been known, so I am assured by a physician who has made a special use of this form of fasting, to have absorbed large tumors, warts, etc. for the body then uses the refuse heaps, so to speak, containing surplus protein instead of food. I have never tried a general fast personally, as I have never seen any need of it. It happens that I am now trying a protein fast because of a blood clot in my eye due to an accident in which I was hit in the eye by a tennis ball. The object is to absorb the clot, and as this consists largely of fibrin, the protein element in the blood, the purpose of the protein fast is to make the blood hungry for protein. This form of fast does not interfere with my regular physiological processes or my daily work.

I admire your openmindedness and willingness

71

not only to change your opinion from time to time with new light, but to declare it openly. I believe that the mind should be a steam gauge faithfully recording changes in evidence from time to time. Only the fool does not change his mind. Personally, however, I feel an obligation not to take the public into my confidence until I am, so to speak, 99% sure of the results. I have, therefore, thus far only published what I feel could be very fully substantiated, and experience has practically confirmed the conclusions which I have reached, the main conclusion being that those living on a low protein diet have far greater endurance than those on a high protein diet . . . .

I quite agree with you that the medical profession have been slow to take up this subject. They are always loath to do anything which bears the stigma of faddism among conservative people, and thus they often miss valuable new ideas, which, like wheat among the chaff, are sometimes misclassified with fads. I believe, however, that the medical profession will take up the subject more rapidly in the future, especially in view of the fact that such physiologists as Benedict in this country and Caspari in Germany have already given some special attention to it.

Your very sincerely,

Irving Fisher

Irving Fisher, professor of political economy at Yale, was the first in this country to undertake scien-

*tific investigation of the effects of diet. His results
supported the low protein diet which I have since
followed for most of a half century.*

JAMES HUNEKER [1859-1921]

New York City
June 22, 1909

Dear Mr. Sinclair:

You did not have to remind me of that poor old
scarecrow, "Melomaniacs," to tell me who you were!
I once called you, whether in print or private, I've
forgotten which—"The bravest man in America."
Col. Roosevelt utilized the phrase later. I may have
heard the opera, its composer says I did, but do not
recall the fact. He is said to be clever, though not
original. There is Harry Rowe Shelley, of the Lambs
Club (his address, I mean) organist at Rockefeller's
church. He has a gift for lyrics and is a capital brain
at the orchestra. Wouldn't it be a sweet paradox
for the Boss' oil-man's music man to make a setting
for a play by U.S. This by way of suggestion. Then
there is Victor Herbert—always busy—or Walter
Damrosch, or a half dozen of the younger crowd.
Arthur Farwell, or Shelley has a light touch, and I
note in the press that he has written incidental music
for a play to be brought out this coming season.
This doesn't mean, of course, that the man you name

73

might not do as well. It's a fluke very often, success with an unusual background.

Greetings from your old friend (in spirit)

JAMES HUNEKER

As author and critic, Huneker took up the duty of making America familiar with the new literature of all Europe. Reference is to a dramatic version of my novel, Prince Hagen, *which I wanted made into a musical comedy.*

KARL J. KAUTSKY [1854-1938]

Berlin-Friedenau,
September 25th, 1909

Dear Comrade Sinclair:

You have bad luck with us Germans. Your letter to the *Vorwaerts* did not get any answer and your letter to me does not get it directly. It was sent after me to the convention of Leipzig, where I read it and had the mischance to lose it. So I have not your address and must ask a friend of mine in America to send this letter to you.

Your manifesto against war I have read with great interest and warm sympathy. Neverthless I am not able to publish it and you will not find anybody in Germany—nor in Austria or Russia, who would dare to publish your appeal. He would be arrested at once and get some years imprisonment for high treason.

But that were not the worst. Sometimes one must take such risk, if something good for the cause comes out of it. But your manifesto were useless if it was only the publication of an isolated individual. Published not by an individual but by the party and approved by it, it meant the destruction of the party by the government. We are here not in a free country. But something worse still: By publishing the manifesto we would instead mislead our own comrades, promise to them more than we could fulfil. Nobody, and not the most revolutionary amongst us Socialists in Germany, thinks to oppose war by insurrection and general strike. We are too weak to do that—in that point Blatchford is right. I hope, *after* a war, after the debacle of a government, we may get strength enough to conquer the political power. But the German government is much too strong, to let us try an insurrection, when it prepares war. That were sheer folly. That's not my personal opinion only, in that point the whole party without any exception, is unanimous.

The only thing we can promise is: To oppose war with all our means that are not beyond our power. And that opposition is not without success. No government risks lightly a war, that is strongly opposed by one-third of the population. You may be sure there will never come the day when German socialists will ask their followers to take the arms for the fatherland. What Bebel announced will never hap-

75

pen, because today there is no foe, who threatens the independence of the Fatherland. If there will be war today, it won't be a war for the defense of the Fatherland, it will be one for imperialistic purposes, and such a war will find the whole socialist party of Germany in energetic opposition.

That we may promise. But we can't go so far and promise this opposition shall take the form of insurrection or general strike, if necessary, nor can we promise that our opposition will in every case be strong enough to prevent war. It were worse than useless to promise more than we can fulfil.

I hope these reasons are strong enough to excuse my not publishing your beautiful and powerful manifesto.

I am dear comrade, yours truly,

K. KAUTSKY

In January of 1907 I published a book, The Industrial Republic, *containing a prediction of war between the United States and Germany, with an analysis of the economic and political forces that were leading to it, and an appeal for measures against them. In 1909 I published and distributed widely a "Manifesto," calling upon the Socialists and the organized workers of Europe and America to realize the peril of a world war and pledge themselves to prevent the calamity by the threat of a general strike in all countries. Among those to whom I submitted this document was Kautsky, editor of* Die Zeit, *Berlin, who was generally recognized as*

the intellectual leader of the German Social De-
mocracy.

My dear wife wishes me to remind the reader
again that there were no Communists in those days,
and the word "comrade" does not have that evil
significance. The Communists have ruined many
good words—including "Socialist," which they use
with no right whatever.

KARL J. KAUTSKY

Berlin Friedenau
December 8, 1909

My dear comrade,

I see how difficult it is for a citizen of a relatively
free country to grasp fully our situation here. By
trying to bring your proposals to discussion here
you would do harm to your own cause.

There are two currents in the German Social Democracy. One is opposed to every revolutionary
movement, also to using revolutionary means in the
case of an outbreak of war.

The other one is revolutionary, but thinks revolutions can't be made artificially, but only by a
spontaneous outbreak of the working population.
If there should be such an outbreak in the case of
war, we think, it were very useful.

Till now we prevented an open discussion of the
matter, because in such a discussion only the opponents of revolutionary measures could speak

freely out. The revolutionary people could not speak freely without compromising not only these persons (that were a trifle) but their whole party in the face of the law.

Such a discussion would therefore only help the opponents of such measures and create among outsiders the false impression as if the anti-revolutionists and the patriots were the majority in our party, which is not true.

That false impression was already produced by the few discussions that took place at international congresses. And it is the same with Austria and Russia as with Germany.

So the only effect of a discussion, brought about by you, could be many protests from the anti-revolutionists, that are opposed to your proposals, and very few, if any, and very reserved consents to those proposals. Things would look much worse for you as they really are.

There is a tacit consent between both sides of the party to have no public discussion of our attitude in case of war, as it would be awkward for both sides. Both sides agree in so far, as we all think, without any exceptions, that it is impossible in Germany to prepare and propagate any organized action in case of war beforehand.

We of the revolutionary side are satisfied, when there is no public discussion of the matter, as that would only help the anti-revolutionists.

There is no fair play in a discussion where the one side is gagged.

This letter is of course a confidential one and not to be used publicly.

I am dear comrade

Fraternally yours,

K. KAUTSKY

VACHEL LINDSAY [1879-1931]

Springfield, Illinois
March 9, 1911

My dear Mr. Sinclair:

It is an honor to hear from you. I have forwarded the Village Magazine under separate cover. If the print is too fine, read the Heroes of Zuire. You will find the same idea there in the verses on Phidias, Michaelangelo and Titian, and the last stanza in the piece.

I hope you can send me something of yours in return. I would appreciate an autographed copy of *The Journal of Arthur Stirling* [one of my earliest novels, published in 1903]. When I was in New York I went through most of that, except I didn't go drown myself and get fished out—a demnition damp unpleasant corpse as Mr. Mantillini might say.

I hope the enclosed newspaper clipping will not

be crowding your attention too much. It shows our common ground, not indicated by the Village Mag.

Yours for the evolution,

NICHOLAS VACHEL LINDSAY

Lindsay was another poet who took his own life. He had given up everything for his muse. He wrote Rhymes to be Traded for Bread, *and went on the road and proved it could be done — all over the Middle West.*

VACHEL LINDSAY

Springfield, Ill.
August 25, 1914

My dear Sinclair:

I am glad you think it worthwhile to put my goods in your collection [The Cry for Justice]. My new book of poems by Macmillan — *The Congo and Other Poems*—is not particularly what you want—being just poetry. But my *Adventures While Preaching* that Kennerley brings out the 19th of September has just what you want in some parts—and just what will make you sore in others. I think you will particularly like the "Kallyope Yell" in the midst of the book—and the five proclamations with which it closes—you will view with mixed emotions.

I am sure Kennerley will send you an advance copy for review if you insist. But he would be more likely to send it on your insistence than mine—I

80

fancy. Be sure to ask him, and I will write today also.

Very sincerely,

<small>VACHEL LINDSAY</small>

Between now and September 23 the *Independent* may bring out a set of anti-militarist War poems. Watch.

VACHEL LINDSAY

Springfield, Illinois
January 15, 1915

My dear Sinclair:

I am sorry to be so long acknowledging *Sylvia's Marriage*. I read it with great interest, and knowing you a little, was interested in discovering as much of you in it as I could, and I am glad to be so much better acquainted. You can say if you want to in your advertisements, that I do not see how a story with a purpose could be more effective. It takes a generous and self-immolating soul to go upon such a thankless crusade as you have here undertaken. It is a chivalrous book all through. And I thank you for the soap-box idea. I have blocked it in, and I consider myself very much indebted to you for it. I will be in New York at the Poetry Society Banquet and make one of the speeches. I will be mighty glad to see you there.

Very sincerely,

<small>VACHEL LINDSAY</small>

81

VACHEL LINDSAY

Springfield, Illinois
February 9th, 1920

My dear Sinclair:

I have no objection to your cutting out any section of the Soap-Box poem you please, giving it a new title and using it anywhere you please.

> Here's to the soap-box
> The soap-box, the soap-box
> Battleship of thought
> The round world over—
> Feared by the chicken-hearted
> Loved by the lion-hearted
> Fair young amazon
> And proud red rover
> Loved by the Lion . . .
> Feared by the fox—etc.

and so on for about six pages. It was first printed in the *Chicago Tribune,* and then in *The Chinese Nightingale* and was entitled "This my Song is made for Kerensky" and was printed at the height of Kerensky's power.

So do not say I am a breaker of promises!

I wish you well. I give you and your wife my most fraternal greeting, and if your paper starts I will be proud to contribute as soon as I have something new—with or without compensation. [The monthly magazine which I had published for a year in the interest of "A Clean Peace and the Internation."]

Thank you indeed for *The Brass Check*. I will read it as soon as I am home again. I am now on the road. The stand-patters still fail to love me, sir!

Very sincerely,

VACHEL

HARRY H. KEMP [1883-   ]

University of Kansas
Lawrence
May, 1907

Dear Sir:

I was very glad to receive a letter from you, for I understand that you are one of the great men of the world who have taken the holy contagion . . . .

You remember the story of the shoemaker in the Arabian Nights—how he was taken into the Prince's apartments and awoke doubting the testimony of the five senses as to the reality of the pomp and splendor in the midst of which he lay? Well, I feel just like that man, in getting the good word from you and Mr. William Allen White and Miss Tarbell and the rest of the "American" [magazine] folks! I am glad that they think enough of my verse on modern industries and the quick vigorous life of today to admit it on their pages. Do not think, however, that I accept the present system as perfect. If God or the Great Unknowable or whatever power there is behind the show of things allows me life long enough to do so, I have a right arm to bare that will deal some tremendous buffets against the tiger-ish system of "the devil take the hindmost" which prevails today. My heart bleeds for the poor un-fortunates in the cellar of life, for I have had a ter-rible time myself, and what a villainous dog I would be to desert my associates. When I was younger—I am now twenty-four—I absorbed through all the pores of my mind the pageantry and the terror of the modern age: I roamed about this country some-what and I was a tramp, but my salvation came through the poets Keats and Shelley as others comes through religion. I have dedicated myself to poetry as a neophyte does to a religious mystery; and the poetry I have dedicated to the cause of the poor and the oppressed. If your eye detects too much smoke and fury in what I write, please ascribe it to my lack of knowledge; I am so ignorant, so ignorant, and I want to learn and need to learn so much before I can do as I feel the God within me demanding of me. I shall come to Chicago within four weeks; I expect a check from the *Independent,* and I have quit school for the rest of the term and will get a job husking corn, and what with the expected check and the work, I shall scrape up enough to see you, because I want to see you very much—you big fel-lows are like demigods to me and I would go to Hell and back to look in one of your faces and learn new things to put into verse. So you can expect

84

me in Chicago within four weeks or maybe sooner. Let me know where you put up there.

Yours most sincerely,

HARRY H. KEMP

Here is the soul of a youthful poetic genius, with all its ecstasies and agonies naively exposed—"the poet's eye in a fine frenzy rolling."

HARRY H. KEMP

University of Kansas
Lawrence
1908

Dear Mr. Sinclair:

You certainly do get about the country! I would be mighty pleased to visit you this summer. But I do not want to put you to any inconvenience. Let me know where you will be, when you are ready to have me visit you, and I will try my best to get thru. There is only one thing, after all, that claims my reverence, excluding God and manhood, and that is the hierarchy of literature. It will certainly mean much to me just to meet you and to talk with you. I intend to take Botany this term; I want to get a scientific knowledge of American flora. I want to know these United States from one end to the other, and when I write of flowers and throw about the purple colors in my verse, I shall sing of sunflowers—and even the jimson weed if need be— rather than prate of hyacinths and the conventional poseys of Greek myth-makers and their imitators.

85

We are having such splendid weather here; the sun is shining and the little English sparrows are chirping and flitting about, outside, on the roof and in the street. Life is a fine thing. I am glad I am alive. Whenever I send a snatch of verse to you, don't think that I am trying to force my stuff upon you and to take advantage of the friendship you have given me; poetry is so much a part of my mode of expression that I can't help dropping into verse or sending on little rhymes to those who are friends of mine.

Yours, sincerely,

HARRY H. KEMP

Is it true that you have whole fields of wind-bending lilies, instead of grass there in Bermuda?

HARRY H. KEMP

1908

Dear Sinclair:

Am out here in the middle of the state, spending the vacation with a college friend of mine. They are going to give a smoker for me here tonight. Wednesday night I am to talk in the opera house, and right after that the Kansas University students living around about are going to give me a banquet (more duck! but I'll be very careful). I have 35 poems, gotten up into suitable shape for a book, if any publisher can be induced to print them! I will work on them a few weeks longer, and then send them to you. I wrote a poem last night, called the "Song of the Dew Drop", a gossamery little thing. My

86

subconscious personality surprises me by taking different tacks every time an inspiration comes on me. I plan to come to California this April.

I hope that your play brings great success [*Prince Hagen,* produced by a stock company in San Francisco].

Accept my belated Christmas greetings, also wishes for a very fruitful and profitable New Year. While here I am reading the Talmud, that thesaurus of dust and diamonds, filth and rubies, and I find in it many of the sources whence Christ derived his parables and sayings. Christ was not as original as most people think. He seems to me to have been a sort of eclectic philosopher—but he always knew the true gem when he saw it, and taking it from the rough, gave it the setting of genius and soaring vision.

Yours sincerely,

HARRY H. KEMP

HARRY H. KEMP

University of Kansas
Lawrence
1908

Dear Sinclair:

I certainly appreciate the honor you confer upon me by letting me read your latest book before having it printed. I will read it and send it on as you direct, and as soon as possible. I wrote a deeply-felt poem on Christ's Death last week, and I am sending you a copy of it herewith. I have sent it to the *American*. My good luck continues; I have just received (last Monday) a check from *Wilshire*, and one from the *American*. Consequently, I spent four days in Kansas City on an artistic "debauch." I saw two art exhibits, heard Lhevinne play the piano, heard Elbert Hubbard and had a light lunch with him, and to crown it all most consummately, I saw Nazimova play in *The Doll's House*. I hardly have slept for three nights, I am so wrought up over the time I had. I speak on poetry here in our Opera House on the 8th, and in Manhattan on the 17th.

When I was down in Kansas City the newspaper fellows gave me the glad hand, and I had dinner at the house of the Editor of the *Post*. But I didn't touch a drop of intoxicating liquors, tho they tried hard to load me up on "high balls." I have the most glorious times! I work and work and work. For the first time I have felt the joy of consecutive determined work and creative effort. Give me a hundred Buddha reincarnations and as many hands as a Hindoo Goddess, that I may adequately express my soul. I might come to see you for a couple of weeks this spring; but when the lakes open up thither must I go, and God prosper you!

Yours sincerely,
HARRY H. KEMP

Got your books from New York O.K.

Am sorry you are not coming back this way, I had planned to show you a good time!

He went to the Great Lakes to earn his bread by a job on an ore-boat. He earned it, and found poetry in the doing.

88

HARRY H. KEMP

1909

Dear Sinclair:

I only wish that your letters were longer. I think
that the Past has us beat in one thing, and that is
in the art of letter-writing. I would that we moderns
had time to practice it more—to write letters to our
sons and daughters, and rounded and ripened in the
garden of leisure and meditation. I wish I were with
you in that quaint old fashioned Florida town. It
must be ancient and quiet—and silence is holy and
it heals the soul. I now, in this fine weather, often
take a boat, and, like Shelley, row far up the river,
and, anchoring in a quiet cove, write till sundown.
I land poems with the *American* every little while.
Am very sorry that you could not come through
Lawrence, but will see you in New York this fall,
I hope. I told you a lie when I was with you. I told
you that I was not in love, but I am and have been
for over two years. And the girl won't have a
damned thing to do with me. She is now away from
here. She was a college girl and was so beautiful
that all the boys went crazy over her—and I was one
of them. She is tall and slender, like one of Maeterlinck's Princesses. My love for her is like a tempest.
I can't forget her. And by God I am going to get
her yet. I hope this confession will make amends
for my lie.

Yours sincerely,

HARRY H. KEMP

89

December 6, 1909

Dear Upton:

I have reached the conclusion that I can never hope to get a long letter from you. Dr. Frederik van Eeden has been here the last week, over-seeing a rehearsal of his play, *Ysbrand*. It is a problem-play dealing with new psychic phenomena, and I am to star in it. It is an all-university affair. Am going to make a hit, I believe. I am the only inexperienced actor in the cast of fifteen persons, all the others having had amateur experience. There is a great spiritual similarity between your plays and those of the Dutch author's; your play which I read this summer is just as good as either of the two of his I have in my possession now. I am to translate one of them into modern English, into blank verse. Have myself written two tiny one-act plays, which have been forwarded to the *American* editors. Have been thinking over your plays and have arrived at the conclusion that they are about twenty years ahead of the American theatre. But van Eeden is doing the same thing in Europe—and Strindberg also! But I would rather be the author of the "problem play" (so genannt) than of the cheap melodrama!

Your friend,

HARRY KEMP

I had given his poems to the Dutch poet and novelist, Frederik van Eeden, who in turn sent Kemp his drama, Ysbrand. *Van Eeden was then in New York.*

HARRY H. KEMP

January, 1910

Dear Upton:

If we can get the faculty to permit it, we will put the van Eeden play on in Kansas City, Topeka and Emporia. But I doubt if we will be allowed to do so—it is so contrary to all precedent, you know! I wonder what our faculty fathers would do if they were in the pre-Adamic state? All the precedent they would find would be to be protoplasms! Enclosed find copy of your prospectus. Several professors here, who are radicals and friends of mine, say that that literary academy would be a great thing—as great a thing as Nobel prizes . . . . . You folks are so perfectly unconscious of yourselves, and naive, and Shelleyan, that it is pleasant to be with you—I wish I were with you now for a few weeks— but I would not want to stay much longer than that; we are too high-strung to stay together longer without quarreling. Even Goethe and Schiller differed. Am glad you are progressing so finely in your new novel. I hope it surpasses *The Jungle.* Yet I am leary of this damned sex-question. I am not going to try to solve it for mankind. I have hard enough work solving it for myself. For my blood is always running riot within me, and I have to wrestle with my nature as one wrestler wrestles with another; yet I

91

am now finally and incurably in belief a monoga-
mist. I will go further than that—I believe that a
man ought to live up to the standard the purest
woman lives up to—it is only then that the finer
mating instincts are preserved. Such a man will
unerringly marry for love, not lust—and then divorce will never be necessary. With love in the
heart it is filled too full then for sex or evil. This is
the kind of a man I vow to be, by God! I exercise
about two hours daily, and am beginning to take on
flesh. I hope to be a real man in all respects, some
day. I want to belong to the true aristocracy, the
aristocracy of God; that aristocracy the members of
which excel in the harmonious adjustment of a complex being to all spiritual, ethical and eternal things.
I want my body and soul to run as regularly together as a Waltham watch. I will in the future to
all letters I write subscribe my bare name.

HARRY KEMP

HARRY H. KEMP

February 11, 1910

Dear Upton:

I received, yesterday, $250 for six months living
expenses, from Mr. Fels. I have plunged now into
a great shining sea of calm, a sea that lifts and
swings and bears me on and on. You don't know

92

how happy I am. I have such a feeling in my heart of consecration to poetry, that I feel positively holy.

How can I ever thank you for this, or repay you? Do you know what you have done? You have saved the life of my poetry—what more can I say! I feel incoherent and smitten down, like a blind man whose eyes are suddenly flooded with the sunlight.

I will write you a longer letter soon.

Thank you!

Harry Kemp

Your friendship toward me is beyond my comprehension as yet—it is almost like the Love of God.

"Fels" is Joseph Fels, soap manufacturer and philanthropist of Philadelphia.

HARRY H. KEMP

June, 1910

Dear Upton:

Another word. Please write immediately telling me where you are so that I can ship on the manuscript of novelette, "Before Bridal." I will ship it C.O.D., and will later on refund what it costs you to send it on to some publisher you know. I think it will make a sensation. I have read it to a half-dozen friends and they like it. Also will ship Fairy Play within two weeks.

Now is the time I'll show you that I haven't been loafing on the job. I have never in my life been so happy, so free, so inspired. Am nearly always like an intoxicated man through the ecstasies of my poetry. Fels, may I say, has never done a thing which he will in the future be so proud of as this.

The whole first act of Judas is nearly driving me mad with joy as it marches about in my brain.

Yours in gratitude,

HARRY KEMP

Poor fellow! All of this joy and gratitude in return for $250 worth of relief from six months of hampering poverty.

HARRY H. KEMP

August 11th, 1910

Dear Upton:

Well, the first six months of my career as a care-free author are over with. I do not know whether Mr. Fels is going to give me further grace or not. If not, I shall be compelled to lay aside "Judas Iscariot" indefinitely and go to work. However, though I do plunge again into the Hell of poverty-stricken poethood, you have in me, I believe, proved your contention that a poet can do better if removed from temporal worries. I believe that my fairy play (which is nothing but a forerunner of what I mean to do) was worth any amount of perishable goods of this world invested in me.

94

I know that my "Judas" will be ten times better. For the former is but my first effort at continuous creative work. Fels is trying to land my fairy play in London.

I have been so happy in my work these few months, excepting the last month, that words can hardly express it. I am going to dedicate that play to Fels, and my books of poems to you.

Six months is hardly an adequate test of your contentions, but yet, I think, Upton, that I have proved you right—that a poet need not starve in order to be a true one.

About apologizing for what you said about the girl. You told the Truth. Truth needs no apology. She was a miserable little snob. A poet should but live for his Art, after all—though it is hard to be cut off from the human things of life because of one's art. You mustn't mind when I write so much about myself. It isn't egotism that makes me do it; I do it because I believe you are my friend, and I must tell somebody of my inner life. Let me hear from my drama as soon as you can; but I expect to hear the worst.

I thank you and Fels for six months rest in an oasis. Now it is perhaps the desert again. But maybe not, maybe I might get another lease on life. Well, let me hear from you soon.

Yours sincerely,

Harry Kemp

95

JULIA WARD HOWE [1819-1910]

Oak Glen
Newport, R.I.
July 1st, 1910

Dear Mr. Sinclair:

I find to my regret that I must ask you *not* to
publish the matter which you have sent me. If you
would tell me for what reason you wish to do so,
I might possibly meet your object by writing something else, but if you only wish to make public the
fact that I have made but little money by my writings, I think it decidedly best not to impart this
knowledge to all the world. I think indeed that I
have made a fair profit on what I have given to the
public.

Yours sincerely,

JULIA WARD HOWE

*In my efforts to get endowments for young crea-
tive writers, I had asked to quote what the author
of "The Battle Hymn of the Republic" had told me,
in 1903, about the very small earnings of her poems.*

EDWIN MARKHAM [1852-1940]

May 26th, 1910

Dear Mr. Sinclair:

I enclose a letter that may serve you in your *Independent* article: but it just comes to me that your

96

plan does not apply solely to poets, and unluckily I do not happen to have your first letter at hand to relieve my doubts with. So let me say that if I have made a mistake in my letter, you must return it to me for my immediate correction.

The enclosed review may have a passing interest for you. You will see that while I have a deep interest in your social gospel, still I am forced to make a gentle protest against the moral purpose when it is pushed a little too far into the front of the stage. But I know how hard it is for us who feel strongly to keep our message toned down to the severe demands of literary art. I am aware also that there is a wide margin for differences of opinion as to what are the artistic demands.

Always faithfully yours,

EDWIN MARKHAM

He had created a sensation with his "Man with the Hoe," and he continued a friend of the oppressed to the end of his long life. The reference is to my call for an endowment for young poets.

GEORGE BRANDES [1842-1927]

Paris
April 17, 1911

Dear Sir:

I am traveling, and no books or printed matters are sent me; otherwise I should have with me the biggest luggage ever seen.

I was rejoiced to see the handwriting of a man, whom I have long time admired, and shall read your book when after months I return.

Sincerely,

GEORGE BRANDES

Brandes, Danish critic, was generally recognized as the literary mentor of Europe.

GEORGE BRANDES

Hotel Astor, New York
June 2, 1914

Dear Friend:

I live for a week in this city exposed to all the tortures of that infernal machine the telephone, worser than any instrument of torture in the medieval times.

Come and take me away from it for an hour, when you are free. I am bound at dinner the fourth, have a little leisure the following days.

Sincerely,

GEORGE BRANDES

When Brandes visited New York he asked Arthur Brisbane to bring us together. At lunch he stated that at the steamer he had told the reporters he considered three American novelists worth reading— Frank Norris, Jack London, and Upton Sinclair. But next morning all but one paper reported him as saying "two novelists, Frank Norris and Jack London." He asked me, "Why?"

98

GEORGE BRANDES

Copenhagen, Denmark
June 25th, 1914

Dear Friend:

I am anxious to know, how the result was of your efforts in Tarrytown. Was it allowed to you to speak publicly? Took they my letter into any consideration?

I thank you very much for *Love's Pilgrimage*, which is of great interest to me. I read almost the half of the book on the ship. I am glad to have made your personal acquaintance, and I don't understand how years ago I have wrote you a postcard as that of which you spoke.

Will you do me the favour of writing only a line or two, a short sentence of yours, for the album of my only daughter. When she was a child her album was inaugurated by Henrik Ibsen. Since all Scandinavians and almost all authors in France, Germany, England and Russia (even the old Tolstoy) have written her. As she heard that I knew you personally, she tormented me for a line of yours.

I beg pardon for the trouble. I try to put a little order in my not too numerous American experiences, but I am only arriving.

Sincerely yours,

GEORGE BRANDES

The Tarrytown reference is to a "free speech fight." He had given me a letter to be read to the town trustees—who paid no attention to it.

99

GEORGE SANTAYANA [1863-1952]

Colonial Club
Cambridge, Mass.
1911

Dear Mr. Sinclair:

Let me thank you for your book, and for remembering the interest which I have always taken in your work.

If the *freedom* of your descriptions in this book is attacked, you will be in the right in defending yourself; if the *aesthetic value* of them is denied, you can only wait and see if they do not find admirers. I will say frankly that I do not care for them myself. I prefer the *Arabian Nights*. Nor am I sure that the moral to be drawn from such a picture of strained and hideous situations would be always the one you would approve. They might seem an argument in favour of celibacy, or of convention.

Yours truly,

G. SANTAYANA

Santayana, Spanish-born philosopher and poet, is referring to Love's Pilgrimage.

GEORGE SANTAYANA

London
August 27, 1914

Dear Sir:

Your project [*The Cry for Justice*] is an admirable one, and I should be proud to think that some

100

chance word of mine should ever come to figure in such a new gospel. The war has separated me from my books, and I have to rely on a most inaccurate memory, but I think in Vol. 7 of *The Life of Reason,* which is entitled *Reason in Society,* and particularly in the chapters on Government and War and on Democracy, some epigrams and sentences might be found that touch upon the ideal of a just society. If you are not in haste, I might in a few weeks (when I expect to be near a friend who—rare phenomenon!—has my books in his library) look these chapters over, and possibly submit a few extracts to your inspection. Otherwise it would be better, if you think the matter worth pursuing at all, to ask some person with a sense for such things, to read the chapters I have indicated—they are not long— and see if he finds anything quotable in them. It is always safer not to let a parent judge of the relative beauty of his children, for he may prefer his ugly ducklings, as most truly resembling himself.

Believe me, with best wishes for your enterprise.

Yours truly,

G. Santayana

101

Villa Des Nefliers
Avon-Fontainebleau
February 1910

Dear Mr. Sinclair:

Many thanks for your letter. I will certainly speak to any managers about your piece that I think likely to be interested in it. I should not however care to meddle with the piece itself. I could not handle this kind of thing. Among my earlier books, the ones I most care for myself are *A Great Man* and *Whom God Hath Joined*. But *The Old Wives' Tale* is better than these, and so is *Clayhanger*.

Believe me.

Yours sincerely,

Arnold Bennett

Bennett, prolific British fiction writer, is referring to my dramatization of my novel, Prince Hagen, *which tells how the grandson of Alberich, the Nibelung of Wagner's* Rheingold, *brought his gold up to New York and took possession of its business and high society.*

ARNOLD BENNETT

Avon-Fontainebleau, France
September 19, 1910

Dear Mr. Upton Sinclair:

Many thanks for your letter and *Prince Hagen*. I found the letter awaiting me after a long absence from home. You have certainly got hold of a great theatrical idea. I am absolutely certain that its radicalism would not stand in the way of the play's production in England. The only criticism that I should venture to offer the piece is that it is too summary, too short, and imperfectly realistic in detail. My notion is that once the central idea is accepted, all the rest ought to be on exactly the same realistic plane as, say *The Jungle*. I should say that quite probably your agents will find a theatre for it in London. Or why don't they offer it to the Manchester Repertory Theatre—which is a first class affair in every way?

Believe me, with best wishes.

Yours sincerely,

ARNOLD BENNETT

Prince Hagen *was produced in San Francisco by a stock company.*

103

ARNOLD BENNETT

Author's Club
2 Whitehall Court
London
March 30, 1911

Dear Mr. Upton Sinclair:

I have read your prodigious and all-embracing *Love's Pilgrimage.* I should very strongly resent its being censored in England. It deals candidly here and there, with sundry aspects of life which are not usually dealt with in English fiction, but which are dealt with quite as a matter of course in the fiction of all other countries except the United States. It deals with these matters in an admirably poetic, lofty, and honest spirit. And no person of real intelligence *and experienced in first-class imaginative literature* could possibly object to this book on this score. Nor could the perusal of it work anything but good in the mind of any person whatever. That there should be any question about its reception merely shows the wrong-headed hypocrisy and provinciality of the English-speaking public's attitude toward art.

Nevertheless I have no sort of doubt that when your novel is published in England it will encounter very considerable opposition, official or otherwise. I shall profoundly regret this opposition, and shall be ashamed of it; and I shall publicly object as I always do on similar occasions.

Yours sincerely,
ARNOLD BENNETT

104

Upton Sinclair and son David,
Princeton, about 1905.

Upton Sinclair and Cornelius Vanderbilt, Jr.,
in the garden at Monrovia, 1957.

Upton Sinclair in his study, the "pink house,"
Pasadena, around 1943.

George Sterling, American poet,
at Carmel.

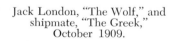

Jack London, "The Wolf," and
shipmate, "The Greek,"
October 1909.

Upton Sinclair selling the "fig leaf" edition of
Boston, Boston, 1928.

H. L. Mencken at home, Baltimore, 1927.
Bettmann Archive.

George Bernard Shaw in his garden.
Indiana University Library.

Sinclair Lewis at the beginning of his
career. *Bettmann Archive.*

Albert Einstein. *Indiana University
Library.*

Thomas Mann. *Bettmann Archive.*

Mahatma Gandhi. *Bettmann Archive.*

ALFRED RUSSEL WALLACE [1823-1912]

Old Orchard,
Broadstone, Dorset
May 3, 1912

Dear Mr. Upton Sinclair:

I think such a "League" as you suggest is wanted, and I hope it will succeed. Later, if you get, say 1,000 members, I will join you, but I can do very little now, either financially or by personal assistance, as I have already all I can do in my ever-increasing correspondence.

Should you, or any one who fully shares your views on Social Reform be able at any time to call on me, I might make some useful suggestions, or at all events discuss them. Things, at length, seem moving. The Railway strike—the Coal strike, and even the *Titanic* disaster, *must* open peoples' eyes, and prove to them 1st—that they are *absolutely* dependent for *their* very lives on the humblest of the workers they so much despise; and, 2nd—that the "Captains of Industry" they are so proud of, and without whose *wisdom* in *organization!* they think the workers can do nothing, are such gross bunglers that they cannot safeguard the *property* or the *lives* of themselves and their fellow capitalists! A Committee of *Stokers* and *Stewards* could not possibly have so grossly blundered as did the owners and the *Captain* of the *Titanic*.

Yours very truly,

ALFRED R. WALLACE

105

Written at the age of 89 in a firm clear hand by the eminent scientist, whose radical political attitude I have never seen mentioned anywhere, who with Darwin was co-discoverer of the theory of evolution. He is referring to the proposed International League which Frederik van Eeden and I were attempting to organize to stave off the impending war.

ISRAEL ZANGWILL [1864-1926]

Far End
East Preston, Worthing
May 4th, 1912

My dear Upton Sinclair:

I have received your programme, but have only time to say now that I hope you realize what it means to form a political party, especially an international one. I have experience of this on a small scale (Jewish) and it certainly leaves me no time for anything else. I think you cripple your chances by pinning yourselves so definitely to Socialism. International Socialism to some extent already exists. What does not exist is the International League defined in your fourth paragraph, but how this paragraph with its welcome to all free thinkers is compatible with your second paragraph I fail to understand. Instead of uniting all lovers of justice you pin them in advance to a single theory, which, important though it may be, is far from covering the whole of life, and taken alone is really materialistic.

106

Will you kindly tell me the name and address of the charming lady who edits *The Syndicalist* and sat at my side during your dinner. I rather fancy that you were living in her house.

With kind regards and hoping your new book will be a success.

Sincerely yours,

ISRAEL ZANGWILL

Israel Zangwill, author of Children of the Ghetto, *was an English novelist whose themes were the Jews of London. He presided at a public dinner given to me in London at this time. Another of his kind letters appears later. The lady was Mrs. Gaylord Wilshire. Mary and Gay were our close friends up to their deaths. They edited* Wilshire's Magazine *in New York, Canada, and London; being Socialist, it had many enemies. It is amusing to compare Zangwill's reply with Bernard Shaw's on the same subject.*

PETER KROPOTKIN [1842-1921]

Brighton
May 28th, 1912

Dear Comrade,

I owe you many apologies for not having yet answered your note about the International League. There were quite a lot of small things in the way; Russian Famine Fund, the Lena Massacres, and

107

finally the affair of my dear friend Malatesta [an Italian anarchist—like Kropotkin, of the philosophic variety—meaning that he used books, not bombs]. You ask me whether I am prepared to represent Russia as the signer of the League's preliminary invitation.

To tell the truth, I don't think that anyone beside the organized labour syndicates themselves ought to come forward with the foundation of a similar league. The duty of us intellectuals, is simply to help by all means their movement whenever they ask our support and to try to spread among them, by our publications and personal influence, the more general ideas of social reconstruction. A separate International League may even be an undesirable source of conflict.

Besides, I don't think that any League of Intellectuals has the right to tell them which methods they have to use in the struggles between Capital and Labour,—the more so, as the methods are usually dictated, not by their wishes, but by the methods resorted to by the rulers of the day.

When are you returning to England? I should be desolated if I missed the opportunity of making your personal acquaintance. I shall be in London at the beginning of June. Kindest regards to yourself and Dr. van Eeden.

Yours sincerely,

P. KROPOTKIN

Russian-born author, scientist, and libertarian, Kropotkin was born a "prince" but dropped the title. His Memoirs of a Revolutionist *became a part of Russian history, and his* Mutual Aid as a Factor in Evolution *is a landmark in both biology and social science. I went to see him in Brighton, England; he kissed me on both cheeks and I can still feel his bushy whiskers. One of the noblest of men!*

PETER KROPOTKIN

> 9, Chesham Street
> Brighton
> December 22nd, 1914

Dear Sinclair:

The work you have undertaken is immense [*The Cry for Justice*, then in preparation], and I don't see how I could be useful in it. Our friend Nettlau, who collects for the last fifteen years anarchist and occasionally social-democratic literature, has already over *thirty thousand titles* in his collection, one title often meaning a paper that was published for twenty-five years in succession. Even in your, more limited field of "literature" which means, I suppose, the belles lettres, there is in Russian literature in every monthly issue of every review some novel, sometimes very beautiful, dealing with a socialist theme. I never attempted to collect such works, so that I really don't know how, with the enormous mass of work at hand, I could help you . . . .

How are you? And Mrs. Sinclair? Does not the thunder of the war reach you in America? I am

109

writing all the time letters in all directions asking everyone to support France and Belgium in their great struggle against the barbarian invasion.

With kindest regards.

Yours sincerely,

Kropotkin

MAXIM GORKY [1868-1936]

Capri, Italy
June 1, 1912

My dear Comrade Sinclair:

I accept the program of "The International League" as it is set forth, and I pray you to have me inscribed as a member of that organization, which could not be more timely than now. According to my forces I will do, without doubt, all my possibility to contribute to the work of the "League."

The program is translated into Russian and has already been sent to be published in Russia.

Permit me, Comrade Sinclair, to communicate to you some thoughts, awakened in me by the program. You will find their resumé on the sheets which I send you with this letter.

Receive my salutations and my fervent hopes.

M. Gorky

The "resumé" was an eight-page letter, also written in French by the hand of his wife. I quote two paragraphs:

110

"I would point out the formidable expenditure of intellectual and physical energy uselessly swallowed up by the militarism of our days; the degeneration, brought about by the conditions of labor, and the lowering of intellectual forces, much affected by the disquieting events, the permanent awaiting of social and national tragedies.

"Living in the atmosphere of events which cause the soul to shudder — something which in recent times has become habitual, as such events follow one another without interval—living in that atmosphere of blood poured out and general intensive animosity, the humanity of Europe cannot be in good health, and right now, when all the peoples of our planet are being awakened by the population of Europe, it would be necessary for them to have a great reserve of physical and intellectual health."

Gorky went on to outline a vast program of activities, wholly beyond the powers of a small group of intellectuals, with no backing and little free time. We had only two years in which to discuss and plan, before the calamity which we dreaded burst over the world.

FREDERIK van EEDEN [1860-1932]

Bussum (N. Holland)
May 18th, 1910

Dear Mr. Sinclair:

Thanks for your letter of April 30. I am very glad to hear you are coming abroad. I hope you will not fail to come to Walden. Write me early in advance that I may make sure not to miss you. I got your *Prince Hagen,* and it is exactly the sort of play I like. I wrote a drama, quite different, but with some of the same motives in it. Of course it will be hard work to make managers see that this is the sort of play they *ought* to perform and make the public appreciate. The public will appreciate it duly, if only well directed by managers and critics. The public will perhaps not quite accept the play at once, exactly for what I consider its virtues, i.e. its conciseness, its abruptness. They will like it more because of what I consider its weakness, i.e. its want of philosophical depth. The great riddle of democracy is not solved. But nevertheless it is a great play. Do not let yourself be fooled by managers. The managers have to listen to you, they always try to make the authors listen to them, which is the wrong way.

Yours truly,

Frederik van Eeden

I first met the Dutch poet, novelist, and social reformer when he came to New York, in 1908. In

112

1912 I visited him in Holland. He wrote at least one letter about every book I sent him. In Berlin we visited Erich Gutkind, poet and philosopher, who had an observatory on the roof of his home, so I called him "Sternengucker" (stargazer). Because van Eeden was bearded and patriarchal, I hailed him as "Urgrossvater" (original or most ancient grandfather) to the glee of a company in Gutkind's home. Both later adopted these titles in our correspondence.

Van Eeden's mind was the most universal I have encountered. He spoke and wrote fluently in English, French and German, as well as his native Dutch. He told me it was discouraging to write Dutch, with only seven million potential readers! He was the most popular poet, novelist and playwright in his country; he had European repute as a psychiatrist; and he established co-operative colonies in Holland and North Carolina.

His best-known novel, both at home and abroad, was The Little Johannes, and its theme a modern Jesus and his experiences in an uncomprehending world; its American title was The Quest. It had great success also as a play. In Amsterdam there is now a van Eeden museum.

FREDERIK van EEDEN

Walden, Bussum, Holland
July 25, 1910

Dear Mr. Sinclair:

What a good idea you had in sending me *Arthur Stirling's Journal*. Now I begin to know what sort of man you are. This is surely the best book you wrote and the work of deepest significance—even without you knowing it—published on American soil. I do not say the most perfect work of art, nor the most important for the present—but of deepest significance. And that you wrote it, in a few weeks, and that you are hardly aware of its significance—shows you more truly a man of genius than *The Jungle* or *The Metropolis*.

After this book a personal interview between you and me I feel as a duty. We must see one another and talk. And that plan of yours will get a better shape after that. I was afraid of the plan because I did not feel sure whether you had exactly those qualities, shown abundantly in this book.

Now, I know that my confederates are also yours.

I wrote a Tragedy in blank verse many years ago [*Ysbrand*]. It is, as a work of art, the greatest thing I produced. It has been translated into English and Mr. Heinemann has now the manuscript. I wish you would read it. When will you come? Gerald Stanley Lee will be here next week. I have to talk to you about wonderful books I discovered, and wonderful men . . . .

Yours,
F. van Eeden

114

FREDERIK van EEDEN

Bussum (No. Holland)
December 6, 1910

Dear Friend:

I finished your MS ["Love's Pilgrimage"] yesterday. Let me speak quite frankly about it. It is surely your greatest book, and very nearly one of the Great Books of the world. But then it ought to stop here. It is very interesting to know it has 90,000 words, and will have 250,000,—but I am sorry to say I do not care for the 160,000. "Birth" is the climax and ought to be the end. You give wooing, marriage, pregnancy, birth in great classic lines. This is general, universal, typical. It is the working of Life seen by a modern temperament. All petty, personal, individual facts are spoiling the monumental structure. Of course you have read Zola's description of a birth. Yours is better because it is more human, more poetical. It is one of the best things in English literature. But it ought to be free from all personal details. I did not find any impropriety in it, not in the whole work.

You must be aware that you repeated much of Arthur Stirling's "Journal" in this book. Now this is all right, because this book is better. We may treat the same subject as often as we like, if we do it to improve. But you have not yet seen why Arthur Stirling was so antipathetic to many people, and your Thyrsis [the hero of "Love's Pilgrimage"] has similar defects which you do not seem to consider as defects. You, the writer, seem to feel sympathetic

115

toward qualities of Thyrsis, that many people cannot admire. He is far more egotistic, violent and ambitious than his poetical mission can explain or atone for. . . . .

Let me give you an idea how this young conceited genius can irritate me. I have been one of the most productive authors in my country and yet I have never been able to live and entertain my family by my pen. I have been obliged to take alms from my relations, to work as a doctor, as a gardener, as a bread-manufacturer, as a lecturer, a.s.o. And I have always found that the less effort I made to write great things and to become famous, the easier it went. I never wrote anything with effort, it all came by itself, in leisure-hours, without worrying or strain—simply because I never hunted for it. I had all the pangs of pregnancy, all the pains of birth—but I never isolated myself from the world, nor wanted everybody to make way and help me. I never made such a terrible fuss about it as this strenuous young man. I took care first of all to do my social duties, to feed and clothe my wife and children and then, if my genius would let me make something beautiful I would leave it to Him. Thus far I was not disappointed. And the more I did practically the easier I could write, the more food I found for my art . . . .

What a pity that you are not near so that we could talk matters over. I do not know whether you are able to stand frankness. In conversation this is so much more easy to find out. You will understand

116

that I would not have written all this if I did not sympathize and admire.

With cordial greetings to you and Mrs. Sinclair.

Yours,

F. van Eeden

FREDERIK van EEDEN

Bussum (N. Holland)
1911

Dear Friend:

I have been reading the rest of your novel [*Love's Pilgrimage*] and it pleased me much better than I expected. It is very long, and I never thought I would finish it all, but I could not stop and stayed up at night, which I hate to do for a book, because it shows that the book is master for the time being, while I want to be master of the book. I congratulate you. There was one name that came to my mind while reading, and that was a great name: Thackeray. But you went beyond Thackeray in many respects. I wonder how old you are, and what we may still expect from you. But it is sure that you are rising marvelously. Now my opinion may be not quite reliable because there is so much personal sympathy between you and me. It is all about things that have interested me too. And I wonder whether the public, that never wrote books, struggled with ideas, quarreled with editors

117

and managers, and staged plays, will be so interested as I am. I don't think so.

But that does not matter. England will soon acknowledge your power, and then you soon have more renown, more power and more influence than I could ever aspire to. Because you are a master of *English* language, while I am only writing in Dutch and dependent on translators. Of course, you will be attacked and decried, but that is all right. This book will make your world-fame. Even the Russians will appreciate it. And then—and then—for Heavens Sake go on straight, like Tolstoy, and give it them hot. I can grow quite excited in thinking what you will be able to achieve.

You see, we are both of royal blood, but what is the use of that so long as nobody believes in us? And the kings of the past generation—Hugo, Ibsen, Wagner, Björnson, Tolstoy—stood alone, had no communion, and did not use their power in an efficient way. The last ones: Tolstoy, Björnson, Nietzsche, were influential, but there was so much lacking in their philosophy, they did not kindle the fire of the immense store of fuel that is waiting for a spark. You will understand me. But you have, like me, the thirst for deeds, the burning love that knows no satisfaction before that great blaze is aflame that will sweep the world.

Thyrsis won my heart by such small things as that deer-hunting to get a railway ticket, and that building of his own house. He is not a whining and complaining literator. And curious was to me the coincidence of small details with particulars of my

118

own life. I have written a big drama, in two parts, where in the *Mondschein-sonata* plays an important role, and comes back at the end of the first part when the hero is dying and later in the second part at the death of his son.

And it was the *"Neue freie Volksbühne"* in Berlin that took up the play *Ysbrand* after its failure in Holland, and initiated its success all over Germany. Surely you knew nothing of this, because it happened only this last season. I wish I could go on writing to you, I feel very fraternal and want more than ever to meet you and speak to you. But I have no time, at present. Let me hear soon from you.

Yours cordially,

F. van Eeden

Ysbrand had been first produced in Amsterdam, Jan. 30, 1808, and in Germany later the same year.

FREDERIK van EEDEN

Bussum (No. Holland)
February 8, 1911

My dear friend,

Did you ever read my two New York speeches? "Practical Communism" and "Socialism without Political Evolution?" I have only a copy left of the latter, which I send you. Perhaps you can get the other in America. As you are reading German now, you can as well read my latest novel in German translation. I send it to you by same post. I read

119

the report of the social conference with interest. Do read *The New Word* and tell me your impression.

What a quaint sort of civilization the American is. A harmless benevolent old little gentleman with white hair and a ruddy face becomes a celebrity by telling people to chew their food and not to eat without appetite. One would take the U.S. for a great Kindergarten. And the author of *Love's Pilgrimage* is advertized as the inventor of a "fasting cure". Surely Health, Prosperity and Long Life are the American Trinity of today.

The other day I was pleased to see a Dutch Paper mention you as "the American Frederik van Eeden".* Of course, you were mentioned as a fasting curer (or curate?). In America my renown rested upon my "mind-healing" achievements.

With kindest regards,

F. van Eeden

*I wonder whether you will be pleased also!

FREDERIK van EEDEN

Bussum (N. Holland)
February 16th, 1911

My dear friend:

Thirty two! Thirty two! I was muttering this morning after receiving your letter. I have been of opinion that no author ought to be allowed to publish his work before he was forty. Present life is too vast and too complicated to be understood without long experience. We may write some of our best things before that age, we ought not to publish anything before we have fully ripened. Yet, I am exceedingly glad of your juvenility. What you want now is to take precious care of your nervous system. Never sacrifice one night's good sleep, when you can help it, even for the most urgent cause. We want your strength and freshness up to ninety.

Now about German books. There is only one great and mighty poet living in Germany—or rather in Switzerland, for he is a German Swiss—and that is Karl Spitteler. He is among the greatest of the world, and I do not know of one other living who is at his level. He is 65 now and not yet fully recognized. But his name is growing. We ought to go and see him someday, you and I, before he is too old. This plan is surging in my mind at this moment and I think it will happen. The two masterpieces he wrote are: *Prometheus and Epimetheus* and *Olympischer Frühling*.

But of course you want men who look into the future, not backward. Spitteler and Max Eyth and Gutkind and you and I are among those. And just the other day I found another man, a first rate one, Allen Upward, who wrote a book called *The New Word* (Fifield London). It was recommended to me by Gerald Stanley Lee and I found it a marvelous book.

I gave your book to a friend of mine who is an excellent translator. When she takes up the work you may be sure of a good rendering, and there will be no difficulty about a publisher.

Are you a friend of Lady Warwick? Or is there only a Socialistic connection? I took her always for a very foolish person and have a special antipathy for those English drawing-room socialists. But I may be quite mistaken.

W. H. Page, the publisher, who encouraged me to write for his magazine and promised to re-edit my books seems to have fooled me. He does not answer a word since three months. I can not help being fond of America and Americans, but your American ways are sometimes exasperating. First the big Drum and then . . . silence. Out goes the flashlight. Your days of misery are sure to come after this prosperity-boom.

Good bye and good luck to you, and may we shake hands soon.

Yours,

F. van Eeden

Lady Warwick was a devoted friend of the Socialist and Labor movements, attending all the conferences and speaking at meetings. I had met her in New York in 1906.

FREDERIK van EEDEN

Bussum (No. Holland)
September 13, 1911

Dear Friend:

I just got word from my lawyer about conditions in Holland in the matter of divorce. It seems that there are no more difficulties about that here in Holland than in Switzerland. The judge in Holland may pronounce a divorce between two Americans, married in America, provided one of them has his domicile in Holland.

The only thing wanted for you is to have an address in Holland duly registered, then the judge will help you. When you come in the district of Amsterdam my lawyer will assist you with pleasure. If the woman in the case does not oppose, the divorce is pronounced without proof. I hope this may be of any use to you.

I may add as an instance that we are in some respects a little ahead in civilization of America, that I divorced myself and remarried and that not one single item about it was in the papers, though you may know that I am in Holland as well-known a personality—and perhaps a more bitterly attacked one than you are. But never, never did my enemies touch on my private affairs. They were most rigorously respected.

With cordial greetings,

Yours

F. VAN EEDEN

Van Eeden wrote this knowing of my two painful failures in New York State. My divorce in Holland was as decently quiet as he had foretold.

KARL J. KAUTSKY

Berlin Friedenau
May 11th, 1911

My dear Comrade,

I am very glad to have written to you on your book [*Love's Pilgrimage*] before I had read the second part of it. I am more free now to acknowledge its beauties and deep thoughts, as I can say, I acknowledged them before I read the kind words you say about my work, and I was not bribed by them.

Your novel is indeed a masterpiece, grand not only from the artistic but as well from the philosophic and socialist point of view. It will create a deep impression and its publication will be of the utmost importance. Only hypocrisy and parasitism have a right to be shocked by it.

I hope you will publish the book in German as well as in English. We want it here too. Unhappily the way in which works of fiction are made accessible to the working people, is in Germany the way of publishing them in daily installments in the newspapers. Your book is not made at all to be published in that way, it would lose very much of its beauty by it. It must be published in the form of a book. But I am sure a publisher will be found easily for it, perhaps even a socialist publisher, although our party publishers are not doing much in the line of publishing novels, as that is done, as I have said, by the party papers in their Feuilletons.

124

Your quotations show me that you have mastered the German language very well. Is it the same to you, whether I write in English or in German? Perhaps you will understand my German better than mine English.

With the best wishes for the success and the speedy success of your beautiful work, I am, dear comrade,

Sincerely yours,

K. KAUTSKY

The novel was published in Germany in 1912 under the title Der Liebe Pilgerfahrt.

HAVELOCK ELLIS [1859-1939]

Woodpecker
West Drayton, Middlesex
April 4, 1911

My dear Mr. Upton Sinclair:

I appreciate your kind words about my work in your letter to my wife. Herewith I send a pamphlet, written at the time, which tells the story of the suppression of my 'studies' at the outset in England [as the English pioneer in sexual studies, Havelock Ellis's career had been one long controversy]. The latest volume of the series has been very well received in England.

Of late I have been very busy, and I have only lately begun to read *Love's Pilgrimage*. I cannot

125

say yet how I shall like the work as a whole, but I really should tell you that I welcome the frank way in which you face the fundamental problems of life. The book is probably destined to have great influence in English-speaking lands in bringing the novel nearer to reality.

Sincerely yours,

HAVELOCK ELLIS

BRAND WHITLOCK [1869-1934]

The City of Toledo
December 6, 1911

Dear Mr. Sinclair:

I hope you will find it in your heart to forgive me for not having written you more promptly about your great book, *Love's Pilgrimage*. Last winter I underwent an operation for appendicitis and I was in the hospital for a month. When I came out I had to take up the task of trying to solve the street railway franchise problem here, and you can imagine what that meant. I worked very hard at it, too hard in fact, so that I was sick again in the summer, and then when I got better I had to go into another campaign this fall—reluctantly, because I didn't want to run for Mayor again, longing as I did for the freedom that would be mine outside of this office, and pretty much filled with disgust, if not with despair by the idea of holding office at all, but I had to run again; it seemed to be my duty because the street railway problem was unsettled, and for me to have dropped out then would have meant surrender to the company. Or at least so it seemed, and so many said, and now I am in office again and rather unhappy over it all, though looking forward anxiously to the time when I can get out, and as I said, be free, or as free as any of us poor mortals can be in this world.

But I did read the book, sitting up two nights to do it, and I must congratulate you on a very sincere and very wonderful and very great performance; many parts of the book are of a poetic beauty, and it is all of the highest significance. It was brave in you to write it, and in writing it you have done a great deal toward setting our literature free, and that is a great thing for any man to do or even help to do.

I wish it and you all success.

Yours very sincerely,

BRAND WHITLOCK

Novelist and political reform mayor, and our minister to Belgium at the outbreak of World War I, Whitlock became a hero to that invaded people. His most widely read novel is The Thirteenth District.

THE BISHOP OF LINCOLN
[1843-1919]

Old Palace
Lincoln
June 24, 1912

Dear Sir:

From a rapid reading of some important pages of your novel *Love's Pilgrimage,* I am persuaded that your aim in writing the story was perfectly sincere, pure, and high-minded.

But I do not like 'Sex-problem Novels'; indeed I am inclined to think the libraries are justified in placing their ban upon them.

I cannot think that the intimate problems and experiences which gather round the marriage-tie can form a wholesome or helpful subject for romance.

Believe me

Yours truly,

EDWARD LINCOLN

The English publisher of Love's Pilgrimage *was in fear of trouble over the book, and I advised him to send a copy to every bishop of the Church of England. I wrote to them and several replied. All the replies were courteous, but in agreement with this example. The publisher had no trouble.*

128

ROMAIN ROLLAND [1866-1944]

Paris
October 3, 1912

Dear Mr. Upton Sinclair:

I send you the *Theatre of the Revolution* (with your fountain pen which I forgot to return to you). These three plays are only a part of the dramatic epic which I should like to write. I have written ten other plays which have been published in part and played.

I have been happy indeed to make your acquaintance, and you will do me pleasure in sending me your novels from time to time.

Au revoir. And believe, I pray you, in my sincere sympathy.

ROMAIN ROLLAND

Rolland, French novelist and playwright, author of Jean Christophe, *added a postscript, inviting me to come again and meet him and his sister at their mother's home, but my schedule in Paris did not permit. I carried for the rest of my life the memory of this benevolent man — a saintly Frenchman, though I know that sounds odd. A dreadful world war lay just ahead, and both of us saw it on the horizon, and labored in vain to prevent it. We corresponded through the rest of his life, and hoped to prevent World War II—again in vain. The letter was written, in French, while I was in Paris.*

129

ROMAIN ROLLAND

Schoenbrunn (Zug) Switzerland
22 August, 1919

Dear Upton Sinclair:

I have written you many times, in course of the months past—from Switzerland and from Paris—but it does not seem to me that my letters have ever reached you. I am going to try again today.

I would like first to communicate to you the text of a "Declaration of the Independence of the Spirit," concerning which I have taken the initiative, last spring, and which appeared just after the peace, in *Humanité*. It has already reunited a great number of Europeans, but almost no one in America—our letters have been intercepted. You will find a copy enclosed. Be so good as to read it and tell me if you give it your adhesion. A prompt response would be very welcome. Since the first list of signatures, a number of others have come, notably the adhesions of Rabindranath Tagore, Edward Carpenter, Leonhard Frank, Fritz von Unruh, etc.

I would like also to present to you an American woman friend who is about to return to the United States and who wishes to make your acquaintance, Madame Helena van Brugh deKay. She will tell you of various intellectual and social projects in which I am interested and which I should like you to know about. One of them, notably, which could have great moral importance: it is that of a New Encyclopedia of the XXth Century, accomplishing

130

for our time what the Encyclopedists of the XVIIIth have done for theirs—that is to say passing under the control of the free spirit of today all the moral and social values established by tradition, and preparing the path to a new humanity freed from the prejudices and the crushing errors which choke its development. The idea is everywhere in the air. One of my young friends in Germany, Wilhelm Herzog, whose review *Forum* has guarded through the war a courageous attitude, wishes to devote himself to it. Other independent spirits in France, in England, aspire also. Perhaps all the tendencies could be associated. I should love, for my part, to have America take the initiative in such a movement. Between the two oceans of Europe and Asia, she is the best placed to attempt to realize the synthesis of the human spirit. And her faculties of organization would be particularly precious in work of this ampleness. If you think that the idea would be of interest in the United States I will with joy put you in touch with the European spirits who would be the best workers in the enterprise. That is only an idea; but I have stopped to speak to you about it, because I consider you one of the spiritual forces of the world most capable of working to its realization.

I have passed some days here with our dear friend Frederik van Eeden. (You will have received without doubt a card signed with our two names.) What a heart, pure, ardent, full of love and of goodness! I love him profoundly. —We have often talked of you.

Goodbye, dear Upton Sinclair. I hope that you

will have some occasion to return soon to Europe. My sister, who shares all my ideas, reads me your new novel (for I do not read English well): it interests us passionately. We see that the struggles are still more bitter in America than in Europe. Patience! The torrent of life will not be arrested.

Affectionately to you

ROMAIN ROLLAND

The "new novel" was Jimmie Higgins, *a name for the humble, obscure worker in the Socialist movement, published in 1919. Rolland's letter is in French.*

WINSTON CHURCHILL [1871-1947]

Tahoe City, California

August 11, 1913

Dear Sinclair:

Your letter has just arrived, and I hasten to answer it. Believe me, I very much appreciate the generous spirit you show. And I have read what you say with care. And I understand, as well as a man can who has not been through your own bitter experience of earlier days, the strength of what you feel and the desire you have to help make things better. That it is an unselfish desire I know well. And you must write the novel you speak of, since, being born of such a desire, and reinforced by the knowledge

132

you have gained, it cannot but have a tremendous effect [my sequel to *Love's Pilgrimage*, never published].

I am sure I have failed to make myself understood by you in *The Inside of the Cup* if I gave you the impression that I regarded the kind of competition which involves the acquisition of property as a permanent and desirable thing. In fact, I have been criticized by some readers of the book for having predicted the coming of a time when property, private property, shall be done away with. And I have called the holding of it un-Christian. I put these words in Hodder's mouth when he was talking to Eldon Parr. It is, of course, not a difficult prediction to make, since evolution so plainly points to it. As to the small investor of the type of Garvin, whose case is taken from life, I cannot but regard him, in the present state of affairs, as more sinned against than sinning.

Of course, in the book, I was dealing with the present state of affairs. And I thought that there was no more room for putting in more theories than I did,—as there are already perhaps, too many. Personally I do not find Idealism, especially as set forth in such modern books as Bosanquet's latest Gifford lectures, in conflict with the great social movement. On the contrary. And I am indeed interested that a new social system shall replace this, one in which there shall be a far greater measure of justice. But I am interested in it for this reason: it is not that those who are now oppressed and starved shall have merely enough food and clothing and fuel, but that

133

they may be given the leisure and the opportunity to *live!* That their lives may flower, and that they, too, shall know the joys of the things of the spirit. Otherwise, to my mind, it were all useless. In this way, of course, they tend to become citizens of the ideal state. It is the business of the state to make such ideal citizens, and when we get enough of them we shall have the socialism so ably sketched by the authors and economists of whom you speak. It is all coming, and the leaven is at work.

You see, my particular temperament and development make me interested in this spiritual side in particular, and perhaps it is just as well that I should stick to it. It is evidently a task assigned to me. It is not, as I told you, that I would ignore the economic, and I have meant to take the first chance to study it. But I am working night and day at present, and cannot do it thoroughly yet. For some years I have believed myself to be a Socialist, as you put it, in the vital sense; and I tried to set this forth in the book,—that is, the difference between political and what I call religious Socialism. Do write me again when you have the leisure. I value your letters.

With kindest regards,

Sincerely yours,

WINSTON CHURCHILL

Of course, in Elom Pain's case, I was thinking of a solution for *him*, and not suggesting an economic solution.

Winston Churchill was, in his heyday, America's

134

best-selling novelist, author of The Crisis, The Crossing, A Modern Chronicle—*always a "C" in the title. I tried to persuade him to my ideas, and this patient letter is a sample of several he sent me through the years on the subject of the best methods of promoting the ideal social state.*

WINSTON CHURCHILL

Windsor, Vermont
April 28, 1927

Dear Sinclair:

Thanks for the book, and it was kind of you to think of me. I read very little now, and then only along certain lines which have come to interest me, and I do not know myself whether I shall be able to write anything complete on the subject—so it is a secret from me, too.

Sincerely yours,

WINSTON CHURCHILL

He had become a complete mystic.

FREDERIK VAN EEDEN

September 26, 1912

Dear brother:

I am much impressed by your saying that *Manassas* was to be a trilogy. You meant to give us the

135

whole war, and Lincoln's death? Brother, brother, this thing ought to be done. It would be a damned shame for a big wealthy nation like America not to give you the opportunity to do this work.

What could I do in the matter? Do speak to any publisher or magazine editor, to Kennerley or Holt or Boyden or Miss Tarbell or Page and show them this letter and say that I think there is a possibility of a great national literary monument, instructive, impressive, solid, aere perennius—say that to have it simply "out of print" and "not continued" because the writer had to write other books that proved pot-boilers—well! That may make later Americans blush over their ancestors—even if they had no better reasons for that.

I—for one—want to read the two next volumes, and I will do what I can to procure myself that pleasure.

Would any magazine take my expression of this demand—in the form of a review of the first volume?

Are you going to see people in New York or not?

Don't lose faith in yourself, Uppie. Hit again! Someday you will hit something better than the stomach, be it nose and eyes, that they cry and bleed . . . .

If possible go and see Kropotkin in Brighton.

Good luck, Brother! May we meet soon again, be it in our castle of Carrabas.

F.v.E.

Van Eeden is referring to my Civil War novel Manassas, *published in 1904; the other two volumes died unborn—of starvation.* Manassas *has been re-vised and republished, 1959, under the title of* Theirs Be the Guilt.

FREDERIK ᴠᴀɴ EEDEN

Bussum (No. Holland)
November 14, 1912

Dear Brother:

I got two letters and two cards, and the enclosed, which I return. Many thanks . . . .

Where are you flopping down, dear Uppy? What do you say about English November weather? Cheerful, eh? London especially. Spleeny gentle-men warming their hinder parts before herd fires with cracking fat coals, and the fog gently creeping in through the doors and windows, making every-thing hazy and unreal. To say nothing of the East-end and the slums.

I liked your article in *The Call* very much. Our minds are working more and more in one direction. I wish I could publish it somewhere on the conti-nent. But there are no papers for it. The S. D. won't take it.

I am just finishing *La Revolte.* I like that man Rolland very much. To see him would feel like meeting an old friend. I know so much of every-thing he is describing, it is such a familiar world to me. I met all his persons somewhere someday. I wonder whether Hassler is Strauss, and who is Jean

137

Christophe himself. What a nice talk we can have, Rolland and I. Does he know English? Do you correspond with him? Has he got some of my books?

He is thoroughly wrong about Brahms, and far too mild for Wagner. I want to talk to him. Yet I won't write before I know he would like the idea.

My congratulations with Wilson. Shall we go and make him a Socialist? More chance with him than with T.R. . . . .

Forgive my queer way of expressing myself. Paul is slowly improving [van Eeden's son]. The little ones are first rate. The lady of the house sends her love. Let me hear again from you and greet the Wilshires.

From your

URGROSSVATER

FREDERIK van EEDEN

Bussum (N. Holland)
February 22, 1913

My dear Brother:

Today came your letter of February 1st. Yesterday, Friday 21 of February, it was Good Friday for my dear son, Paul. His death was to me at the same time the worst sorrow and the greatest blessing in my life. His long illness had made out of an unruly, willfull, sensitive but ill-tempered boy a saint and a hero. I have seen many death-beds, but none like

138

his. His face was more beautiful than any Christ picture I know, and his kindness, his patience, his self-denial was angelic. His agony lasted from Thursday evening till Friday afternoon, and his only complaint was for us, because we had no sleep, and it was "so tiresome for us." He could not help, he said, that it lasted so long. He was fully aware of his situation and prepared everything with the tenderest love. "Do not send these cards with an ugly black rim. Rather give them a golden rim."

Until the last second he was fully conscious and kept into contact with us. His senses were wonderfully refined in the last hours, he heard every whisper, and answered every slight token. When the heart had entirely stopped beating and no pulse to be felt, he had still the force to whisper to us: "Now it must happen, now it must come," then he folded his hands, shut his mouth, opened his eyes wide, prayed and died in ecstasy, without a sob, without a convulsion. The expression of his face was so radiantly happy and beautiful that it left us all in gladness. We could not feel sorry, it was too great. You will understand what this means to me, brother poet, it is what a man wants more than anything in my career and at my age. I am walking in a trance today, and slept quietly this night after so many weeks of suspense. Forgive when I speak only of my own affairs this time . . . .

You will soon hear again from your brother,

F.v.E.

139

FREDERIK van EEDEN

Berlin
May, 1914

Dear Brother:

I am plotting again with the "Sternengucker" in Nicolas-see. I think I have found the right way at last . . . .

This last plan of mine is generally considered feasible and promising. We drew up a little expose whereto collaborated Gutkind and another man of practical insight and free mind. The idea is to give representative people, not celebrities but really noble, generous and powerful people of all nations who are not bound by prejudice—the opportunity of meeting, in a pleasant place, without any formality, during a few weeks of the year.

They will be invited and have the position of guests, but are expected to pay a small sum for board, when they can afford it, quite voluntarily. We will pay their railway ticket when they want it. Men of experience agree with me that the whole thing, including about 30 guests can be financed with a guarantee fund of about $8,000. And it will not be difficult to find this money. Mr. Kiebitzei—you remember him—will be glad to be of the party. I include a copy of the scheme.

I fervently hope that when the thing comes to realization you will leave your dear Bermuda for awhile and come with the H.E.

I am now looking for the man who can do the practical things, look out for the building, be treas-

140

urer and so on. I will be glad with any suggestions you make.

Have you received the second volume of *Sirius*? I ordered a copy to be sent to you, but I did not know you left Arden for good . . . .

With love

F.v.E.

"Kiebitzei," plover's egg, was my name for Walther Rathenau, the powerful German industrialist, who had invited van Eeden, Erich Gutkind (Sternengucker) and me to lunch at the Kaiserliche Automobile Klub and served us this delicacy—one of mine having a young bird in it. The "H.E.," himmlische Engel (heavenly angel), was Mary Craig, my second wife.

FREDERIK van EEDEN

Potsdam, Germany
June 14, 1914

Dear Brother:

A great marvelous thing has happened. The circle has been formed, it *is* there. Hardly can we trace the wonderful way of its realization. But each one of us feels that something great and wonderful has happened which nothing can undo. We all feel that the thing that came into existence is as powerful as a phenomenon of nature, and that its

141

creation was not the work of one of us or of our scheming. We feel to have been instruments obeying a power more mighty than the individuals. Yet each individual feels that he is losing nothing but only gaining. I will not try to tell you more in writing. You can only know the full truth by coming in our midst. We are expecting you. You belong to us and all the others accepted you by the confidence they have in Gutkind and me.

We are at present eight: Martin Buber, Däubler, Paul Bjerre, Henri Borel, Florens Cristian Rang, Gustav Landauer, Erich Gutkind and me. Further may the following be counted as belonging to us, though they have not yet attended a meeting: Hjalmar Wijk, Ernst Norlind, Upton Sinclair.

Moreover we are going to invite for the next meeting in Autumn: Romain Rolland, Walther Rathenau and Rabindranath Tagore.

The next meetings will be held in the fortnight beginning September 20th, the members gathering perhaps a few days earlier. The meeting place is *Forte di Marmi*, not far from Pisa on the seashore. This name is also determinating the name of the circle. The fortress of Marble is a place on the feet of the Carara Mountains where Michel Angelo built a castle to protect the shipping of marble for his statues.

This place offered so to say itself without our arrangement. We can have a house there on the seashore, all for ourselves, well attended and cheap. Board and lodging at 7 francs a person.

142

You are invited to come in that fortnight, and we shall be delighted to see Craig also. But it is to be understood that the invitation is personal in so far as membership of the circle is concerned and that the meetings can *not* be attended by any man or woman on the right of being a spouse of a member. Yet the meetings will take only a few hours every day, and there will be plenty of occasion to meet socially in the other hours of the day. We want all the members to bring their wives and we will try to find room for all. As to the financial question, this was solved easiest of all, and we did not give even ten minutes to its discussion.

One of us will guarantee that no difficulty of money will hinder the realization of the plan. Everyone is expected to pay his ticket and board when he *can* do so. When he is not able to do so he is requested to mention the sum he wants and we will send it to him. This is all, and we know already that the total expense will be much less than we can afford.

Of course, we want women to join the circle, but they are not so easily found. Membership will not be a sinecure, for it is a deadly serious matter to all of us. But I am sorrily in want of an Anglo-Saxon representative and so I hope fervently you will come. Until now we have three Swedes, two Hollanders, one Italian (Däubler) of German origin and the rest Germans, which is not a fair relation. And they all want in the first place other nationalities.

143

Write me soon, dear brother, I have plenty to do, of course. But it is glorious work, after what has happened. I had no greater time in my life.

With love,

Yours,

F. VAN EEDEN

P.S. Pray to avoid all publicity about this matter!!. We don't want to have any rumors whatever to come into the press!!

And just seven weeks later their world fell apart.

FREDERIK VAN EEDEN

Bussum (No. Holland)
July 25, 1914

Dear Brother:

I am grateful for your letter, but sorry you will not come. Let us hope you will change your mind. As I consider you one of us I can send you a copy of my notes concerning the meeting at Potsdam. Mind it is only meant for members! I am not conscious of any fear about Craig's breaking into the circle. I was only afraid of being misunderstood. It is very charming to read that she is so sure about her seducing power . . . .

I read with greatest interest what you have been doing in Broadway and in Colorado. It could make me envious.

Is Croton a little town and how far is it from

144

New York? Why are you staying there? Let me hear from you.

Yours,

F. van Eeden

I had not come, because I foresaw what was coming to Europe, and had warned him. On the day this letter reached me, the Kaiser's armies were on the march. Alas, for the poor human race—and especially for its poets and dreamers of social justice!

What I "was doing" refers to our so-called "Broadway demonstration," walking up and down in front of the Standard Oil building on lower Broadway, in protest against John D. Rockefeller, Jr.'s, treatment of his striking Colorado coal miners. It had the effect of completely reforming his labor policies; and it provided me with material for the novel King Coal.

WILLIAM DEAN HOWELLS
[1837-1920]

York Harbor
August 13, 1914

Dear Mr. Sinclair:

If you could find time to go through my books of the last thirty-four years, you might find something to your purpose. There are only about thirty-four of them.

Yours sincerely,

W. D. Howells

Howells, novelist and editor of the old generation, is referring to my query concerning The Cry for Justice, *the anthology for which I was collecting material.*

WILLIAM DEAN HOWELLS

New York
January 26, 1915

Dear Mr. Sinclair:

I find the Harper's still unwilling to let you use extracts from my books and under the circumstances I cannot press the matter. I am sorry I cannot meet your wishes in it.

Yours sincerely,

W. D. Howells

So the very charming early novel, A Traveler from Altruria, *is represented by only thirteen lines in* The Cry for Justice.

146

ARTHUR STRINGER [1874-1950]

Cedar Springs
Ontario, Canada
August 25th, 1914

Dear Sir:

Your letter of August the Tenth has been forwarded to me here at my summer home. Since I know of no individual who has done more than yourself to cheapen and sensationalize a profession which I prefer to follow in my own quiet way, I must ask to be excused from cooperating with you at any time or for any cause.

Very sincerely,

ARTHUR STRINGER

The sons of the Canadian poet graciously permit me to include this letter. They think that time makes a difference; and so do I. I grant every man the right to speak his opinions and to disapprove of mine. His letter was occasioned by my request to include one of his poems in The Cry for Justice.

ELLEN GLASGOW [1874-1945]

One West Main Street
Richmond, Virginia
October 8th, 1914

My dear Mr. Sinclair:

I am so sorry I can't help you about your anthology but I am so busy just now that I can't stop to look over my books. Several of them were written to express such a protest, and the verses called "Justice" in the book *The Freeman and Other Poems* give voice somewhat emphatically to my feeling about it all. They were written when I was very young—about eighteen—and when one comes to know more of life what one *thinks* about it seems to make so little difference to what it *is*.

Sincerely yours,

ELLEN GLASGOW

I am tempted to argue with the spirit of this keen-eyed and broad-minded Southern lady and novelist of both the old and the new Virginia. Yes, but is it not equally true that what Life is has been determined by what men and women of the past have thought *about it? Consider how much the thoughts of Washington and Jefferson—and the present Senator Byrd—have determined what Virginia is.*

MARGARET H. SANGER [1883-   ]

The Woman Rebel
New York City
September 23, 1914

Dear Comrade Sinclair:

Keep the copies, do. I am glad to have you have a set just to see what foolishness has possessed the P.O. officials.

148

Following are the articles on which I am indicted:

"Prevention of Conception" (March), "Open Discussion", "Can You Afford to Have a Large Family?", "Abortions in U.S." (May) "Marriage Bed", "Are Preventive Means Injurious", "Birth Control League", and the "Defense of Assassinations" in July issues—August issue held up on Birth Control League. If you should care to read them—you will be highly amused—I 'specially requested the inspection to wait a few weeks so that I could give them something to really indict me on—

Thank you for your interest.

Fraternally,

Margaret H. Sanger

The career of Miss Sanger, a lifelong advocate of birth control, has been a series of controversies.

MARGARET H. SANGER

International Planned Parenthood
Federation
Tucson, Arizona
February 17, 1957

My dear Upton:

So you, like me, "are there". We are tough ones, you and I. Certainly I am pleased if you have found any of my letters interesting enough to publish. Go ahead!

Yes, Upton, the "world do move," if we care to push hard enough and care to have it move. It is interesting to see how readily the idea of spacing pregnancies or controlling or limiting the size of the families has taken on in Japan and India. Japan within two generations may be the most cultural and eugenic of all nations. If she employs her 22,000 midwives to go into the homes of the fishing, farming, mining areas to teach and instruct the parents-to-be regarding birth control, her population will slow down in numbers and improve health and eugenic factors. Slums will be no more, transmissible diseases will be controlled, a finer nation will be developed. Watch it.

Affectionately yours,

MARGARET

Contrast this letter with the one forty-three years earlier, when she was welcoming indictment and arrest in New York.

LOUIS UNTERMEYER [1885-   ]

January 4, 1915

Dear Sinclair:

I have just returned the manuscript of your book [*The Cry for Justice*] . . . . I think it is one of the greatest anthologies ever attempted. Embodying as it does, many of the greatest utterances of the most inspired, it should rank with the very noblest works of all times. Not only for what it says but

150

for the manner in which it is said. Its qualities as literature are no less than its quality as Revolution. "A Socialist's Bible" is an excellent term for it. And you could scarcely have improved on its contents —it is remarkable in variety and scope. For one thing your very divisions give the volume color as well as contrast. With a few exceptions, it is all in one ringing key; buoyant but never blatant, power-erful and passionate. It has the spirit of a challenge and a battle-cry. I congratulate you again.

Sincerely yours,

Louis Untermeyer

Poet and anthologist, Louis ought to be a judge of anthologies, having produced so many of them, and more books on literary subjects than any other man I can think of. Always and everywhere an alert and liberal mind.

LOUIS UNTERMEYER

New York
August 12, 1915

Dear Upton:

The Anthology just came from the *Chicago Evening Post*. Thanks—and good luck to it. I had already begun a review (or, between us, a smuggled and badly disguised advertisement) of it for that same paper, and I'll send you a clipping when it appears. That won't be for a few weeks as I have some earlier stuff on the galleys out there.

I notice that several papers are fattening their columns with selections from *your* book—*without* credit. One in Philadelphia, (the name of which I forget), The *N.Y. Evening Mail* (a clipping from which I enclose) and, most inexcusably and most uncomradely, the *N.Y. Call.* Considering the time, expense, brainwork, etc. that you spent on the volume there's something exasperating (possibly because its so petty) in that mean kind of thieving. You ought to give the *Call,* in particular, a word to that effect.

I'll bet it's no hotter in Gulfport than it is here in the Sweltering City. "O Thalatta . . . Thalatta . . .". and similar apostrophes to the same cooling effect.

Again my best wishes and hopes for your fine achievement. Also, I hope you're all over your recent trouble.

Cordially,

Louis Untermeyer

SHERWOOD ANDERSON [1876-1941]

Taylor-Critchfield-Clague Co.
Chicago
December 12, 1916

My dear Sinclair:

Your letter set me thinking. It was a cold snowy afternoon in Chicago. I left my office at four and

152

started to walk home across the city. A man with a withered hand ran down a stairway out of a tenement. He had no overcoat and his clothes were thin. The blue veins on the back of the withered hand were ghastly blue. He saw me looking and stared into my eyes. His lips mumbled words.

A middle-aged policeman came along the street. A young girl came out of an office. The cold made her cheeks glow. She was alive with life and something in the stolid figure of the policeman tempted her. Their eyes met and he stopped and stared. He perhaps had a wife and family at home but he was stirred by the sight of the young girl who was not unwilling to flirt with him. His lips also mumbled words.

And so I went along seeing things and thinking. I also muttered words. I kept thinking of you and what you had said to me about socialists.

Man, you seem to see and feel them as things apart. You ask me to pity and understand socialists as you might ask me to understand the Arabs or the Chinese.

Truth is, Sinclair, I'm married to a socialist and when I vote I vote that ticket myself but if I thought the fact of my doing so set me apart in the way your letter suggests I'd quit in a hurry.

Really I'm tempted to go at you hard in this matter. There is something terrible to me in the thought of the art of writing being bent and twisted to serve the end of propaganda. Why should we as writers be primarily socialists or conservatists, or anarchists, or anything else?

153

Here is all America teeming with life that we haven't begun to really cut into or to understand. We aren't making our fellows understand it. It's wrong, man, terribly wrong.

Here is this man I shall go to lunch with tomorrow. He is rich, is piling up more riches daily. And he is becoming brutalized. Dimly he knows it. He wants to know about himself. God, he don't want me to preach at him.

I have a book coming next year called *Marching Men*. I hope you will read it and like it. But it also finds nothing of great value to the world in the socialists. My man McGregor meets and knows socialists. At one place he cries out to his marching men "If men preach at you from a box knock them down and keep on marching."

Sinclair, your letter was something like a cry to me. Can I not get into this letter the beginning of a cry to you?

I do so want to see writers quit this drawing themselves apart, becoming socialists, or conservatives or whatnot. I want them to stay in life. I want them to be something of brother to the poor brute who runs the sweatshop as well as to the equally unfortunate brutes who work for him.

Won't we serve better thus? We are so terribly young. We haven't even begun to understand our own American life. As writers can't we leave politics and economics to the more lusty-throated ones and run away, one by one, into the streets, the offices and the houses—looking at things—trying to write them down.

154

Damn it, you have made me go on like a propagandist. You should be ashamed of yourself. Come see me won't you when a wind blows you this way.

Very truly yours,

SHERWOOD ANDERSON

An American businessman who wanted to be a writer, Anderson one day walked out and left his business to write books about other men as unhappy and bewildered by life as he was.

In Money Writes I *have discussed his* Marching Men, *a whole tragic book telling men to march and march, and giving them no idea where to go or what for.*

SHERWOOD ANDERSON

Taylor-Critchfield-Clague Co.
Chicago
January 26, 1917

My dear Sinclair:

Answering your letter of December twenty-second. Perhaps my letter seemed impertinent. Did it? I was honest in it and I did so keenly respect and value your interest.

However, your last letter, like the first, has left me confused. My conception of an artist's attitude toward life about him is that he shall at all costs keep himself open to impressions, that he shall not let himself become an advocate.

155

To me there is no answer for the terrible confusion of life. I want to try to sympathize and to understand a little of the twisted maimed life that industrialism has brought on us. But I can't solve things, Sinclair, I can't do it. Man, I don't know who is right and who wrong.

Can't you believe that a man can sympathize with the revolutionist, hope for his success, pray for his success and find himself utterly unable to engage in propaganda? I simply haven't faith in my own conceptions of what is to be done.

When you are in Chicago you must see my wife whether you see me or not. I hope you will want to see me.

Yours very truly,

SHERWOOD ANDERSON

HARRY CARR [1877-1936]

Los Angeles
February 12, 1917

My dear Upton Sinclair:

I like you so much—and you make me so damn sore.

Sincerely

HARRY CARR

Thanks for the Play.

In passing on this handwritten missive to a friend, my wife has jotted in pencil: "If I live to

156

write Upton's biography I shall use this as best de-
scription of Upton!"

There is a curious story behind this and other
similar letters from Harry, then editor of the Los
Angeles Times. *I met him socially soon after my*
moving to Pasadena. We took an immediate "shine"
to each other. He knew everything that was going
on in the world, and was completely frank about
himself and his job. He would do me any personal
favor that I asked; and he took for granted my un-
derstanding that as an editor he had to "take policy."
For a quarter of a century the Times *pursued me*
with ridicule and misrepresentation; and to the day
of his death its chief editor remained my smiling
friend.

FREDERIK van EEDEN

> Bussum (N. Holland)
> "Walden"
> 15 August, 1914

Dear Brother:

I enclose a letter from one of our German friends
with my own answer. We are like the whole of
Europe in a terrible condition. [World War I had
begun six weeks before]. Communication between
our friends seems to be cut off. I got only one letter
from one of them, namely Rang in Coblenz, probably because he is a Regierungsrat [state counsel-
lor]. I am in anxiety for the sake of our poor Gut-

157

kind, who lives in the middle of German militarism in Potsdam, the most warlike centre in the world. I am so afraid they will compel him to serve and they are very quick in shooting people now. The nervous tension of all people has risen to an incredible height.

Thus far the effect on Holland has been wholesome, all small quarrels are forgotten. I never saw my countrymen so united, so alert, so energetic and so confident. The soldiers behave well, the organization of the army is splendid. Drink is forbidden. It may be that this great war is the moral convulsion of monarchism, autocracy and militarism. At least it would be too bad if the majority of thinking people would not see the ridiculous stupidity of this struggle, which nobody [is] said to wish for and which can bring no good to any of the participants. The greatest victories could not save Germany now from an economical ruin. Perhaps only America will have the advantage of this madness. Heaven deliver us from any more Siegfried Mayers [a reference to the Kaiser]! That will be the prayer of mankind, after all is over. After my view the tactics of all the free nations must be to isolate economically any nation that shows again symptoms of aggressive militarism. This is what I also wrote to your Ambassador Page in London and I think your President Wilson would be the only man at this moment, able to bring about a coalition of that sort.

The atrocities now going on in Belgium, are beyond description. Never has mankind had such a fit of warlike mania. And all for nothing, all without any advantage for the strugglers. Let me hear as soon as you get this letter. I suppose our mail to America is going regularly.

Love to Craig.

Yours ever,

F. van Eeden

FREDERIK van EEDEN

Bussum (N. Holland)
August 30, 1914

Dear Brother:

We are all in the utmost state of indignation at the devastation of Leuven and Mechelen and the attack on Antwerp. I think this invasion of modern Huns in poor Belgium is something so awful, so appalling that it would justify an intervention of America. This would be really a blow if it were only a menace, for the German public opinion is still very sensitive for the sympathy of neutral states, especially America. Of course, you have read the letter of H. G. Wells. It is in accordance with my letter to you. Write me soon after you got mine. Tell me whether you will be able to do something.

Fraternally,

F. van Eeden

159

FREDERIK van EEDEN

Bussum (N. Holland)
January 30, 1915

Dear Brother:

Excuse me for not writing sooner . . . . I am very much occupied. Rehearsals of the drama, lectures in different towns and then the weekly paper and a lot of correspondence make a rather crowded program. Your article is still waiting for room but it will not be less true for waiting a few weeks. Do you get the weekly regularly as I ordered it to be sent?

As to the war, things have come to a standstill, yet the tension is greater than ever. The Germans are just as mad as ever and there are only very slight instances of a change of feeling. A group of Social-democrats from Germany have issued a manifest from Rotterdam to all the comrades in the world. Carl Spitteler has published a wonderful lecture on the Swiss point of view. With Romain Rolland I am in lively correspondence. We have come very near each other. My idea is to publish all the contributions to the international tribune, later on in a separate volume, translated in four languages. Don't you think that would find a large public in America?

I can tell you that a friend of mine has been to Hamburg and heard a German General, just from the front tell in a family-circle that he had ordered not to take notice of the enemy throwing up his hands. Order was given, not to give quarter and to kill with the bayonnet, not with shooting. This was told in such a way, that the Dutch lady had to leave the room. What can you expect from the soldiers, when the generals are like that? I know from another gentleman, who was in Cologne, that machine-guns are standing on the cathedral-towers and have been standing there since the beginning of the war in defense for air-ships. Italy and Roumania are announcing quite openly that they will join in the fight next month. At the same time England is doing wonderfully in sending out new troops, perfectly drilled and equipped. So perhaps the spring might bring a great change . . . .

Let me soon hear from you again.

Yours,

FREDERIK VAN EEDEN

FREDERIK VAN EEDEN

Walden, Bussum (N. Holland)
April 23, 1915

Dear Brother:

What a success! The "Berliner Zeitung am Mittag" and the "Frankfurter Zeitung," first class German papers, reproduce Craig's Sonnet with great relish, in a rather weak translation! It was sent to me by triumphant German friends as a crushing blow, the conversion of Uppie to the Kaiser. You are called the world-famous author of the great book *The Jungle*!!! Now we see how this "Kultur" can be led around by the nose of its vanity with a string of flattery, like Bottom by the fairies. It would be a good cartoon Uppie—Puck

Craig—Titania
Kultur—Bottom
Well done, brother,

Yours,
F.v.E.

When World War I broke out, my wife wrote a sonnet satirizing German Kultur. When I read it I said to her: "Be careful. The Germans will take it seriously." She wouldn't believe it, so I sent it to George Sylvester Viereck, whom I had known for a decade or more. He printed it in New York in his pro-German propaganda paper, The Fatherland, *with the happy announcement that the wife of a writer well known in Germany was a supporter of the Kaiser.*

EDWARD M. HOUSE [1858-1938]

New York
April 11, 1918

Dear Mr. Sinclair:

Your recent telegram was forwarded to me while I was in Washington and I happened to be with the President when it arrived. I read it to him and I hope some result may follow.

Sincerely yours,
E. M. HOUSE

162

My wife and I had just started a monthly maga-
zine, Upton Sinclair's, *with a program "For a Clean*
Peace and the Internation." The post office authori-
ties in Washington refused us the "second-class
entry," on the ground that the magazine was "sedi-
tious." This meant, in effect, suppressing the maga-
zine. My wife wired to the Mississippi Senators
Vardaman and Williams, the latter being her cousin.
I wired Colonel House, author and publicist and
President Wilson's most trusted advisor. We had
already sent the magazine to all three. John Sharp
Williams wrote that he had prepared "a 13-page
brief" for the Solicitor of the Post Office Depart-
ment. This letter and brief has been misplaced, but
I recall one sentence: "I told him I would under-
take to read every word of those passages to the
President and I would agree to eat my hat if he did
not endorse every one of them." The "entry" was
granted, and the magazine continued for a year.

SIR ARTHUR CONAN DOYLE
[1859-1930]

> Windlesham, Crowborough
> Sussex
> March 29, 1918

Dear Sir:

You have sent me a copy of your paper [the first
issue, April 1, of *Upton Sinclair's*], but much as I
admire your books I cannot in such days read your
public views with patience.

If England has approached this question in the half-and-half limited liability way in which you talk, it is certain that the Germans would now be absolute masters of Europe and that America would have been next on the list. I do not see how any sane man can deny this.

And yet in our battle for freedom we have continually been hampered by all sorts of socialist cranks who, according to their own views should have been champions of extra-democracy and yet by some queer twist have made themselves the chief ally in actual fact of the most autocratic tyranny ever seen. It is not clear to you that German Socialism so far as it is not militant has no power at all, and that we can only release it by smashing the military party. That that can only be done by wholehearted culturiasm and sacrifice which cannot be got by luke-warm words. When we have done it then a clean peace by all means. I never heard anything else suggested, nor does England want anything in the world for herself. Our Empire is already too large and yet if we quitted it, it would throw a fifth of the world into barbarism.

Your former essay as quoted should show you how blind you have been. You talk of England having "a perfect craze for battleship building." There was a margin, I believe, of four dreadnaughts between Germany and England in 1914, and that was the margin which preserved the clear seas and all that it meant. You ought to be thanking England instead of nagging at her. All this talk of Capitalism is perfect madness in face of the taxation cheerfully borne.

Yours truly,

Arthur Conan Doyle

I am very much with you about the gaols.

Sir Arthur, creator of Sherlock Holmes, was troubled by the same thing that troubled the Solicitor of the Post Office Department, my call for "a Clean Peace and the International." We did not get either, so we got World War II instead.

SIR ARTHUR CONAN DOYLE

Windlesham,
Crowborough, Sussex
1920

My dear Sir:

I read your book [*The Brass Check*] with interest and sympathy. I certainly take off my hat to you for the long unselfish fight you have made for what you believed to be the right. As to your literary reputation what you say amazes me, for no American stands higher in this country.

As to the abuses of which you speak I am sure that we shall never get them remedied, or we shall find the remedy brings fresh abuses, until we come on a real religious basis which will be practical and make people realize that they really cannot go wrong with impunity and that life is so short a thing that it is madness to imperil ourselves for such a

165

trifle. In spiritualism in its higher forms I see such a development and from the time I understood it I have devoted my life to spreading it, meeting in a small way such oppositions as you describe. I think the cure, or one part of the cure, lies there.

With all best wishes,

ARTHUR CONAN DOYLE

On the subject of spiritualism, my attitude has to be, wait and see.

SIR ARTHUR CONAN DOYLE

15 Buckingham Palace Mansions
London S. W. 1
July 25, 1929

Dear Upton Sinclair:

You must have about the most mixed post bag of any man in the world. Here is one more addition to it.

You know how highly I think of your work. I have just completed a book *Our African Winter* in which I express my sentiments. I allude now to your literary work in which you are supreme. As to the social I admire and yet I always feel that you weaken it and provoke sympathy for your victim by your over-emphasis.

I am reading your *Profits of Religion*—brave and strong, and good. I am myself writing a small one shilling book upon the R. C. Religion so I appreciated it.

But don't run down Spiritualism. It is the one solid patch in the whole quagmire of religion. Of course there are frauds, quacks, tho that has been exaggerated. Dr. Austin of Los Angeles is a worthy exponent. There is a much "exposed" and beaten up medium named Dickson or Dixon across the bay from San Francisco if you are in that quarter, who is I believe one of the great phenomenal media of the world. But it is not the phenomenal but the religious side that counts. It comes from higher wisdom and knowledge than ours, and is the first really reasonable system ever given to the world.

I run a book store of psychic books at 2 Victoria Street, London S.W. at great loss to myself. If ever I can send you any books let me know. Take a course of psychic knowledge.

With all respect and greetings,

A. CONAN DOYLE

In an inscribed copy of Our African Winter *Sir Arthur wrote: "With all kind regards. Vide p. 229. Remember us when you want books." His statement on page 229 follows:*

"I have been agreeably occupied in reading Upton Sinclair's Boston *[my novel dealing with the Sacco-Vanzetti case, published in 1928]. I look upon Sinclair as one of the greatest novelists in the world, the Zola of America, and his power of detail and of marshalling facts leaves me amazed. I think he has become almost monomaniacal in his reaction against*

167

our settled law and order, but his high, unselfish soul shines through it all."

SIR ARTHUR CONAN DOYLE

Windlesham
Crowborough, Sussex
December 21st, 1929

My dear Upton Sinclair:

I sent your MSS [I cannot recall the title] back to your literary agent and now I am sorry to say I cannot remember the agent's name. I am now returning your cheque.

In judging the probability of a life after this or its desirability, I recall the words of my dear mother who used to say very quaint and wise things. She said, "My dear, this life is so utterly extraordinary and so entirely different from what one would expect that I can believe anything of the next one." There is a lot of sense in that saying. Our own approval or endorsement has certainly nothing whatever to do with the matter.

Concerning war, I am not at all convinced that Jesus Christ would have been anti-war where a good cause was concerned. He had those traders out of the Temple in record time, and his opinion about the Pharisees was a fairly robust one. There are great improvements in the world which can only, so far as I can see, be acquired by war. As examples, the anti-slavery war of the United States, the war by which France and England with their allies pre-

168

vented Germany from obtaining the predominance of the world. I would certainly avoid the beastly thing as far as possible. I do not think it has a place which can be filled in no other way. I agree that the Mohammedans are more logical in this matter than we are, but Christianity has always been the least logical and least intellectual of all religions. Yet in working practice it produces, I think, the finest result.

I quite understand about the immaculate conception, so you must have misread that paragraph. I am an ex-Romanist myself, so I am not likely to go wrong on their theology.

As to the subconscious mind being an explanation of psychic phenomena, it does not seem to me to be a possible one. How can the subconscious mind produce a loud independent voice talking in the air or an ectoplasmic figure which walks and talks, or the mould of a materialized hand or a pyschic photograph? The theory to which Charles Richet still clings has been riddled with criticism and seems to me to be quite impossible.

William James put forward the theory of the universal soul which seems to attract you, but it seems to me that the road is perfectly clear and straight and that there is no necessity of inventing all sorts of round-about by-paths.

Never fear, my dear fellow, that you hurt me by plain-speaking. I love to give and take and I always respect your honesty even when I think you are far from truth.

With my kind regards to your wife, who must, I think, be a powerful latent medium,

Yours very sincerely,

ARTHUR CONAN DOYLE

P.S. I have suddenly developed angina pectoris, so I am tied to the house, but I find my spiritual knowledge to be the immense help in bearing what would otherwise be very sudden disaster.

LUTHER BURBANK [1849-1926]

Santa Rosa, California, U.S.A.
September Twenty eight, 1918

Dear Mr. Sinclair:

I shall be pleased to give you my opinion as to the new book which you propose publishing and I think the subject is the best that I have heard of late.

I think the brief poem by Mrs. Sinclair in the last number is the finest thing of the sort ever born of the human mind.

Faithfully yours,

LUTHER BURBANK

Burbank, the "plant wizard," is referring to The Profits of Religion, *and to the sonnet called "Love," reprinted in the pamphlet* Sonnets *by M.C.S. and also included in her memoirs,* Southern Belle. *The miracles this kind and gentle man wrought all live after him.*

LUTHER BURBANK

Santa Rosa, California
November Fifth, 1918

My dear Mr. Sinclair:

I took my earliest opportunity to finish *The Profits of Religion*. I could have been much quicker about it but I am harassed at the present time with thousands of other matters which require my careful attention.

I inclose my opinion of the work which I hope will please you; if not let me know and I will try again.

Faithfully yours,

LUTHER BURBANK

It pleased me; but it might be too flattering to please the reader, so I omit it.

LUTHER BURBANK

Santa Rosa, California
November tenth, 1918

Dear Mr. Sinclair:

Yours of November 8th received. Although I have some eight thousand visitors each year not one in fifty of whom I can meet personally, yet I shall be very glad to have you come sometime when convenient to you, and will guarantee that you will be treated with the consideration which is so well

171

due you. *Come anytime* but if you want to see the Places in full working order July is the best time; but that is too far away.

Your son seems to be a genius too. Full specifications were not given however regarding the new fruit tree wanted. I should specify a white fig of excellent quality which will bear the year around and also it should bear a few oranges, bananas and ice-creams at the proper seasons. I am like him, *I like figs* and think them about the best fruit that ever grew. We could not very properly make the figs as large as cocoanuts for they would probably in falling from the tree be mush instead of figs when they arrived.

Faithfully yours,

LUTHER BURBANK

P.S. You will not find so many cranks to the square yard in this end of the state as there are there.

Meaning, in Southern California, where we lived.

LUTHER BURBANK

Santa Rosa, California
July 24, 1923

Dear Mrs. Sinclair:

Yours of July 17th received while I was away for a few days. I thank you for your kind letter. We enjoyed meeting the party of authors very greatly—

though I was never so "combusticated" or felt so downtrodden as I did under the gaze of the eyes of your select party. No, I am sure there was no idle curiosity in the group.

No, we do not forgive you, we thank you.

The copy of *The Parlor Provocateur* [a volume of letters by Kate Crane-Gartz, published by my wife] just received and will be read with interest as soon as we can melt a few of the big stacks of letters which have gathered unmercifully on my desk.

With kindest regards to yourself and Upton and to all the friends whom I had the pleasure of meeting,

Faithfully yours,

Luther Burbank

P.S. We had 126 teachers from the summer school the next day.

FRANK HARRIS [1854-1931]

67 Lexham Gardens, W.
London
January 11, 1912

My dear Upton Sinclair:

With the sad superiority of the Senior I drop the "Mr." as being no distinction to either of us: You'll follow suit, I hope.

I've wanted to meet you ever since I read *The Jungle*—and now I'm delighted to seize the opportunity.

173

Will you lunch with me on Monday next, the 4th inst; if so come to the office of *Hearth & Home,* 10 Fetter Lane, off Fleet St. at 1:15, and we'll go together. If there's anyone you'd like to bring, bring him or her. If Monday doesn't suit you choose any other day you like save Tuesday and drop me a line here to say when I may expect you. Then we'll make friends, I hope.

Meantime a hearty welcome to you.

Yours,

FRANK HARRIS

Born in Ireland, a cowboy in Texas, a student at eight universities, editor of a leading English weekly and then of an American monthly, Frank Harris was one of the three most extraordinary talkers I met in England—Bernard Shaw and Hilaire Belloc being the others. I said then that Harris was a strange combination of man and devil. When he talked about Shakespeare he sounded like Shakespeare, and when he talked about Jesus it might have been Jesus; then, when the conversation turned to someone he thought had done him wrong, it was Satan pouring out hate . . . I am putting a number of his letters into this book, because, whether they are right or wrong, his views are always lively. I met him only this once, in London. The reader will sense that I held somewhat aloof from him, because of differences not merely in ideas but in temperament.

That lunch lives in my memory. I brought no one,

174

but he brought a newspaper lady and paid five pounds for the lunch, which was $24.25 in those days. It filled me with dismay.

FRANK HARRIS

> 3 Washington Square, North
> New York
> January 4, 1916

My dear Upton Sinclair:

First of all, I did get the *Cry for Justice* and thank you for it; but there was no word in it from you so I do not specially love it. If you have a *Jungle* to spare and would write a few words in the front page and sent it to me I should be grateful and put it among my treasures . . . .

I got some articles on Wall Street that would have made a sensation but I am told that they are too dangerous; in fact I have to walk gingerly along a very narrow path that is said to span the abyss but may well land me in a bog of ruin on the other side.

I do not quite agree with you about London. I think you over-estimate him. I prefer your *Jungle* to all he has written, and surely *The Pit* and *Sister Carrie* are higher than his work because they go deeper.

I hope to see Dreiser tomorrow night and talk of you with him. You are often in our thoughts but why do you live in Pasadena? . . . .

175

I want to see what you think of Shaw and my answer to him. I will send you a copy in a day or two.

Ever sincerely yours,

FRANK HARRIS

At this time Harris had come to America and was editor of Pearson's Magazine.

FRANK HARRIS

New York City
November 13, 1916

My dear Upton Sinclair:

I wish you would sign your letters in full because your initials are the same as these United States and I mistake them for official communications from the Most High!

In spite of my interview with Captain Koenig and my work on the "Deutschland" for the January number I have read two of your [ms.] books of "King Coal!" Very good indeed. I cannot say yet how good.

I sent you a copy of my book on Oscar Wilde on October 30th. I hope it has reached you. Bernard Shaw says "it wipes out all other biographies" and he has besides sent me a long letter telling of all his meetings with Oscar Wilde and his view of O.W. He wants it to be an "appendix" to any future edition I may publish. I invite you herewith if you see fit, to do the like. I want to know really what

176

you think of this biography of mine. By the bye it is almost sold out here in America. You and Dreiser are the only two people in America whom I would ask to tell me what they really thought of this book. But I want the truth, the whole truth and nothing but the truth. Will you give it to me? . . . .

I am going to publish your address on "Truth". That needed saying and you have said it well. Thank you for sending it!

Tell me what you think of the magazine—*Pearsons*? The sale on the newstands has increased sevenfold in my four months—Hurroo!

Yours ever sincerely,

FRANK HARRIS

FRANK HARRIS

Pearson's Magazine
New York City
May 19, 1917

My dear Sinclair:

I could write a volume on this letter of yours and your wrong-headedness in regard to Germany.

I was a student in Germany for more than six years and think I know it. What do you mean by saying that you would have to spend thirty years in military preparation if Germany should win? When has Germany shown any aggression towards the United States? What could she do with her fleet against your stronger fleet in the way of attacking you? I never expected to read such moon-shine from your pen.

There may be a revolution in Germany. No one would welcome it more than I should, but when you talk of Germany's reserves of man power not outlasting this fall I am glad because that pins you to a definite statement that time will make ridiculous. If the war continues you will have to give in that that statement is pure absurdity.

I think a revolution is much more needed in America than anywhere else.

Again you say that the English allow you to read anything and the Germans do not. I beg your pardon but the reverse is the absolute truth. The English won't let you read *Pearson's* and won't admit any German paper or other paper uncensored into their country. The English *Times*, the *Daily News*, the *Nation*, and other papers are on every hotel table in Berlin as they were before the war. You are bitten with the German bug like Charles Edward Russell. His is of ignorance. For the life of me I can't understand why you rave.

At the same time I feel nothing but the keenest interest in you. You are right about Thoreau, but I only put him in to show how small in my opinion Jack London was; and you will never put over your Mark Twain on me. *Huckleberry Finn* and *Tom Sawyer* are good boy's books and nothing more. You put him among the world's great humorists. I deny him any quality of greatness.

A man told me once here that I had not read his *Joan of Arc*! I must read that; and so I read it.

178

The difficult thing about a biography of Joan of Arc is that there are not shadows enough to match the high lights. No biographer has told us of any weaknesses in her—any faults of temper or insight. There are one or two hints that she was very impatient, as people of intellect usually are when dealing with fools, and that she became seduced a little by the honor paid her at court and her success, and so lingered when the "voices" called her to go back to Domremy.

Now a man who writes a biography of Joan of Arc would have to ransack the literature of the times and find faults enough in her to give reality. In Saint Beuve's little essay he has set forth a coarseness of speech attributed to her and one or two other little faults that give a sort of reality to his sketch. But Mark Twain sits down and writes 500 pages of treacle. She is as pure of mouth as a Yankee schoolmarm or a Howells' heroine. She has every virtue and every grace. In fact Mark Twain simply writes himself across 600 pages—"I am not an artist."

I will not admit such a man among the great. I would rather admit Rudyard Kipling.

I am beginning to fear that this world, especially in America has lost the very notion of what greatness is.

But there I won't bother you with any more of my opinions and will allow you to think yourself much broader if it pleases you. But you have told me nothing of your views on sex which I had hoped to get from you when I opened your letter. I cannot make bricks without straw. I want to know,

179

not only your views on sex, but also if you believe at all in a personal immortality. Do you believe at all in what Shakespeare says:

"There's a divinity that shapes our ends
Rough-hew them how we will."

Is there any clear unfolding purpose in the world to you?

These questions I beg you to answer. They are the stuff out of which I shall make the picture. And do tell me how *The Jungle* came to you: that is one of our "possessions forever" as Thucydides said of his history.

Yours ever,

FRANK HARRIS

Still in bed with this malaria and pleurisy: forgive pencil. Had a patronising letter from Mr. Jack London and replied!

FRANK HARRIS

3 Washington Sq. No.
New York City
June 6, 1917

My dear Sinclair:

Madness can go no further; when Mr. A. M. Simons writes: "I do think we can afford to demand the overthrow of the Kaiser as a *sine qua non* of peace", the limit is reached. It reminds me of the

Welshman in Henry IV. calling the spirits from the vasty deep.

"Yes", says Henry; "so can I and so can any man; but will they come?"

You can afford to demand what you please, but the person who does not know that the Kaiser is even stronger than before the war knows nothing of Germany and does not realize what Germany has achieved.

On that line you will spend the lives of two or three millions of Americans and after some three years of useless slaughter you will be where you are now. America cannot do as much as even Russia and Russia is out of the war. Russia was attacking on a boundary of thousands of miles in length and all America has to attack is the north-western corner of Germany which is not two hundred miles long. If in three years you get the Germans back to the Rhine it will be all you will be able to do and you could get that today with peace.

I am beginning to think that the Americans are madder than the rest of the world.

Send me your sex stuff and anything formative in your early life; any incident that counted in your development or any early love episode before even fifteen. It will all be much more interesting to me than your views on war or my own.

Sincerely yours,

FRANK HARRIS

181

FRANK HARRIS

Tannersville in the Catskills
August 28th, 1917

My dear Sinclair:

I suppose you approve the President's message—
idiocy gone mad I call it, promising as it does
five years' more of war, unless we rouse these United
States against it before the Congressional elections
of 1918. For God's sake, think, Sinclair; many of
us miss you, cannot understand how you can be on
that side. Suppose I'm right and we can't win!
Russia is out of the war: in relation to Germany
we are not as strong as Russia. Russia had 12 million trained soldiers at first: 3,000,000 in the first
line as fast as any soldiers in the world: she had
a frontier 2,000 miles long and at one point only 230
miles from Berlin, and yet Russia failed. Now, can
America hope for a decisive victory? It is not to be
had, I fear: and I would wish Germany beaten
rather than that this war should continue another
2 years.

I wish we could meet and have it all out: there
is so little between us and so much. If I've told you
the harsh truth about "The Coal War" forgive me:
I want you to beat *The Jungle* to write the biggest
book yet written on this class-war. I like your little
warning immensely, "Government by Gunmen," and
there are superb sentences scattered all through,
sentences of insight and thought. (I only ask you

to be as frank with me about my books; I don't want sugar but fact.)

Yours ever in The Grand Army

Fr.

"The Coal War" is a sequel to King Coal. *I could not find a publisher for it. No one was interested in social reform in wartime.*

FRANK HARRIS

Nice, France, A.M.
September 28th, 1925

My dear Sinclair:

Your letter of September 10th amused me. You say that I glorify my past life and its worst faults and make a Crusade out of it. Not one word of truth in this. You construct your facts to suit your prejudice. Again, you repeat that I make a glory and a boast out of my sin. Give me chapter and verse, will you, for the boast and the glory.

But as you say you are going to publish this letter, you won't mind my using it and publishing an answer to it: a careful corrective of your false statements.

I thought that you at least would see that the book [the first volume of his autobiography, *My Life and Loves*] was an effort to tell the whole truth even when it told terribly against me. Shaw

183

said, I believe, that I confessed to murder in the book, and after that there was no more to be said. But Shaw would not say that I gloried in the murder and made a boast of it. This is to misapprehend everything I have done.

One conclusion you should have drawn, or at least an able man in your place would have drawn from the whole thing. "He is a man," you would have said, "who has outraged all my fine sentiments; he has written a book I consider most vile at 70. He will pay for it and pay terribly. One does not throw up a position and undergo tremendous pecuniary loss at 70 to gratify boyish lusts or boyish vain-glory." And then you might have gone on— but this is merely to say that you are Upton Sinclair. And by this I mean that you are not only below Shaw, who wrote me that he would have defended the book, were it not for the inartistic pictures, but below a high English journalist. Filson Young, of the *Saturday Review*, wrote to me regretting the sexual parts of the book, but he went on accepting all my articles and praised very highly the non-sexual chapters in the book. You find nothing in the book but vileness, like the pig who can nose out a truffle though buried feet deep in good, sweet earth; you are some 500 years behind Filson Young, that is what I mean when I say you are Upton Sinclair.

Sincerely yours,
FRANK HARRIS

I burned the copy he sent me, so I cannot check; but I don't recall that he "confessed to murder,"

184

and I think that Shaw was merely using a playful phrase. The book was banned, not merely in the United States, but in France, where it was published.

GERTRUDE ATHERTON [1857-1948]

New York
February 25, 1918

Dear Mr. Sinclair:

I enclose $5 for five years' subscription to your paper [*Upton Sinclair's*] because I think you have the right idea.

I hesitated at first for two reasons: You quoted Frank Harris, whom I believe to be a pro-German and a spy and a rotter generally (I hear he has recently been interned, and I hope he will be shot).

I look upon the Bolsheviki as the maniacs of democracy—those that are not tools and sellers out. Their tyranny would be several times worse than that of the Romanoffs, and I surely hope the Germans will eat them up and discredit them for ever. We can attend to the Germans later. With all good wishes,

GERTRUDE ATHERTON

I had entered into controversy with this American novelist as far back as 1902, in an article called "Our Bourgeois Literature" in Collier's Weekly,

185

making all kinds of fun of her social ideas. From the time of this present letter I sent her all my books and always got lively replies.

GERTRUDE ATHERTON

New York
August 7, 1918

Dear Mr. Sinclair:

I have taken this hot day "off" to write some letters, and am glad not to delay longer in telling you how much I enjoyed *King Coal*. I have plodded through a number of propaganda novels on the question of capital vs. labor, but I never applied the word enjoyment before, however much I may have felt instructed. But there is a curious quality of light in your brain which would not only illuminate but impart fascination to any subject; and although you certainly do not mince matters in describing the horrors of the mining camps one reads on with the same enthrallment that one does a great romance. This it seems to me is an achievement peculiar to yourself. I do not think any one else is capable of it.

I have not the slightest idea that you have exaggerated anything, and hope now that we are growing so virtuous, and possessed with the desire to be unlike the Huns in every possible respect, that the Government will get round to your problem and abolish it. In spite of the war, which has crippled the sales of most fiction, I fancy it will be read in the right quarters.

I hope you are quite well again.

GERTRUDE ATHERTON

GERTRUDE ATHERTON

New York
August 20, 1918

Dear Mr. Sinclair:

I do not care to say anything further on the subject for publication, but in reply to your letter will decline to meet any more I.W.W.s. If I have not met any but that unspeakable Haywood personally I have heard a lot of them speak, and my curiosity is satisfied. I saw Giovannetti one night at Carnegie Hall when he was so terrified he could hardly articulate. The sheriff, or perhaps it was the mayor, had appeared unexpectedly with several policemen on the stage, and the man's white face and shaking body were really pitiful. There was another blatherskite—a fat Italian, whose name began with E. [Ettor]—who got through the ordeal better, merely by spinning out phrases with nothing in them; although people were so bored they left by the dozen.

The complete failure of Bolshevikism (they behaved exactly as I predicted and hoped) has averted the danger of similar trouble in the U.S., but after the war there certainly should be legislation to improve the conditions of the working class, if they

187

have shown patriotism. But merely to increase wages, or even give them a co-operative interest is not enough. They should be educated. How on earth are people to improve without education, whether they get three or ten dollars a day? The reason they have accomplished so little is because they are stupid through ignorance.

I will take back one thing I said. Not for anything would I have those 100 I.W.W.s executed and made into martyrs. I would have them put to hard labor—we are a million men short industrially—and God knows, no punishment, not even death itself, could be as bitter as that.

While I want to see poverty eliminated from the world, because it is the darkest spot in civilization— far worse than war—and would do anything I could toward a more equable distribution of wealth, and toward the possibility of comfort and happiness for all, still I am frank to say that if it came to a show down,—that is to say civil war—I'd stand by my own class. My reason might protest, but my instincts would be stronger. I cannot understand any one going back on his class any more than I can find any sort of excuse for a man going back on his flag . . . It may be a good argument that we should not be expected to show allegiance to natal conditions in which we had no choice, but our brains were made by our ancestors, and whatever we may choose to put into or take out of them the form remains the same.

GERTRUDE ATHERTON

188

P.S. I don't mean to say that in ordinary times the working class should be rewarded for patriotism or anything else. Their business then was to stand on their rights, it was the business of all fair-minded people to support them. But in this war every single person who does anything to hamper speed and delay the result should be punished in any way it is possible to reach them. Laborers or profiteers, it is all one and the villainies of one do not excuse the crimes of the other.

The "unspeakable Haywood" was William D. Haywood, president of the Western Federation of Miners. He was accused, and acquitted of murder in connection with a labor war.

I have forgotten how I came to introduce her to any I.W.W., but apparently I did so. They were Syndicalists, calling for "One Big Union," and were cruelly persecuted during World War I. I have portrayed them in my drama Singing Jailbirds, *1924.*

GERTRUDE ATHERTON

October 21, 1918

Dear Mr. Sinclair:

If you had ever run a war relief organization and were expected to write propaganda every fifteen

189

minutes you would know that there is not much time to read or write letters. I am taking a morning off in bed with a cold as I have two committee meetings this afternoon, and that means a few letters.

I have been intensely interested in *Jimmie Higgins* [portions of my novel, then appearing serially in my little monthly magazine], as it gives me a progressive point of view that I could not get elsewhere, and I get the whole picture owing to your skill, with no effort on my own part. *The Profits of Religion* is both erudite and courageous—aside from its compelling interest—but I am afraid the newspapers will be afraid to take it up. I think you would have strengthened your case by an attitude of cold impartiality and given credit to the hundreds—possibly thousands—of priests, who are fighting in the French Army. Also to the great work of the K. of C. are doing. People who are no more Catholic than I am give them the highest praise.

I have not gone to Fall River on account of the epidemic, as I want to see it in normal conditions. Also I have been getting off a unit of women to Paris—dieticians for Le Bien-Etre du Blessé—and that is more trouble than three books. It looks, honest, as if those cussed Germans knew they were beaten.

All good luck

Gertrude Atherton

190

GERTRUDE ATHERTON

2101 California Street
San Francisco,
July 10th, 1927

Dear Mr. Sinclair:

I hope that biography of you by Floyd Dell [*Upton Sinclair. A Study in Social Protest*] will be widely distributed, as I find it the very most interesting biography I ever read of a contemporary. In fact it stands comparison anywhere. You may not agree with his estimate of your work in some cases, but you must appreciate the fact that if this book were widely read it would put an end to all prejudice save among the rabid.

I had a lot of extra work to polish off after I finished my novel, but I have got round to *Oil* at last. I find it extremely interesting and no doubt it will be absorbing later on; the signs are all there! I doubt if any one else could have written it but Balzac.

I hope it is not true that your wife is ill. I saw a statement to that effect the other day. Anyhow, I hope she will soon be all right again.

> With best wishes,
> Very sincerely
>
> GERTRUDE ATHERTON

Why don't you make an arrangement with booksellers here to exhibit your book? They told me at one of the lending libraries that there was an immediate demand for it as soon as it was verboten in Boston.

The demand for Oil!, *my novel published in 1927, was so great that the publishers couldn't keep up with it. The book was translated into 29 languages, to my knowledge. The banning in Boston was due to a mention of birth control.*

GEORGE D. HERRON [1862-1925]

San Domenico, Florence, Italy
September 20, 1915

Dear Sinclair:

I am glad to get your note of August 26th. I have been wondering what you might now be at work upon. The Colorado novel [*King Coal*] ought to be greatly worth while, both as a social dynamic and as a drama . . . .

I think I have already told you what I think about the war, and have also sent you things that I have written about it. I think the outcome will be social revolution in every country and the sweeping away of all the old institutions of government, perhaps of religion also, with new conceptions of morality and of social responsibility. There will be a wholly new and nobler world, but it will come only out of a great tribulation. The freedom of the world will be bought with an unreckonable price, and I imagine that half a generation will pass before we settle down to a chosen and orderly course of social revolution.

Lovingly,

GEORGE D. HERRON

Formerly an Iowa Protestant minister, Herron divorced his wife and married another woman—something which was considered unforgivable in those days. The newspapers made it such a scandal that he moved to Italy. When World War I began he became a confidential agent of President Wilson. His first book was Christ or Caesar, *his last* The Defeat in the Victory.

GEORGE D. HERRON

Le Retour
Geneva, Switzerland
December 4th, 1918

Dear Upton:

I have read your book, *Profits of Religion,* with profound interest and I have been deeply stirred by it. It is one of the very few books I have taken time to read during the past two years of my strenuous activities here.

I wish you had said more on the positive side. I wish you had made clear what I think must be a real belief on your part, of a belief in Christ as the supreme expression of God's humanity and man's potential or essential divinity. However, what you have done has been well done and thoroughly . . . .

193

The war may be ended and it may not be. We have defeated the German Army but we have not defeated the German mind or pro-Germanism. The so-called German Republic is merely the old Germany in new clothes, without even having taken a bath, and as spiritually dirty and devilish and dangerous as ever—if not more so. As a result of all that is now going on, Europe, if not the whole world, trembles in the balance as never before. The next few weeks will decide whether the world takes a long step forward or goes back into the melting-pot. It is indeed a time for fasting and prayer.

My book about Wilson is soon to be published in German, in Italian, in Russian, and in Japanese. The whole world is turning to Wilson.

Give me news of yourself.
Lovingly yours,

GEORGE D. HERRON

The war was over and he referred to the coming peace settlement.

GEORGE D. HERRON

Le Retour
Geneva, Switzerland
April 22nd, 1919

My dear Sinclair:

It would take long to tell you what I think of the present situation [following the Versailles Peace Treaty]. Perhaps I shall be able to do so in June or

194

July. I hope to return to America for the summer and to see you.

I do not in the least share your fear that the Allies are forcing the Germans into the arms of the Bolsheviki; it is exactly the contrary that is happening. The Allies are forcing the Bolsheviki into the arms of Germany. My own conviction is that as a result of all that has happened at Paris, or rather as a result of all that has not been done in Paris, the Germans have won the war. There will be a period of complete chaos in Europe for a time, during which the old regime will come back into power in Germany, and Germany, or at least Prussia, as the only centre of order, will proceed to reorganize Europe and to Germanize it at the same time. That is my prophecy as to what will happen in the course of five years at farthest, and may happen within two years.

In any case we are at the "End of the Ages". I mean that Europe, or our Western civilization, is upon the verge of a disintegration which seems to me inevitable. What I said in the letter which Marion Wentworth published in the *Times* becomes every day more true. The disintegration of civilization and a great current of faith that seems something like a resurgence of primitive Christianity are proceeding together.

I shall be very glad to see what America looks like once more—I mean inwardly looks like—and to learn if America shall be able to take up the burden of the world which is being laid upon her.

Affectionately yours,
GEORGE D. HERRON

195

GEORGE D. HERRON

Le Retour
Geneva, Switzerland
June 2nd, 1920

Dear Upton:

The Brass Check certainly gets in its righteous and deadly work here in Europe everywhere I have given it out. I told you the profound impression it made upon a Monseigneur of the Catholic church who came to borrow other of your books. I gave a copy to a former Russian minister under the Czar. He told me that for four nights after reading the book he could not sleep. He insists that the moral horrors of our public life and press in America counter-balance the physical horrors endured in Russia under the Czars.

I am glad to see that you have broken through the conspiracy of silence and that your book is being widely discussed now in America.

Send me a line and tell me how you are.

Affectionately yours,

GEORGE D. HERRON

Some American newspapers have improved since those days.

196

GEORGE D. HERRON

Ragaz, Switzerland
August 30, 1920

Dear Sinclair:

Professor Singer of Vienna who was for twenty-five years editor in chief of the *Zeit*, the most powerful political journal of the old Austro-Hungarian Empire, and who is also one of the most distinguished publicists in Europe, has just written me a note to inquire if he can translate *The Brass Check* into German and supplement it with experiences of his own regarding European journalism. Professor Singer's name carries great weight in Europe, and this might be worth while. I don't know that there is any money in it. It would probably be purely a work of political propaganda. Professor Singer has become a thoroughly-going socialist.

You might send me a cable simply addressed, Herron, Conova, with one word "Alright", if you agree.

Affectionately yours,

GEORGE D. HERRON

The German translation of The Brass Check *was published in 1921.*

GEORGE D. HERRON

Florence, Italy
May 16, 1923

Dear Upton:

I thank you for your good thought of me indicated by your letter of April 23rd. I still hope that I may write the book which really expresses all that I have within me, and I hope my health will be such that I may begin it in the coming winter. It has been more or less in my mind these twenty years, but it always seems to have been my destiny thus far to be called from one thing to another with nothing ever completed, and my life spent in fighting lost battles. It was my long poem that I was at work upon when you were with me in Florence, but that was put aside at the beginning of the war, and I have never looked at it since. I have three things that I would like to do, so far as literary accomplishment is concerned. First, to write the book which really sets forth my philosophy and prophecy of life, second, to complete the long poem in one form or another, third, to write out the whole story of the work I did for Wilson and our State Department during the war, and to disclose the real inner tragedy of the war and the truth about many hidden things, based upon my own experience. The original documents, some two hundred in number, will probably go to the Hoover War Memorial Library at Leland Stanford. Hoover wants them there and they have promised to observe any condition I may make regarding them.

But as to writing out the story of my life and of all the things that happened regarding the early marriage or even some of the inner things that happened between myself and Wilson and Balfour during the war, I do not think I could ever bring myself to do it. I have an intolerable shrinking from laying naked the false lives of others and of taking any advantage of that for my own justification. And how could I bring myself to tell the truth about a woman whose soul was the very essence and genius of falsehood and evil. Even Balzac could not tell the story if he were alive and knew it. And, besides all that, my whole life has been such an incredible, such an unbelievable thing, that I don't half believe it myself. It has indeed been a fool's life, and the truth of it is an absurdity so impossible that nobody would believe it if it were told, not even myself. It is curious how many times I have practically had the world in my hands to take anything I wanted and then have deliberately thrown the world away in order to be true to something within me that seemed more imperative.

I am perfectly aware that, as you say, my personality has made no adequate impression upon the world, and that the powers within me have been baffled of any effectual exercise. But does this really matter, after all? So far as I myself am concerned personally, I would not walk across the street to have it different. It is only a question of whether or not it would be better for the world itself to know the

199

truth, whether the things I care about would be better served by having the truth told.

Lovingly yours,

George Herron

For years I had urged him to write his memoirs; and now I plead for some scholar to take up the task.

GEORGE D. HERRON

La Meta
Florence, Italy
March 5th, 1924

My dear Upton:

I have often pondered the question of writing out completely my personal experience with Wilson and the different governments of Europe during the war, and of setting forth the whole heart of the matter according to my own actual contact with it. I should have liked especially to set forth the times and ways when peace might have been had during the war, and how it was always prevented. I could certainly tell a strange story running through the years of the war and the two years following the armistice, and it would be real history. I have always intended to do this some time or other, even if the story were not published during my life-time. It is something that I could not do in a day nor probably in a year. It would take a good deal of time.

But several reasons have withheld me from undertaking this now. The first was the breakdown of my health as a result of all that happened. For two years previous to last autumn I had really been a pretty sick man. Every attempt to live over again the events of the previous six years have been disastrous. Now that I am better, there is another book which I shall soon begin, which I think ought to be done first.

But there is another problem that would confront me immediately, were I to write the book which you propose now or soon. It would be the whole problem of holding my own with such a book against the world. If it were a question, let us say, of my word against Mr. Balfour's or my word against Clemenceau or my word against Col. House, in negotiations with which I had to do with these men, or in things in which I had the interior responsibility impinging upon my reports, you know perfectly well whom the world would choose to believe and what a storm I would have to meet in the press of the world. Again, there is so much that would have to do with Wilson who is now gone. There would even be the question of what worth while publishing house would take my book in the first place. Even my book, *The Defeat in the Victory*, and my later book about Italy have had a sorry time in America, though being translated and widely read in Europe. Even in France an edition is now asked for, much to my surprise.

Who would publish such a history as I would write at the present moment and what publishing house would stand by the book after it were published and the inevitable storm arose?

The question of personal obligation no longer detains me. Of that I can assure you. Every passing event between the nations shows me how I was bridled and saddled and ridden to opposite ends from those to which I intended to go. My own good faith was used to accomplish the opposite of what I believed in and worked for. In this the British Government used and betrayed me even more shamefully than the American Government— or at least the British Foreign Office.

Above all, what publishing house will permit me through its press to expose the sheer brute economic forces that have bought and sold the people like sheep for the slaughter from the beginning? It is not enough even to call them economic forces. It is the now parasitic super-finance which is taking the life out of industry itself. Even today the French franc is being desperately held up by certain great banking houses in New York City, until these banking houses can unload their French national securities, many of them upon American school teachers and small professional and business people.

I need not go into all of this. I am only pointing out to you the exterior difficulties of getting the truth of all this matter before the world at the present time. Even the awful truth about what is happening in Germany is either very lightly touched upon or generally suppressed. In fact, truth is left without any organs wherewith it may now communicate itself to the peoples of the world.

But I am heartily glad that you feel as you do about the matter, and I shall be glad to have any further suggestions from you, at any time you are moved to make them.

I wonder if you know that the originals of my war documents to the President and to the Government are now with the Hoover War Memorial Library at Leland Stanford. There are some six hundred of them, all told. I still have a good many to arrange and send on through the Embassy here at Rome. They are deposited there for safe keeping and for the use of historians and research workers in the future. But I reserve for my lifetime the right to write the history or to publish any of the documents. You might be interested when you are there in looking over some of these documents.

Affectionately yours,

George D. Herron

My letters to Herron are in the Hoover Library at Stanford University, and my copies of them are in my collection of papers in the Indiana University Library.

GEORGE D. HERRON

La Meta
Florence, Italy
June 11, 1924

My dear Upton:

Very well, God willing, I will write the book. As you know, of course, it will have to be done according to my own nature. I don't think I could produce anything that you would call "chatty", but I think I can tell in a straightforward yet dynamic way the story of what actually happened. Nor do I think I am likely to overload it with preachments. I have enough of the dramatic sense to avoid that. I think the story will move to its own lesson in the end. The little books I have hitherto written have all been candid preachments, not pretending to be anything else. But this is different. It will in a sense be my Apocalypse, emitting its own lightnings and thunders as it goes along.

Above all things, I want to tell the truth as nakedly as it can be told, and yet with as much conviction of righteousness and judgment to come as is possible, and especially of the human possibility that yet remains. This does not mean any sort of a propaganda book. All that must be avoided. Nor must it be written with any thought of establishing a case merely against capitalism or against or for any class or party, but merely as an attempt to tell the inclusive truth about the whole matter, so far as that truth came within the realm of my

204

experience and observation, and with the hope that that truth will have a saving meaning.

It is only the apostolic motive, and the hope which you and others have held out to me that now is the moment for the play of that motive in such a book as we have discussed, that induces me to write. Or perhaps I do it because it is one of those predestined things that are forever coming upon me and which seem to have given me so little choice about my life, at any time. In any case I don't think any personal hope or motive could quicken my reluctance into action. I am deeply touched, I am indeed profoundly moved, by your always urgent and affectionate wish to have me set right before the world. But somehow, dear Upton, I don't seem to be able to work up any interest in that. I sometimes wonder about myself. But, actually, I don't seem at bottom to have any concern or care about what the world thinks of me, but only a care as to how I may somehow contribute to getting the world out of its ancient scrape. Maybe this is abnormal. Maybe it is, as Mary Wilshire once said, a deplorable lack of any personal ambition in my psychic constitution. Or maybe it is just a deep fatigue of soul resulting from the fact that I have spent my life trying to get other men—or else groups or parties or churches— to do their work, instead of doing my own work.

And mayhap the writing of this book will start me to really doing the work that it lieth within me to do and which I never have done.

But this is more than enough about the matter. I only want to show my gratitude to you for your devoted urgency in the matter, and to make your heart glad by saying I will set about clearing the way for the writing of the book and aim to have it ready by spring.

Affectionately yours,

George D. Herron

GEORGE D. HERRON

Florence, Italy
May 10th, 1925

My dear Upton:

I am afraid it is quite useless to expect anything from me, prose or poetry, not more or less steeped in Christian symbolism—and *more* rather than *less*. You see I was always a sort of "early Christian" in my faith. And all my experience with the world has been based on a deep underground of that early faith—now renewed and clarified, only more certain and apostolic than ever . . . .

Lovingly,

George D. Herron

Herron in spirit was an early Christian saint and martyr who came into contact with modern social thought. He died a few weeks after this letter was written. He had made promises on the authority of Woodrow Wilson in Switzerland during the war, and the Versailles settlement which broke those promises also broke his spirit. I owe it to his mem-

ory to record that he saved my life as a writer, by giving me thirty dollars a month for the year 1903, in which I wrote Manassas.

KING C. GILLETTE [1855-1932]

Los Angeles, California
March 14, 1919

My dear Mr. Sinclair:

No more conferences for me of either labor or capital—I do not believe it tells anything whatever —it simply results in unwelcome publicity. It puts the whole proposition in a false light for the reason that no one—and in particular no one chapter can put forward a clear presentation in form of outline and give a reasonable basis for argument.

I have met the type of men like your newspaper man and banker many, many times—and they all travel in the same groove—and the groove is so deep —none of them ever see over the edge.

I will see you someday early next week—and we can go over this together; but no more, no more plutocratic—Socialist or proletariat gatherings, never again. I am willing when time comes to court publicity. If I am left alone in my tower nothing doing —if I must face a pack of wolves—

With best ever

KING C. GILLETTE

P.S. I have never expected to convince or secure the support of the type of men whom I met. I don't go forth to educate those who have no desire for change—I hope to reach those of every class who are looking for a way out and who will seize the opportunity when a plan is presented that is right— whether it be mine or someone elses, makes no difference.

K.C.G.

This elderly, kind-hearted multimillionaire, the inventor of the safety razor, first presented himself at my office with his calling card attached to a brand-new hundred-dollar bill. Perhaps it was for the secretary, in order to break my rule not to be disturbed when I was writing. The purpose of his visit was to persuade me to work with him on his manuscript, "The People's Corporation." I accepted the task, and while we were writing it, I invited a group of Southern California's business leaders to our home to discuss his program with him. They came—and gave him a most unhappy time.

JOHN REED [1887-1920]

Croton-on-Hudson, New York
June 19, 1918

Dear Upton:

I received your letter, and appreciate your generosity in taking my estimate of Gorky in lieu of Gorky's estimate of the Russian Revolution.

I feel very doubtful of being able to make you see Gorky as I saw him—or at least as I read him; for although I dined at his house, I didn't succeed in getting any nearer to him than a violent quarrel with Marie Andreeva. But besides his written word, I also had intimate reports of him from the Russian novelist, Eugene Tamiatin, for one of whose books Gorky was writing a preface, and from others of Gorky's close friends.

Gorky, it is true, stood with the Bolsheviki until the insurrection was in full swing. His party, the *Novaya Zhizn* group (United Social Democrats Internationalists), remained with them afterwards too. Avilov, one of Gorky's best journalists, was minister of Posts and Telegraphs in the first Soviet Cabinet, and others of Gorky's supporters and of the *Novaya Zhizn* staff were also members of the insurrectionary military Revolutionary Committee and of the Executive Committee of the Soviets. The editor of the *Novaya Zhizn* himself (name for the moment escapes me), became editor of the Soviet organ *Isvestia* just before I left.

Gorky took an original and characteristic attitude. He violently opposed the suppression of the bourgeois and moderate Socialist press, operated by the Bolsheviki in the heat of insurrection, and lifted later. He was horrified at the early arrests which occurred at the same time. But more than all else, he was shocked at the bloodshed.

Now everybody who was in Russia at the time knows that there was almost no bloodshed. The Bolshevik revolution was the least bloody uprising in history. At Moscow there was severe street-fighting, it is true, and about eight hundred persons lost their lives. Gorky was in Moscow during the fighting. He has written, in his paper, an illuminating series of reports on what he saw. It was evidently the first time Gorky had ever seen fighting. He was astounded and revolted.

For example, he tells this story. He came upon a soldier, standing in an arch-way near the Kremlin, watching. A man darted out of a cross-street and ran across the square. The soldier immediately threw up his gun and fired—at the running figure, bringing him down. Gorky asked the soldier why he had shot. "Why", answered the man, "he was running."

This was, remember, during the street-fighting, which lasted for six days.

Later, in Petrograd, Gorky saw a mob seize a thief and beat him to death—which I think is a method of summary and elementary justice indulged in by most peoples in time of Revolution—isn't it?

Well, from such things Gorky made up his mind that the "Russian people", as he said, were "the cruelest and most bloodthirsty race of savages in the world."

That is his premise, so to speak. The Bolsheviki were determined and efficient in their plan of proletarian dictatorship. Cruel, however, they were conspicuously not; nor bloodthirsty. Russians in Revolution are laughably merciful and forgiving, to a Westerner. Gorky bases most of his indictment of the Revolution on that ground, but almost anyone

210

who was in Russia last fall can testify as to the lack of bloodshed, if he wanted to tell the truth.

As to my analysis of the attitude of the Russian bourgeoisie and the "moderate" Socialists, I stand where Gorky stood all last year. In what followed, I think perhaps I was in a better position to overlook the violence and injustice which cannot help going on in times of Revolution, and see beyond them to the beauty and bigness of the thing as a whole.

I have noticed before the quotation you send me. This is not the first time most of these accusations have been hurled at the head of the Soviet government. When I was in Petrograd the Menshevik and Socialist Revolutionary and bourgeois journals were then saying that the peasants were fighting over the distributed land, that the soldiers were massacring wholesale, that industry was disintegrating into utter chaos. It was not true then; it may be true now. But if it is true, from what I know of Russia I should say that it was not lack of organizing ability, or the power to work together, or any lack of proof that the thing would work, which caused these things, but the ceaseless and desperate efforts of the ruling-class to regain its property by the help of foreign bayonets, coupled with imperialistic foreign invasion from the front, and the threat of the same thing from the rear, and no help or sign of effective sympathy from any quarter of the world.

In my experience, however, the Soviet government was doing phenomenal creative work in industry, and the peasants were dividing the land and getting to an agreement about it. Fights undoubt-

211

edly go on in the villages; the poor peasants were urged to combine against the rich peasants, so as to prevent the rich peasants from hogging more than their share.

Those "monstrous rumors" are in line with the quantity of legends which find a ready receptacle in Gorky's ear. He already thinks that Russians are monstrous, you see.

The dreaded Mr. Bleichman's advocacy of massacre is nothing new. As in all Revolutions, there is always somebody around Petrograd urging wholesale slaughter. If the bourgeoisie keep on sabotaging and calling upon Germans and Japs to come and save their property, it might even happen. I can't somehow see Russians cold-bloodedly resolving to do it.

The Soviets and the workers' democratic organizations are *always* urging the workers to get busy. So much for that.

Maxim Gorky is a very sick man. Moreover, he is very much under the influence of Marie Andreeva, who is beautiful, theatrical and romantic, who wants to manage things herself for the ignorant workingmen, and who finds the Revolution disappointing.

Oh, that Russian intelligentsia! How profoundly it misunderstands and disapproves of the Russian mass!

Yours,

JOHN REED

Please do send the paper. I don't think your optimisms are justified, or that you are right, but I do recognize that you are honest as the devil.

I publish this letter from the correspondent and author of Ten Days That Shook the World *for its historic interest. I had known Reed during the Paterson silk strike and had called him "the playboy of the social revolution," and learned later that this had hurt his feelings. The revolution turned out to be a tragedy for him; he died broken-hearted over the later developments in Russia. And what would he have made of Hungary in 1956? As to my "optimisms," they were for a "clean peace" at Versailles. What was actually achieved there is pictured in* World's End, *the first of my Lanny Budd books.*

EUGENE V. DEBS [1855-1926]

Sunday, 7th, 1918

My dear Comrade:

The report is being circulated here that Upton Sinclair sold the copyright of *The Jungle* to the Beef Trust, that the book has been suppressed, and that it is not now on sale anywhere. As soon as I heard of it I vehemently denied and denounced the charge. The man who made it said that Sinclair himself would not deny it as "he had admitted it in Los Angeles the day he had his trouble at the Hotel Alexandria"—I quote his exact words. Now I wish you to write to Upton and ask him to write

213

me here and deny the charge over his name, and at the same time let me know if *The Jungle* is now on sale and where it can be had—I said I would stake my head it was a lie, and that I would at once write and get the denial and produce it in evidence —Please write at once as I want to stamp out this falsehood and put an end to the mischief it is doing.

EUGENE V. DEBS

Debs, Socialist candidate for President, was in Atlanta Penitentiary for opposition to the draft. This note was passed on to me by his brother, Theodore. Not only was it false that I ever sold the copyright of The Jungle *to anyone, or that it was ever suppressed, but I certainly never had any "trouble at the Hotel Alexandria." A man posing as Upton Sinclair gave a party there and got drunk. Viking Press and Harper's are still selling their editions of* The Jungle.

EUGENE V. DEBS

Please write in answer and say to Upton that I have squelched the story here about *The Jungle* so it will not raise its head here again. The circular you sent me about the new edition was sufficient to stamp out the lie, but I am glad to have Upton's letter to make it emphatic and final, and at the same time show how the silly and malicious falsehood originated. Please say to Upton that I fully appreciate his prompt response and note with care and interest all he says. He need not have sent the free copies of *The Jungle* but if they are admitted, which is not at all certain, I will place one copy in the Prison Library and make the best possible use of the rest. Tell him *The Jungle* circulars he enclosed did *not* reach me—they were taken out.

I will autograph the books of the Poets as promptly as possible when they come. Tell him I shall not now attempt to say how lovingly and lastingly grateful I am to dear, noble Ruth Le Prade for this inexpressibly beautiful service, and to the gifted friends and comrades who have contributed their gracious and flattering tribute, and to him who has been so extremely kind as to take over the work of editing and publication, but that deep in my heart I am conscious of it all and that the loving service thus rendered and the high honor thus shown me will be remembered with the profound gratitude and affection to the last hours of my life.

Tell Upton also that I am very sorry not to be able to send him the testimonial to his new book as requested on account of restrictions placed upon me by the rules which prevent me from doing many things I would be most happy to do under other circumstances.

Please say to Upton that I do feel honored, very greatly so, by this coming book compiled by dear Ruth Le Prade, and to which so many gifted writers have so generously added their tribute, and that I feel further honored by his editing and publishing the book. Tell him we employ no clipping bureau but that our many comrades and friends see that we get them. Tell him if the Warden grants permission I shall most gladly autograph the 500 copies as requested. Please send Upton my sincere thanks and my love and the same to Ruth.

Ruth Le Prade was a crippled girl who was heartbroken over Debs' imprisonment. A great many poets were moved by the event, and Ruth collected their tributes. I was asked to edit and publish them, and did so in a volume entitled Debs and the Poets, *but did not please Ruth because I left out most of her own.*

VICENTE BLASCO-IBANEZ
[1867-1928]

New York
June 22, 1920

My dear Sinclair:

I am leaving tomorrow in the steamer *La France*.
My last letter from New York is for you.
Some days ago I have sent my two novels (author's edition,) to Mr. Guillette.
Here is my card with my address in Paris.
Write when you have need of me.

Very amicably

VICENTE BLASCO-IBANEZ

This recalls an amusing episode. In my first talk with the Spanish novelist and author of Mare Nostrum—*in his French, as bad as mine—I happened to speak of a "millionaire Socialist." He expressed incredulity, having never heard of such a phenomenon. I told him playfully that I would give him*

216

a dinner party in Los Angeles to which I would invite only millionaire Socialists. I produced half a dozen of the species, male and female; and that is why he is sending autographed books to a "Mr. Guillette"—that is, King C. Gillette, the "razor king," whose picture you still see on little packages of razor blades. All Blasco's letters to me are in French.

VICENTE BLASCO-IBANEZ

Menton (Alpes Maritimes)
November 25, 1921

My dear friend Upton Sinclair:

I love you very much, always as a friend and as confrere, and the motive of my long silence is other than you believe.

When I returned to Europe I found my personal affairs very much mixed up, and I had need of much time and great efforts to arrange them. Afterwards I passed some months in Spain, to attend fetes and manifestations in my honor.

Finally, when I had returned to the Cote d'Azur in the month of June last I launched upon the adventure to buy this Villa Fontana which is a great property, with vast garden and three buildings, where I have installed my library and performed some other important work. At this moment I have almost finished my installation, but I believe I shall still have to work up to the end of the year.

When you make a voyage to Europe, you will come to spend some days in this place which is more

217

beautiful even than Pasadena, and even on the shore of the sea. For me and for my artists, Menton is the most beautiful and poetic corner of all Europe. My house is close to the border of Italy, and right close also to Monte Carlo and Nice. When you come, that will please you much.

Now that I am installed and more free, I give you my word to reply to all your letters, and I beg your pardon for my silence which was produced more by circumstances than by my will.

My affectionate recollections to Mrs. Sinclair and to all the sympathetic friends you caused me to know.

You may count on me as friend and as literary comrade. You have erred in your last letter, for I cherish you and the days that I passed at Los Angeles as one of the best memories of my life. I desire to return to the United States, simply to live some weeks in California. Perhaps you will see me arrive some day, on motion picture business.

Receive dear Sinclair my very friendly salutations.

VICENTE BLASCO-IBANEZ

MAX EASTMAN [1893-   ]

New York
November 30, 1919

Dear Upton:

You'd better typewrite this for the printer:
There are few sweeping statements to which I

218

like to sign my name, but one is that American popular newspapers and magazines are false and unreliable to the core. American journalism is a monstrous and malignant growth, which if it continues uncured will destroy every honest and straightforward and hopeful thing in our civilization.

Upton Sinclair, in *The Brass Check,* proves this statement for the first time. He backs it up with the unanswerable facts and documents. He illustrates it with living tales from a wide field of observation, and with a swift and candid narrative of his own experiences which can only leave the reader in a state of amazed indignation.

He points to a cure, which I believe is the only possible one—organized effort by the employees of the printing and publishing industry. They are the only people whose economic interests would be served by the regular and reliable publication of the truth, who occupy a position of power. But in their effort they will need all the sympathy that is available, and therefore I can wish nothing better than that every honest-minded American should stop reading his newspaper long enough to read this book and find out what his newspaper is.

MAX EASTMAN

Author of The Enjoyment of Poetry *and a score of other books, Max founded and edited* The Masses, *and then years later became a senior editor of the* Reader's Digest. *But in spite of this we have remained friends for half a century. The above letter was written to serve as preface for my book* The Brass Check. *Some newspapers are not as bad as they used to be, and I venture to hope it is because the editors and reporters read this book.*

MAX EASTMAN

Chilmark, Massachusetts
June 22, 1948

Dear Upton:

I deeply appreciate your "casting your vote" for my book [*The Enjoyment of Living*]. It means a great deal to me.

I have *American Outpost* in the original Farrar & Rinehart edition. In fact I bought and paid for it and read it with pleasure and admiration. I thought the mood of humorous candor in which you wrote of some of your intimate life was delightful. If I had been a little more energetically generous I would have written and told you so as I should.

I'll pass along the Haldeman-Julius copy to someone who deserves to have it. *Our Lady* has come and is on the table beside my bed—also *A Giant's Strength*.

Your sustained creative energy and excellence is wonderful to me. I remember how hard it always was to cut a word or two out of anything you wrote when it wouldn't fit into a column.

220

My best to you, and very happy Thanks for your letter.

MAX

I just reread the charming account of your meeting with Inez.

American Outpost *is my book of reminiscences of the first thirty years of my life, published in 1932. Our Lady is my novelette telling how the mother of Jesus fell victim to enchantment and found herself in her own city of Our Lady the Queen of the Angels, and failed to recognize it as hers.*
A Giant's Strength *is my play about what the atomic bomb did to America. Inez Milholland was a beautiful suffrage leader; I tell her story in* American Outpost.

JOHN BURROUGHS [1837-1921]

Pasadena, California
February 24, 1920

Dear Mr. Sinclair:

Thank you for the copy of *The Brass Check*. I am reading it. I am not a socialist and know little about Socialism, but I am always in favor of the Square Deal. You cannot paint the Hearst papers too black. I will not even touch one of them. But most of the other papers try to deal fairly with the public. They have got to be run on a paying basis, or cease to be. If we could endow them all, we might get ideal Journalism, but until we do they

221

dare not offend their supporters. I am in favor of Government ownership of all our natural resources, such as coal, oil and of the R. R. In this world good and evil grow on the same tree. Out of great good comes great evil also. Capitalism is a great good or a great evil also, but the good greatly predominates. Religion is a great good and a great Evil also—I mean Ecclesiasticism. This great good rain we have just had has been an evil to many things. Strikes and lockouts bear both good and bad fruit. Great good came out of the War and out of nearly all wars, in the downfall of tyrants and overthrow of despots, but behold the evil also. I dare say Socialism has its good and its bad side also. Unmixed good we cannot hope to get in this world.

I have had a happy life and have done my work [Burroughs was a widely-beloved naturalist and prolific author] and have let the other fellow do his and have helped him when I could. But you will not care for my philosophy. I would say come and see me, but I am so full of engagements to go somewhere, and to receive some one, that I do not know when you would find me in.

Sincerely yours,

JOHN BURROUGHS

P.S. I am in Sunday evening. We leave on the 1st or 2nd.

WILLIAM JENNINGS BRYAN
[1860-1925]

Miami, Florida
May 20, 1920

My dear Mr. Sinclair:

I have just found your book *The Brass Check* on my return from a two months' absence. Pardon delay in acknowledging. I have read enough to know that it is interesting. I shall take it with me tomorrow and read it on the train. You may be interested in the enclosed. I see no way of getting the necessary information before the voters except by bulletin issued by state and federal governments.

Thanks for book.

Yours truly,

W. J. BRYAN

Three-time Democratic Party candidate for President, Bryan was known to his time as "the silver-tongued orator."

FREMONT OLDER [1856-1920]

June 15, 1920

My dear Sinclair:

I have your letter in which you ask me to let you know the inside of what I am reported to have learned in the Mooney case.

The trouble is I haven't learned much yet, that is, not in sufficient detail to make any kind of a statement about it. What I am striving to do is to get the perjured witnesses who convicted Mooney and Billings to face about and tell me the truth. I am right in the midst of it at this moment and may or may not succeed. It looks, however, as if I would learn practically all there is to learn of the truth concerning the way in which the State handled its perjured witnesses—how it suggestionized them into becoming the perjurers they were.

Altogether, it is the most amazing story I have ever had anything to do with. It seems to me if you are going to write another novel or another book, it should be the Mooney case pure and simple, and the title of it should be "An Illegal Murder". For when all is known that I think can be known, it will be shown clearly that the State before an open-eyed community was able to murder a man with the instruments that the people have provided for bringing about justice. There isn't a scrap of testimony in either of the Mooney or Billings cases that wasn't perjured, except that of the man who drew the blueprints of Market Street.

If you think well of my suggestion it will be necessary for you to saturate yourself with the case. It would take some time, but you could do it, and you would have a book that I think would be worth while.

I am sorry that I haven't anything to give you

other than what has already been published, but within the next two weeks perhaps I may have.

With best wishes,

Sincerely yours,

FREMONT OLDER

Fremont Older was editor of the San Francisco Bulletin *and a friend of justice. Mooney and Billings were two Labor men convicted of having thrown a bomb into a "Preparedness Day" parade; neither was executed. Mooney remained in jail until 1938, when a Democratic governor, elected by our "Epic" movement, freed him.*

WILLIAM JENNINGS BRYAN

The Bellevue-Stratford
Philadelphia, Pa.
1920

My dear Mr. Sinclair:

I am still reading your book as I have leisure—not consecutively but as the chapter heads attract me. Your quotations are valuable for reference. . . .

I think your remedy, while a help, is wholly inadequate. I see no escape except a *national bulletin* (and also one in each state). Government ownership of all natural monopolies would help but we

225

need the bulletin to get government ownership or any other reform.

Yours truly,

W. J. Bryan

The Brass Check called for a union of newspapermen—which we now have—and a "National News," which we do not have.

OSWALD GARRISON VILLARD
[1872-1949]

New York

March 17, 1920

PERSONAL

My dear Mr. Sinclair:

I have been meaning to write to you for some time to tell you with what great satisfaction we printed your article in *The Nation* and congratulate you upon the remarkable results it has achieved. No article has appeared in *The Nation* this winter that has attracted more widespread comment, and letters are still coming in about it. I forwarded one to you the other day. I have been wondering what financial response you have received.

Had I not been ill I should have written to you promptly to say that I think the great weakness of your proposal is the financial provision. You have tremendously understated the amount of money needed. My experience with *The Nation* has been very discouraging on the financial side, and I am now compelled, after having put in more than double the amount you call for, to go among my friends and see whether others can be found who will help to put *The Nation* across; otherwise, *The Nation* will disappear at the end of this year or pass out of my hands as *The Evening Post* did. I anticipate that it will take $125,000 for three years more at the very least, before *The Nation* can break even. It is a circulation problem largely, and with us the answer is that we must have 100,000 readers to break even. I would have believed no one who might have told me when I started that it would take such a large sum because we are not extravagant. I take no salary myself and every editor on the staff is underpaid, and we are paying less for contributions than any other periodicals in this class.

That is the disheartening side of all these proposals—the enormous amount of capital needed. It will interest you to know that we are paying eight cents a pound for our paper and shall probably be paying twelve or fourteen cents next year, and that wages have increased 25% since the strike of last fall. This is the way the thing goes. Advertising is extremely difficult to obtain until one has 100,000 readers, and even then it is difficult to get it at a rate which is really remunerative.

Most newspapers fail because they do not know their own business—just what their advertising pages are costing them, for instance, and how much the getting of a subscription costs them. An accurate cost accounting system, however expensive, is essential in all such undertakings and will be in yours.

These facts *are for your own eyes alone,* but I shall be grateful if you have anyone to suggest who might subscribe to the new *Nation* stock which we are issuing in order to insure its living for three years, but, of course, I don't want you to handicap yourself in any way with your own undertaking.

Yours very sincerely,

OSWALD GARRISON VILLARD

Editor of The Nation *for many years, Villard is referring to my project for a national newspaper to be conducted as a public service.*

H. L. MENCKEN [1880-1955]

1524 Hollins Street
Baltimore, Maryland
February 26, 1918

Dear Mr. Sinclair:

Thanks very much for the first issue of your magazine [*Upton Sinclair's*]. There is excellent stuff in it, and I am delighted to see you start it. What we need in this country, beyond everything else, is absolutely free discussion. At the moment, of course, it doesn't exist. You will be barred from the mails if you are not very careful.

The war discussions in the newspapers make me

228

doubt that any sane men are left in America. But I doubt that your Clean Peace is possible. In the end England and Germany will compromise, divide the loot, and leave all the others to suck their thumbs.

Sincerely yours,

H. L. MENCKEN

In the course of the next thirty years, Mencken, author, social critic, and editor of The American Mercury, *wrote me 186 letters, and no doubt many more which got into my files unsorted.*

H. L. MENCKEN

Baltimore, Maryland
August 19th, 1918

Dear Sinclair:

You state your case neatly and cleverly—but can the *Felis pardus* change his spots? I labor under a bilious distrust of all forms of improvement. The world is already too damned good. Surely not one man in a hundred deserves his luck.

But why should it have surprised you that I subscribed to the magazine? I take my own beliefs very lightly, and am always eager to hear the other fellow's. For many years I read the *Maryland Methodist* regularly every week. But now I am down to a short list—E. W. Howe's *Monthly* for pleasure, and yours and half a dozen other magazines for instruction.

I see no chance for the Internation you talk of. The end of the war will see national animosities more bitter than ever before. Worse, even the present alliances will not hold up. The Germans and Austrians will fall out (Germany cultivated Austria in Bismarck's day simply because she needed help against Russia), and the French, Italian, Japanese, British, American bloc is obviously quite as unsound. I look for at least 25 years of wars.

But this is not for publication.

Yours in st.,

MENCKEN

H. L. MENCKEN

Baltimore
January 28, 1920

Dear Sinclair:

Will you please have paper-bound copies of *The Brass Check* sent to the addresses on the enclosed list, and forward the bill to me as above? I can't figure out the exact cost, including postage.

You have done a good job in the book. I have read it with great care, and find nothing in it that seems to me to be exaggerated. On the contrary, you have, in many ways, much understated your case. For one thing, you have not gone at sufficient length into the relations between the newspapers and the war-makers, including especially the munitions purvey-

230

ors and the British press service. Again, you have barely touched upon the newspapers' part in the extraordinary persecution of heretics that went on during the war.

Here, I suppose, your belief in the Wilson balderdash hampered you. Well, every man to his own delusions! As it stands, the book is a valuable piece of work. You will be denounced as anti-Christ, but you will open many an eye.

To hell with Socialism! The longer I live the more I am convinced that the common people are doomed to be diddled forever. You are fighting a vain fight. But you must be having a lot of fun.

Sincerely yours,

Mencken

H. L. MENCKEN

Baltimore

February 23rd, 1920

Dear Sinclair:

Howe, Plumb and Company are surely not laboring men [reference is to the "Plumb Plan" for the American railroads]. I grant you that the cause of democracy attracts a number of able and honest men, but I fear that most of them (like you yourself) make the error of overestimating the sense and decency of the actual proletariat. Consider, for example, the soldiers. Most of them are true proletarians. They were conscripted, in the majority of cases, against their will, and forced to fight in a war

231

that few of them could understand. While they were in France there was much tall talk about their determination to clean up the country on their return. Well, what did they actually do? They succumbed instantly to the most ridiculous blather, and began raiding and beating up the very men who were trying to save them from another such war.

I by no means argue that the capitalistic case is good. On the contrary, it is infinitely unsound. Capitalism in America is much worse than even you make it out to be, just as journalism is much worse (as I shall say in my *Smart Set* review). But I am convinced that you will never do any execution upon it—that the proletarians you sweat to save will succumb to capitalistic nose-pulling and so stand against you. My personal interests are on the side of capitalism. I admit it openly. Don't ask me to have any sympathy for idiots whose interest is *against* capitalism, and who yet permit it to make them its dupes, slaves, butts and janissaries. The newspapers fill you with indignation. They fill me with agreeable amusement, for they convince me that, as a capitalist (small but tight) I am quite safe.

Your bout with Conan Doyle interests me a good deal. You have jockeyed the poor fellow into a fearful position. But I half suspect that you are in the same boat yourself. You succumbed to Wilson's tosh—maybe not thoroughly, but still publicly. Surely you don't maintain today that he was honest! The theory that he was an idealist undone by scoundrels is really too much! And now you propose to establish the truth by such experts as Rabbi Wise,

Frank Vanderlip and company. Your case against the newspapers is perfect, but your remedy makes me weep.

Some time ago I ordered some copies of *The Brass Check.* They have not come in. Perhaps the American Legion objects.

Sincerely yours,

MENCKEN

The boycott of the book extended even to the wholesale paper dealer. For months I could not buy book paper, and I bought a carload of brown wrapping paper and printed some sixty thousand books on that.

H. L. MENCKEN

Baltimore
March 4th, 1922

Dear Sinclair:

The manuscript [of my novel *They Call Me Carpenter*, published in 1922] has gone forward to Dr. Holmes. It is tart stuff, and will get you denounced by patriotic men. I file a caveat to one of your assumptions. You take it as granted that Christ, if He came back to earth today, would be regarded unfavorably by the chief living Christians. This is only partly true. As a theologian and political economist, true enough, he might cause eyebrows to lift, but as a Jew he would be warmly welcomed by the Christian Scientists and Episcopalians. I hear that

233

one of the most fashionable "Church of England" mosques in New York now has a vestry that is 80% Ashkenazim.

If you want to do it, say that I read the book and liked it. Every Episcopal bishop in the Republic ought to be jailed until he can prove that he has read it.

By the way, if you will send me a couple of dozen of the circulars announcing your book on education [*The Goose-step*] I'll see that they get into the hands of learned and very sore men.

Sincerely yours,

MENCKEN

H. L. M E N C K E N

The Smart Set
New York
March 21, 1923

Dear Sinclair:

Enclosed is a proof of my review of *The Goose-Step* to be printed in the *Smart Set* for May. Please don't make any use of it before April 14th.

I doubt that any of the jades you have galled will seek a remedy in jurisprudence. They all know very well that getting into court would lay them open to even worse exposure. I think you did a very neat job. I read page after page with my heart in my mouth, fearing at every moment that you would presently introduce a boost for the San Francisco quack, Abrams. George Sterling tells me that he still believes in Abrams. I begin to suspect that you yourself have begun to suspect that there is some reason for suspecting that the amiable doctor is a bit suspicious.

My best regards. When are you coming East again?

Sincerely yours,

H. L. MENCKEN

H. L. MENCKEN

Baltimore

August 24th, 1923

Dear Sinclair:

"The Goslings" [my study of American schools, published in 1924], unluckily, finds me in an unexpected situation. I am leaving the *Smart Set* next month to start a new serious review, and hence cannot buy a serial for the former. And the new review probably will not begin before January, and so it could not use any substantial part of "The Goslings" before the publication of the complete book. The Los Angeles section, as it stands, would make, of course, far more than one instalment, and in view of the plan upon which you have written it I see no way to cut it materially without grave damage to it. So the whole scheme seems to blow up. The enclosed stuff is excellent. I have read every word of it, and with constant interest.

Now to the new review. Knopf is to be the publisher, and it is to be a genuinely first-rate monthly, well printed on good paper. I shall try to cut a rather wide swathe in it, covering politics, economics, the exact sciences, etc., as well as belles lettres and the other fine arts. I have some promises of stuff from men who have something to say and know how to write, and I hope to stir up the animals. In politics it will be, in the main, Tory, but *civilized* Tory. You know me well enough to know that there will be no quarter for the degraded cads who now run the country. I am against you and against the Liberals because I believe you chase butterflies, but I am even more against your enemies.

Nothing would delight me more to have a roaring article from you in the first number. I go further, and suggest a subject. Why not a sort of reminiscent and autobiographical chapter, "aus meinem Leben", rehearsing realistically your adventures as a reformer—not the objective facts and struggles, but the psychological adventures and observations. Isn't it a fact that the majority of people, even those who are most obviously oppressed, are quite devoid of any comprehension of liberty—that they are contented in their wallow? Haven't you, as a matter of actual experience, found them apathetic and even hostile? It is my own observation that liberty seems dangerous to all ordinary men—that respect for it and love of it are confined to small classes. Think of the doings of the American Legion!

But maybe this notion doesn't appeal to you. If not, what other ideas have you? I needn't point out that this new review would get you before an entirely new audience—a cynical one, perhaps, and

236

impatient of exhortation, but nevertheless one with a keen relish for wit and a decent attitude toward opponents. Give the matter your prayers.

Yours,

MENCKEN

The magazine was The American Mercury, *and during its long career I was able to write only one article that its editors considered "safe." That was my memories of Edward MacDowell, the composer, whose pupil I had been.*

H. L. MENCKEN

Baltimore
December 12th, 1923

Dear Sinclair:

At first blush this play [*Hell*, my blank verse drama] seems hopeless for the stage, but on second thoughts I believe that it has a very good chance. All sorts of novelties, chiefly from Central Europe, are now making successes in New York, and so the odds begin to be in favor of another one, instead of against it, as in the past. Finish the thing and give it to some good agent. I think the fact that it is in blank verse is against it. Why not put it into prose, which is much harder to write but much more effective? The idea is good, and it seems to me that you have launched it with skill. Think of the money awaiting you, if the play is a success. Poor old Don Marquis is now getting $1,500 a week from "The

237

Old Soak". I hear that he is afraid of banks, and is keeping the whole amount in an old collar-box. He receives 150 circulars from oil-stock and Mexican mine promoters every day. But he is saving the money to invest in an expedition for recovering the buried gold of Captain Kidd.

The play is not for our great moral periodical. We use only one-acters, and very few of them.

I am trying, by the way, to get some satirical articles on prison-life under the Republic from men who have been in the great American institutions of reform, e.g., Sing Sing, Atlanta, Leavenworth, Moundsville, Joliet, San Quentin, etc. Do you know any such criminals who can write, and have a sense of humor? If so, who are they?

Yours sincerely,

MENCKEN

My wife thinks I should state that the remarks about humorist Don Marquis are merely kidding!

H. L. M E N C K E N

The American Mercury
New York
November 6th, 1924

Dear Sinclair:

I have been ill and in a hell of a state, but am now recovered by God's grace. For three days I had hiccoughs. I know what you suspect, but the fact is that I had not had a drink for days.

238

I wish I could get more stuff about the doings of the Polizei in California. I like to print it in Americana. Let me have anything that comes into your hands. My best thanks.

Your failure to send me that sure-cure birth-control formula is having evil effects in New York. At least 250 babies will be born next year who hadn't ought to be.

Sincerely yours,

H. L. MENCKEN

H. L. MENCKEN

Baltimore
December 10th, 1924

Dear Sinclair:

I like the "Jack London" chapter [the manuscript of my "Mammonart"] very much, but its onslaughts upon alcohol make it impossible for us. We are committed to the revival of the saloon, exactly as it was. America misses it, and is much the worse for the lack of it. London, sober, would have written nothing worth reading. Alcohol made him.

The other chapters seem to me to be feebler. In fact, most of them, e.g., the ones of Clemens and Howells, say only what has been said before, and is obvious. I am holding the MS. at your order.

The news that the *American Mercury* is "lacking in constructive points of view" is surely not news to me. If any such points of view ever get into it, it will only be over my mutilated and pathetic corpse. The uplift has damn nigh ruined the country. What we need is more sin.

Twenty barges in tow of five tugs set out from the Bahamas for Baltimore last Tuesday. It will be a Christian Christmas. God's hand is in it!

Yours,

MENCKEN

H . L . M E N C K E N

The American Mercury
New York
December 28, 1924

Dear Sinclair:

I assume that, like all other literati, you occasionally get tired of your job. Why not abandon propaganda and fiction long enough to do a book of character sketches of the salient men you have known? You have known many, and you could do a corker. I needn't add that the suggestion is inspired by the fact that it would delight me to print some of these sketches in the above periodical.

I send all the usual insincere and idiotic good wishes for the New Year.

Yours,

MENCKEN

This letter led to a controversy. I could not "do" Jack London because I was forbidden to mention

*his drinking; and then the same for George Ster-
ling. And they both took their own lives because
of drinking. What a fantastic idea, to try to conceal these facts in the interest of the anti-Prohibition
crusade!*

*Because of the relationship of Mencken to George
Sterling, it seems advisable to break off the for-
mer's letters at this point and insert the second lot of
Sterling's.*

GEORGE STERLING

San Francisco
April 16th, 1918

Dear Upton:

You are generous, and I'd not take advantage of
the fact if I'd not just got a bill from the tax collector
for $22.44 taxes on my book-rights, etc. Down with
civilization!

I'll throw in another poem, for good measure. I
fear I've none you'll care for, just now. I shall have,
though.

Craig's sonnet *is* good. I don't quite "get" that
"drink my blood." And I think "your hounds of Hell
and Death" is an improvement on the last line.

If she goes on with that habit of waking up to
write sonnets, she'll be in the bug-house someday.
I know from experience that's it's a bad thing to
do and a hard thing not to do.

241

I've finished "Lilith," and suppose the Comstockians will jail me as soon as it appears—next autumn. And still I think that Craig ought to write to me!

Yours ever,

GEORGE

"I drink my blood in secret grief" is a line from a war sonnet, published in our magazine, Upton Sinclair's, *and later in my wife's* Sonnets by M.C.S.

GEORGE STERLING

San Francisco
August 20, 1923

Dear Upton:

It was characteristically kind and impulsive of you to rush to my defense, and I'm grateful. However, I'm able to do my own fighting, and shall write to the *Freeman* [a reactionary magazine of the period] myself in a day or so. Fletcher's article [belittling George's poetry] was too idiotically unjust to bother me. What can he, or even you, know of my inner life? Even my "corroding scepticism" is a milder thing than you imagine, and more speculation than conviction. I *want to know what's what,* but even if things are as bad as they seem to me I shan't let it make a sterilized misanthrope of me. I'll send [Van Wyck] Brooks my verses "Here and Now". That ought to settle something.

242

I wish you'd not "rung in" that absurd "Abalone Song". ("God deliver me from my friends," eh!) It merely gives them a chance to become successfully sarcastic. But you have stuck up for me finely and kindly, and I shan't forget it.

I had it all fixed to speak to [President] Harding about those I.W.W. boys—and he died!

Affectionately,

GEORGE

He lived at Carmel, and, a tireless swimmer, he could dive for abalone at Point Lobos. Then his friends would come at night and build a campfire, make a stew, and sing new verses of the "Abalone Song." George had started it, and others contributed new stanzas.

GEORGE STERLING

San Francisco
June 7th, 1924

Dear Upton:

The matter you bring up [in "Mammonart," then in progress] is one to which I've given but scant thought, supposing it to be relegated to the outer darkness littered up by other Victorian sentimentalities. Also, its discussion presents the difficulties common to all vague generalities. But certainly the end of art is not technique; *that* is merely an accessory. The end and aim of art is to transmit an emotion, and the stature of the artist may depend

243

both in the power of the emotion and the competence with which it is transmitted.

The matter has always been in need of clear thinking. To put it concisely, I may say that some folk claim that it is not enough that the artist charm; his work should also convey a lesson. In other words, he must charm and preach simultaneously. I've certainly no objection to his doing so, provided that the two qualities do not nullify each other. I dare say it all depends on the man; one artist may have the ability to charm, but go all to pieces when he tries to preach. Another may have so sound and vital a theme to put over that his art is an accessory in comparison, a sort of sugar-coating. Witness much of [H.G.] Wells. As for my own negligible self, I've usually "let Nature take its course," and written as the ideas were presented me by (perhaps) the subconscious mind. That's what's meant by "inspiration," and I may seem vain to claim it, with no better results to show. However, so it is: it's easier for me to write than not to write, and when I put myself *deliberately* to setting forth a theme in verse, as in the case of the "Exposition Ode," "Yosemite" and a few others, the results have fallen, *poetically*, below some of my other work. Perhaps one has to take one's choice—either to charm or preach. And it is hard to say from which action the world would reap the greater benefit or the artist the greater fame (if that latter "infirmity" matters; I don't think it does. I think fame is a joke and, what very little I've had of it, a damned nuisance!) It seems to me that Coleridge in his "Kubla Khan"

244

and Keats in his "Eve of St. Agnes," "Ode to a Nightingale" and "Hyperion" have given far more value to the world than if they'd deliberately tried to put over "a message". The best work of almost all poets is that which contains least preaching.

And yet I'd not say a poet should neglect any valuable thought that came to him, even though his pen spluttered a little in putting it down. As I've said, it's hard to generalize: I'd want to know the man and the thought, before passing judgment; and even then that judgment would be merely one man's taste in the matter. "Invictus" is pretty purposeful, isn't it? Is it preferable to "Ode to Melancholy?" Who's to decide such a thing? The world likes to be charmed and dislikes being preached to. But God knows it seems to need a lot of preaching! Well, if a man feels called on to preach, let him turn loose; and if it helps him to use a sugar-coating on an otherwise neglected pill, let him do so. He has his choice, and I don't think the pure artist should berate him. On the other hand, let him not abuse the pure artist for doing good as *he* sees it. The latter may not be consciously trying to do good at all— he may be delighting in the exercise of his natural and ineluctable function, or merely in a glory-chase. Nevertheless, despite himself, if he has functioned finely as an artist, he has given value to the world. As no generation is final or perfect, each has a right to its natural pleasures, and even so unearthly a thing as "Kubla Khan" has its use *aside* from pleasure, as a quickener of our imaginations. Shelley didn't want to be a poet, at first. He wanted to write

245

pamphlets in the cause of Irish freedom! Would the world have gained if he'd stuck to that instead of going in to the "Ode to the West Wind", "The Skylark" and *Prometheus Unbound*? Of course it's impossible to decide such a problem, in this swirling chaos of inconsequentiality and meaninglessness. So I'm for letting each of us do "as the spirit prompts" and, as Carlyle says, "let Fame and the rest go prating"—"the rest" including "bad" art and poor preaching. But you'll never preach poorly, Upton.

Now see! I've written you a whole essay on the subject, and I ought to be writing a poem! Which shows that even a minor poet will sometimes prefer laying down the law to the exercise of his legitimate function. If you can make out from all the foregoing where I stand as to "art for art's sake," you'll be lucky. It seems to me I've no bone-bound convictions on the subject, but prefer rather to let each man follow his natural bent, and to judge only by results. I've heard it asserted, more than once, that you "spoilt *The Jungle* by its ending" (as I "spoilt the Yosemite Ode"), but *I* don't think so in *your* case. Can such things ever be definitely settled?

I'm immensely interested in your present work, and hope you'll send me installments early and often.

Love to you both!

GEORGE

GEORGE STERLING

San Francisco
July 2nd, 1924

Dear Upton:

By all means let me see the complete manuscript [of "Mammonart"]. When I see a friend about to make a world-ass of himself, I feel that I should do what I can to lessen the infliction.

I never wilfully try to hurt you, but you are so colossal an egoist that one has to hit hard to make you even "sit up and take notice." However, I may be of use in errors such as the "generation" one.

Your book should create an uproar, and I think that that's what you're really desirous of. But let me prophesy an odd thing: the folks that'll whack it hardest will be the radicals! Not the stupid ones, but such chaps as ran the *Freeman* and are running the *Liberator*, the *Nation* and the *New Republic*.

For you know not the soul of the artist.

Your apprehensive friend,
GEORGE

Poem

And I shall ask for a piece of your skin
To bind my copy of "Lilith" in!

G. S.

San Francisco
August 8th, 1924

Dear Upton:

It's good to find you taking my meaner remarks in so good part—though maybe you're only saving me up for a final commination!

As to Charmian's life of Jack [London], her chapter inclusive of his death was written carefully to camouflage the fact of his suicide, which was not exactly a compliment to her! And there was the insurance! she fairly *rushed* him to the crematory.

If Poe and Keats are not "great artists" then you and I don't even live on the same planet—and I fail to find the slightest "reforming impulse" in either of them. Maybe in one spot, in "The Pot of Basil."

As to Rousseau, I meant that I doubt if *any* man will tell *every*thing. He'd always hold back a few items. (I'm aware, too, that he confesses to masturbation.)

It's long since I've read *Gulliver's Travels,* and my notion as to the size of the Lilliputians was got from the pictures in the book, which gave them a height of about an inch. As to Goethe, I was including his *work* with his "character". Of course he'd have had no trouble finding a woman as *moral* as he!

Yours ever,

GEORGE

248

GEORGE STERLING

San Francisco
August 21st, 1924

Dear Upton:

Just a line en passant. Take a look at what Halde-man-Julius has to say about Conrad. I'm interested to see what you'll make of him, our dead King of Pessimism (not excepting Hardy), who seems to me blood-brother of the Greek dramatists in their depiction of man's helplessness in the clutch of Fate.

As I say, I wonder how you'll react to him, for in *The Nigger of the Narcissus* there is a satire on altruism (unnoticed except by me, so far as I can see) that makes me angry, for *immediate* altruism is my religion: I can see less good in the postponed and dubious effects of the reformer.

Will you say, because his philosophy cuts like acid into your theme, that he's *not an artist*? You did some marvellous wriggling in the case of Keats: I give you Conrad as an equal quandary. . . .

Yours ever,
GEORGE

H. L. MENCKEN

Baltimore
September 21st, 1926

Dear Sinclair:

The notion that business corrupts politics is like the Methodist notion that the saloon corrupted poli-

249

tics. The fact is that politics corrupted the saloon. Such laws got on the books that no saloonkeeper could obey them and survive, so he naturally went into politics. Business has gone in for the same reason. The government is the common enemy of every decent man. Its form is of small consequence, though I believe that it is worst when it is democratic. But all that I discuss in my coming book, *Notes on Democracy*. An early copy will reach you.

If any newspaper reporters ask you why I am coming to California, tell them it is to play the part of Pontius Pilate in the new DeMille Biblical movie. I am to receive $5,000 a week.

Yours,

MENCKEN

On his way to San Francisco Mencken stopped off for a short visit and a luncheon with us.

H. L. MENCKEN

Hotel St. Francis
San Francisco
November 16th, 1926

Dear Sinclair:

I am sorry indeed that I didn't get a chance to go down to the beach. With [Joseph] Hergesheimer in active eruption, one thing led to another.

Poor George Sterling is in bed here, and seems

250

to be very ill. He accumulated a large supply of bootleg liquors against my coming, and incautiously tried some samples. The result was a dreadful drunk. He looks to me to be in a really serious condition. I am thoroughly glad that I wasn't here when he began.

I shall return to Los Angeles Friday. On Friday I expect to start back for the East.

Yours,

H. L. MENCKEN

Sterling took his own life November 17, 1926. I have always been moved by Edwin Markham's tribute, and I quote here the concluding lines of his poem "Sarpedon," published in the Overland Monthly, *November, 1927.*

How can I call you back, O stormy lover,
    Since you have turned and dropt the mask of time?
    I have no power, none but this flying rime
And these wild tears; but these cannot recover
    That look of light, that step of gallant grace,
    That lyric laugh, that old-young wistful face.
What can I pour now as a last libation,
    What scatter on thy mortal dust, O friend?
    What thunder loosen at the road's last bend?
Let it be clarion, paean, exultation;
    For it must be thanksgiving for your song,
    Your laureled head above the applauding throng,
Your lyric voice the kingliest in our choir.
    The mightiest voice that ever shook the West.

251

H. L. MENCKEN

The American Mercury
New York
January 14, 1927

Dear Sinclair:

If I attempted any prohibition propaganda in
the *American Mercury*, it would ruin the magazine.
I am usually not against free discussion of debatable
ideas but the readers I am trying to reach do not
think that prohibition falls within that category.
They regard it as completely insane, just as Method-
ism is completely insane, and they'd no more tolerate an argument for it than they'd tolerate one for
chiropractic.

I think you could do an article on George Sterling
without mentioning his drinking but unfortunately
Mary Austin is already at work on the subject.
Whatever George told you in moments of katzen-
jammer, I am sure that he got a great deal more fun
out of alcohol than woe. It was his best friend for
many years and made life tolerable. He committed
suicide in the end, not because he wanted to get
rid of drink, but simply because he could no longer
drink enough to give him any pleasure.

I'll be delighted to see the [Floyd] Dell biography of you. A book on you should have been
written long ago. I incline to think that Dell will
make an excellent job and I'll certainly review his
work in the *American Mercury*.

I am trying to pull myself together to start a new book.

Sincerely yours,

H. L. MENCKEN

H . L . M E N C K E N

The American Mercury
New York
February 2, 1927

Dear Sinclair:

The news that George [Sterling] was a prohibitionist is news indeed! If you will put it into the form of an affidavit before a notary public I'll be delighted to have one million copies printed. If George was actually guilty of such treason to the noblest of human inventions, he was the damnedest scoundrel ever heard of in Christendom and deserves to be held up to eternal infamy. But I console myself with the hope that perhaps you, yourself, have been dallying with the wine-cup.

Don't miss Sinclair Lewis' new book [*Arrowsmith*]. It is ten times better than *Babbitt*. I have been reading the page proofs.

Yours,

H. L. MENCKEN

Affidavit of Mary Craig Sinclair: George Sterling was prohibitionist at that time—maybe all the time. Jack London was also, and several of my hard-drinking friends in the South. All drank to excess, however.

H. G. WELLS [1866-1946]

London
1922

Dear and only Upton:

That Bible idea is yours. I got it from your previous book of elegant extracts. I say so somewhere in these lectures, which, since I couldn't come and spout them, the *Saturday Evening Post* is giving in homeopathic doses to a slightly indignant world. You have just saved a bit of your property by getting ahead with your *Book of Life*. I should have been at that in a year or so. I may do it still in spite of you. Why do you always think of things first? I am older than you. I have read both your books. I won't say anything about them except, "Fine!" If I start on anything more I shall use up the whole morning, and meanwhile you will be getting ahead.

Love,

H. G. WELLS

In a series of articles in The Saturday Evening Post *the English journalist, historian, and fiction writer called for a new Bible, containing, first, a collection of the world's most vital literature, and second, a guide to modern conduct. I wrote him that I had tried to supply the first in* The Cry for Justice, *1915, and the second in* The Book of Life, *1921-22, which I sent to him on the day of publication.*

254

His tribute to The Cry for Justice *did not appear in the* S. E. P.

H. G. WELLS

Chicago, Ill.
November 23, 1940

Dear Upton:

World's End is a great and well-balanced design and it's kept me vividly interested from Los Angeles to Omaha. I think it the completest and most faithful portrait of that period that has been done or is likely to be done. But maybe the title should have been *Painful Gestation.*

He did not leave himself room for his signature; but I knew his very difficult handwriting. I had published in facsimile a letter from him in my little magazine during World War I, and a subscriber had written to ask me, "Please publish a translation."

When this card was written he had just been on a visit to Los Angeles and we had been to dine with Paulette Goddard, then the wife of Charlie Chaplin. I had there given him an autographed copy of World's End, *the first volume of the Lanny Budd series, just off the press.*

255

H. G. WELLS

Regent's Park, London
September, 1943

Dear Upton:

I liked your *New York Times* article [about neutralization of Central European territories] very much and I'm glad Eleanor [Roosevelt] got going about it. The Lanny Budd books have come to hand and have been greatly appreciated. I keep pretty fit and I am much stronger than I was three years ago. Here is some stuff which may interest you. Do you feel disposed to line up with these ideas and start a group of revolutionary nuclei over there?

Yours ever,
H. G. WELLS

He was a diabetic, with only three more years to live.

I do not recall what the enclosure was. The word "revolutionary" must have been playful for neither of us was in that mood.

FLOYD DELL [1887-   ]

The Masses Publishing Co.
New York
1916

Dear Upton:

I find here a note of yours to [Max] Eastman, which he must have received the day he left for France. He has noted on it that he hasn't any clippings on the Colorado strike.—It's good news that you are writing a novel about it [*King Coal*]. I think I shall like it. You know, when you published the *Metropolis* you lost the pedestal you had had in my youthful admiration, and it wasn't until I re-read some of *The Jungle* that I became certain again that you could write first-rate stuff. I fancy that you have a mind in which the sense of humor is chained by the foot in some dark corner (I know from *Sylvia's Marriage* that you have one about you which if let loose is the real stuff!)—and that in consequence of its suppression you do not do well with any except a really tragic theme. When you take the attempted seduction of the youth in the *Metropolis* by the fine lady tragically, and have him look at the church spire as he goes home and know for the first time why church spires exist, why then I weep and forswear you.

And in spite of the many splendid things about *Love's Pilgrimage*, your attempt to make out the life of a man of genius in this coarse world to be a tragedy, when it really is (say I, dogmatically) a comedy, a satirical comedy,—that spoiled the book as a whole for me. The fact that you could see the delicious comedy of an aroused and rampant wife shocking all the poor Southerners to death by insisting on telling them about marriage and syphilis, the comedy of a loving and conventional family that has to face an utterly bewildering, inexplicable, incredible, impossible, inescapable fact like their lovely, tongueloose and mercilessly truth-telling daughter—that book [*Sylvia's Marriage*] suggests to

257

me that you may yet do the tragedy and comedy both at once in a book that will be simply splendiferous. But I won't expect all that at once in your Colorado story. But I shall expect something very good . . . .

Yours faithfully,

FLOYD DELL

Dear Floyd: I look back on The Metropolis *after just half a century and I am truly sorry. I had paid off the debts on the Helicon Home Colony and I was "broke." The stage version of* The Jungle *was a "flop"; my first marriage had became a long torment; and I was far from well. One cannot produce a good novel under those circumstances.*

My friendship with this editor, novelist, and playwright began early, in Greenwich Village, but we corresponded only after I moved to California.

FLOYD DELL

1920

Dear Upton:

I'm sorry, I don't like your new book [*100%*]. I've just been reading the glowing praise of it in the *Nation,* and that makes me feel a little better about not liking it. What I don't like is precisely what that critic likes—the dry, repressed manner. It affects me like Flaubert's *Sentimental Education* or *Bouvard and Pecuchet.* The lack of emotional repercussion from any of the events upon the characters or author is supposed, I believe, to increase such repercussion upon the reader. But it always fails in my case in works of fiction, and leaves me with a sense of unreality—as if a man were painted in strong sunlight without a shadow. He can't really be there! I think if your book had stopped short after the Jennie episode it might have made a tremendously effective short story—as some of Maupassant's are tremendously effective. But when it goes on with no relief, I feel as I do about Maupassant's longer things, *Bel-Ami* and *Une Vie*—which I understand are worshipped by many people but which I cannot see. This is just to express the hope that you haven't permanently committed yourself to that manner of writing. To which I suppose your reply well might be that folks are damned hard to please! They object to your being emotional, and they object to your being unemotional. Well, put me down as voting for everybody being a regular human being in his writing—not a tear-squeezer like Dickens nor an inhuman lidless eye like Flaubert.

I hope you've received my novel [*Moon Calf*], and that you will find something to like in it. I am fulfilling a promise made a long time ago to myself— to write a novel which I woudn't be ashamed to send to Upton Sinclair. It has taken me more time to do it than I thought it would, but I now feel embarked upon a literary career, and I can't help expressing my gratitude to you for the example of your honesty and courage, of which I only hope I haven't fallen too far short.

Faithfully yours,

FLOYD DELL

259

FLOYD DELL

Croton, New York
1921

Dear Upton:

B. Marie and young Anthony are flourishing, and I am finding it very exciting being a parent. There is nothing like it!

At last I have read *The Book of Life.* I am very much pleased with it on the whole. I do think you lay rather too much stress on economic factors and not quite enough on psychic ones; and that your anthropology is rather old-fashioned and questionable; but in spite of these things the book attacks the personal problem very vigorously and helpfully. In the latter chapters, which I like best, you formulate, I think, your scheme with too much precision, it begins to look cut-and-dried at just the point when it had carried emotional conviction and opened the imagination to happy vistas. I wish you would stop short of giving, so to speak, the dimensions of the room in which the young people are to meet. And where, except from the depths of that same inner consciousness from which the German evolved his picture of the giraffe, did you get the age of—was it 12 or 14?—for the first lecture on sex? That is just about 12 (or 14) years too late! And it can only be defended upon the ground of not shocking your

260

readers. But while we are being Utopian, why not do the thing right. A child can acquire quite a lot of poisonous misinformation about sex between the ages of 2 and 12.

The absolute confident definiteness with which you propound this arrangement for early marriages —an idea of which I enthusiastically approve, but one which meets with other obstacles than the plain economic one—provokes me to this inquiry. What about the *character-forming* aspects of a marriage economically supported by the parents? What about the mother-in-law problem? Economic independence helps any marriage—economic dependence will damage any marriage. And what if the young couple *do* have babies? Are they to be *forbidden*? A girl who found her lover-husband growing *away* from her in the ages of 16 to 19 would be pretty likely to have a baby to hold him—and there are ways of getting a baby even from a cautious husband.

Is this first stage really an experimental stage? Is it a trial marriage, entered into with complete confidence that it will last, but kept childless for reasons of economic insecurity due to youth? Then it is an institution which used to exist all over Europe, and which is already beginning to exist in America, hampered by the necessity of secrecy and the lack of comfortable domesticity. There are thousands of young people having such trial marriages today, and managing them on the whole with honor and idealism. I think the wisest course of the older generation would be to recognize these trial mar-

261

riages, give them the opportunity of domesticity, and socially accept the private engagement of those couples as having all the binding force of the formal marriages you propose.

You believe too much in law, I think. The law is always an ass. Tradition, bad as it is, is better—and the best thing to do is to shape and change the tradition—and when you find a new tradition springing up, or an honorable old one being revived, give it encouragement. The strengthening of the bond of engagements, and the inclusion within it of the old-fashioned marital privileges which it used to have and after a brief Puritan interlude is beginning to have again—seems to me infinitely better than artificial marriage and divorce reform by law. My point being that a marriage is not a real marriage until children are in prospect, or some other *actual* (as distinguished from an ideal) *task* to hold them together; also that it isn't a real marriage until the husband is economically able to support the wife while she is by reason of having children unable to support herself. Any sexual commitments previous to this condition do not need the sanction of *law*; they need the sanction of public approval, and encouragement in their honest idealism. I think two young people could break such an engagement after a year or two with less psychic injury to themselves than would attend upon a divorce of however easy a sort.

Do I make my attitude upon this at all clear? Anyway, your attitude, as distinct from certain specific formulas, seems to me admirable, and such

262

would have the best effect upon the public to which you address yourself.

Faithfully yours,

FLOYD

The above refers to the first half of The Book of Life. *The next letter refers to the second half, published a year later.*

FLOYD DELL

Croton, New York
1922

Dear Upton:

The Book of Life, both editions, arrived . . . .

What I am getting at is this: Do Americans generally object to being lectured at moralistically? I imagine they don't. I imagine that they will take your book, so far as they get a chance, quite seriously. The fact that you have never been on a jag will not disqualify you in their eyes, from discoursing on the evils of drink. The young intelligentsia, however, as I know them, are avid of experience: and the only reason my moral attitudes are at all tolerated is that, as I gather, my vast experience in iniquity gives to these moral attitudes a certain piquancy. I raise this question because I want to be reassured. I feel that I am getting even more moralistic, and I wish to believe that even though the young intelligentsia regard me as they do the picture of an ichthyosaurus, I shall still find a public

263

willing to listen to me. I like your book precisely because it is a serious endeavor to tell people what they should and should not do. I don't regard you as the best qualified person in the world to give such advice, it is true.

Your account of the difficulties of making the stomach attend to its work sounds more like an exciting and complicated mystery-and-crime story than like the prosaic and on the whole dull affair which, in spite of a few romantic episodes, it is for most of us. Nevertheless, so long as you are honest about that stomach, I am willing to read about it; and on the fundamental proposition, that it matters extremely that we put the right and not the wrong things into the stomach. I quite agree with you, I can't see why the stomach shouldn't be taken seriously. In the same way, it seems to me that your experience of life is in general likely to be a special one, and that your conclusions may not have, in specific details, a wide validity; but you can testify only of your own experience, and I want to hear your testimony.

I still like the Book of the Body better than the Book of the Mind; I cannot get interested in the question of survival after death, and in regard to other psychic matters I have a smugly superior feeling—I know, I feel, more about these matters than anybody except Freud! I know how to do everything I want to, except stop smoking cigarettes, and some day I shall work that out—

B. Marie sends her love, and says she is waiting for you to write a book on how to bring up babies.

264

Is it possible that she doubts my wisdom in that matter? She is blooming, as usual . . . .

I trust you have received *Briary-Bush* [a novel by Dell], and I very much hope you like it. Re-reading parts of *Love's Pilgrimage* the other day, I realized how deeply that book had sunk into my mind, and become the groundwork, as it were, upon which any story of marriage that I might write would inevitably be built, whatever differences there might be. So you see, even if you don't like it, you are in some degree responsible for it!

FLOYD

FLOYD DELL

Croton-on-Hudson, New York
1923

Dear Upton:

I have just finished reading *The Goose-Step*. It is magnificent. I don't think there has ever been a better job in the history of literature. It is so rich with facts, so brutally rich with them—and yet, with all its historical value, it ripples, and sings, and laughs, scornfully and pityingly—it is so full of the truest and finest human emotions, so aware in every line of the best values of life. And—befitting to subject, it even has a Rabelaisian touch. Surely the monstrous and comic and horrible crudities of our Carthaginian civilization have never been better

265

pictured. If you had done nothing else; if you left only this book as your literary monument, readers of a future age would know that here was a spirit like Voltaire's, like Swift's, like Anatole France's—having that "holy rage"—

 With which the prophets, in their age,
 On all its decent seemings trod.

I cannot tell you what a wonderful book you have written; but it is one of the books that mark an epoch.

Faithfully yours,
FLOYD DELL

FLOYD DELL

Croton-on-Hudson, New York
1924

Dear Upton:

I got the *H.*[*aldeman*] *J.*[*ulius*] *Weekly* in Sconset, a little irregularly, and read a considerable part of *Mammonart*—I sent a post-card asking them to change the address, but haven't received it here. Of what I read, I liked very much the parts showing the economic determinism of literature—much of it being splendidly stated, and ringing all the bells. I thought you overstated the propaganda point, and that it would serve the purpose quite as well if you showed (as you did) the propaganda *aspect* of certain classics, but *without* asserting or implying that they were written *for* that purpose as an exclusive or even a main purpose. There is a difference between Aristophanes, for example, and Virgil: A—was a

266

real propagandist; V—one only in a secondary sense. The propaganda is there, even in V—, and you point it out very neatly; but it isn't as prime a purpose as it was in A—. And I think these distinctions should not be blurred—because they will be important when you come to the Ivory Tower stuff, whose propaganda is even more remote from what people ordinarily think of as such. You tend to confuse an important and true argument by the implication that *all* writers are *first of all* propagandists.—

The Author and Wife foolery seemed to me rather too long drawn out and over-labored. I parted company with you when you came out for Christian art as the only proletarian art. What kind of art will we have in the happy poet-revolutionary society?— Won't it celebrate beauty and joy? Must it go on celebrating misery? Doesn't what you think of as master-class art have something in it for the workers, even now? If the master-class can get satisfaction out of art founded on working-class life, can't the workers do the same thing in return? The paintings of Rubens might be considered as propaganda to the effect that after all we have bodies, that we live now, and that earthly happiness is to be desired. (I don't like Rubens, but if I had seen nothing but emaciated Christs and Virgins, I should welcome him, I am sure!) If art is to represent life as a vale of tears, without any natural joy in it, how are we to get the idea that the world is worth having a revolution to get possession of?—It was at some such point that the paper stopped coming, so I can argue no further. In general, I found

267

much of it saying something that needs to be said, and saying it splendidly, so as to arouse a deep enthusiasm in me; some of it rather feebly and fictitiously humorous; and some of it marred by a one-sided preoccupation with the pitiful aspects of life—by a Christian psychology in the worst sense. I don't suppose you will believe that, however; and I am glad that you are doing the job—it is, particularly in this period, a pretty thankless one. Art has become so divorced from the realities of life that a recognition of its bases gives pain.

By the bye, have you read Jane Harrison's *Ancient Art and Ritual* (Home University Lib)? It contains some important matter bearing on the relation of art to life. Robert Graves *On English Poetry* (Knopf) contains a jaunty and breezy statement of some important things too, though they may be too special for your purview. I should like to see it all.

Faithfully yours,

FLOYD

P.S. In all of this argument you may feel that I am distorting the picture of your early life by leaving out the robustness, the grit, the doggedness, the superior abilities, the triumphs. I know the "suffering boy" was also—(strangely enough, in his way!) a "go-getter", a cock-sure, impudent, independent, proud, snooty, resourceful, ambitious and immensely able lad, a million miles from having any of the psychology of failure (thank Heavens for that!)— but to my mind that only gets a young idealist into deeper hot water (as for example, in his sheer inability to admit that a bright lad like himself could have made a silly marriage, and his ruthless determination to *make* it a success, thereby prolonging his agonies!) Only an able, resourceful, superior boy could *possibly* suffer as much as you did; only a bright lad could *be* such a God damn fool! Am I right?

F. D.

Floyd's postscript refers to Love's Pilgrimage.

FLOYD DELL

1924

Dear Upton:

I have been reading *Mammonart* with profound admiration. I could quarrel with you on points of theory, interpretation, and judgment; but the fact remains that it is a great work, greatly accomplished.

I wish every young writer in America could read it—and every boy or girl who dreams of some day becoming a writer. It would knock that pious nonsense out of their heads that they are taught in school—the notion that true art is tame art, art made safe and harmless for the bourgeoisie! That nonsense, poisoning the minds of our finest, bravest, most clear-seeing young people even before they have learned how to write, muddying youth's purpose and degrading art's meaning for them, is robbing us of the great and vital literature they could create tomorrow. Your book is the best antidote for that spiritual poison.

Faithfully yours,
FLOYD DELL

FLOYD DELL

London, N. W. 3
July 22, 1925

Dear Upton:

I am—as I suspected—not a good traveler. I don't
like to go around looking at things, and I have maintained a reasonably good temper only by working
regularly every day at a literary task. London has
put me into an 18-year-old mood. It is, above all,
the citadel of two things both of which I hate—the
surviving remnants of feudalism, and the—what
shall I call it to distinguish it from our sort of high-
way robbery?—aristocratic finance; and most of the
monuments I see here are so full of the associations
of both, that I cannot enjoy their beauty (if they
have any, which I deeply doubt), but am filled with
a childish and helpless rage. Nothing in America
except your damned romantic picturesque, pious,
slave-holding, aristocratic South: I am glad every
time I see, in Central Park, that statue of Sherman
on his implacable and deadly march to the sea!—
affects me like that. American wealth is too recent,
too jerry-built and frail and uncertain in any case,
too piratical and accidental, too much like a stroke
of gambler's luck, too vulgar, too much of the
peddlar grown rich over night, to be angry at; in fact
in the strictest sense of the word, Capitalism seems
an English thing, a thing more odious and hateful
than our reckless American exploits in money-mak-
ing, just because it is more cold-blooded and respectable and hypocritical and frigidly "Chinese". We

270

haven't, it seems to me, any class quite correspond-
ing to the class of English people who live on their
invested capital; we have a lot of hopeful and occasionally successful, and often ruthless, gamblers.
Even the frantic ruthlessness of the Merchants and
Manufacturers Associations in the States seems to
me a less depressive thing than the whited-sepul-
chral dignity of the gentlemanly investors here; and
the jailing of wobblies than free speech in Hyde
Park. Well, I didn't intend to run on this way,
but only to say that for once, under special auspices,
I did enjoy a glimpse of one of these British monuments, when we dined at the House of Commons
with Ellen Wilkinson, a left-wing Labor M.P., and
saw David Kirkwood and others, and later listened
to a debate in that queer and cosy club, The House
of Commons itself. But enough!

We are all well, except that I've a cold.

FLOYD

FLOYD DELL

Croton-on-Hudson, New York
1926

Dear Upton:

I went to see your mother the other day, and I
really like her very much: a nice, hard-headed, conventional old reactionary—don't you tell her I said
that! She is the very antithesis of you. If the world
were made up exclusively of people like her, there

271

would be no progress; if it were made up exclusively of people like you, it would prematurely explode! I like, as a matter of fact, both kinds of people, and I think it very amusing that you should be her son. Such people, too, are usually right about half the time.

And so to work!

FLOYD

At this time he was getting material for his biography of me.

FLOYD DELL

May 25th, 1926

Dear Upton:

Mame is delightful, and I enjoyed it thoroughly. All the same, I think you missed a good bet in keeping the gal so pure. It would have been even funnier, and a better all-rough satire, if her profoundly patriotic emotions had let her go to bed with her gentleman friend as occasion required; she would have had reasons for doing it of the same quality as the reasons for all the rest of the political farce so delightfully exposed here. And I daresay she would have been truer to a certain type that Washington affords. Your affection for her seems to me to have mixed your motives a little bit, so that you don't turn the final edge of your satire on her. It is

272

possible that if you had conceived her as less virtuous you would have treated her less kindly; and that would have been unfortunate. But I really cannot see that Mame's chastity is up to the author of this satirical skit to preserve so conscientiously. I don't see what point is gained thereby, in truth or effectiveness. Must Mame be a working-class heroine too, and are none but the idle rich ever to fornicate in your fiction? I decline to accept her as working-class, she seems to me to belong to a class that deserves just a little more exposing than you give her. And her earnestness, her moral earnestness, would be so delightful, on top of the rest of her career. I really think you have just missed making a character as good as Pangloss or Candide, and as destined to last, as a picture of certain aspects of our hypocritical civilization. But that chastity of hers, so carefully preserved by the author, keeps her from ever quite coming truly alive as a person. Well, doubtless you had your reasons. But, whatever they are, I think they were wrong! . . . However, as to the literary dispute that I believe I am to adjudicate between you and your son, I cast my vote for you, or at least the book. It *is* funny, and it is good.

FLOYD

Floyd is referring to my The Spokesman's Secretary, *published in 1926. In the days of Coolidge, the President never gave interviews; the "White House Spokesman" spoke for him. The absurdities they put off on the country are exposed in my skit subtitled "The Letters of Mame to Mom."*

273

FREDERIK van EEDEN

Bussum (N. Holland)
July 6, 1921

My dear good Brother:

I have finished *The Book of Life* which you gave
me to read. Of course, I have the greatest appreciation for your work. It is exactly what I could expect from you. It is sincere and upright. It will
make thousands of people think. But I fear it will
not be read as your last novels. It is a bit . . . tedious.
I finished it because you wanted me to read it. Had
it not been for you, I would have struck half way.
And then I must explain my remark that I had no
confidence in you as a philosopher and a prophet.
That is because you are still too young. As an author, you are in full bloom, and one of the best on
earth. But as a thinker you are not yet ripe. And
you will not be so before you are sixty or seventy.
Your religious part is still undeveloped. You have
never felt as concrete facts those religious truths
that William James described in his *Religious Experiences*. I know quite well that you are a Christian and a religious man—as all your works are full
of the religion of deeds. But you do not yet know
the super-natural life, just as I had to discover it
some years ago. I want you to read two books. Perhaps I mentioned them already to you. *Saddhu
Sundar Singh*, and *The Light Invisible* by Benson.

But all my words are powerless, when you have
not the experience yourself. My stay in a Benedic-

274

tine Monastery has had the most wonderful results and the days there are the most glorious of my life.

O, my dear brother, how I wish we could talk. I don't think you will ever understand me, before we have seen and embraced each other.

And there is so much going on, inward and outward, and so much to talk about!

On the whole my life is more gay and prosperous than ten years ago. The mortgage on my house and ground is paid off, and Walden is well-groomed and prosperous. The only loss I had was my dear mother and my son, Paul. I am not however bereft of their presence. I am getting wonderful messages in Automatic script (not mine!) and these are published in two volumes . . . .

There are lots of books now coming out, in Germany and England and Holland on the same subject. It seems the great Shock loosened the ideas.

Good bye, and God's blessing on you.

van Eeden

He had not seen me since 1912. We never met again.

FREDERIK van EEDEN

Bussum (N. Holland)
May 31st, 1923

My dear Uppie:

I got your long letter of May 11th. It is rather funny, that you end by saying that we cannot argue, while you have been arguing on five pages. I quite agree that we cannot argue and this because for arguing fruitfully it is necessary for both parties to have the faculty for reason, and the sense that is beyond reason. We are not on equal terms, because you lack the mystical streak, that I—thank God—possess. You are in my view an invalid—lacking this supreme faculty. And with all your knowledge of historical facts, your understanding of them is very poor.

Never fear to hurt me, for I must do the same to you. I must do it out of love. And so I consider this long hopeless letter from you as a token that you love me after all, and so I do you.

When you wrote me some years ago, that you were going to write a "Book of Life" I told you at once frankly that this was beyond your power. You are a wonderful novel writer, a genius in your sort, but your mind lacks absolutely any deeper philosofy [*sic*] or profound sense of superior matter. You have a "streak of blindness" and your grasp of reality is feeble and confused. Your wisdom is more infantile, I should say, than oriental wisdom of two thousand years ago.

The wisdom of the ancient Indian sages, the wisdom of Upanishads and Rigveda is much more profound than yours. And your talk of "Hindoo mystics looking at their navel" is child's talk.

You are not only behind the ancients, Hindoo or Christian—but you are behind your own time. Your talk of "reason" and "blind emotion" is superannuated for perhaps a century. The age of materialism

276

and naturalism has passed for good, and America is still in Goose-step to it—probably because of the slow advance of philosophy in your big, badly educated nation. The debacle of pure reason by Einstein's logic, is in Europe so generally known that your talk seems to come from some obsolete period, passed long ago.

But how this super-reason, this super-natural wisdom will develop and whether it will be the Catholic or the Hindoo wisdom, that will realize it and bring it into everyman's life—that is subject to discussion . . . .

Good-bye, brother, write me again.

Urgrossvater

van Eeden

FREDERIK van EEDEN

Bussum (No. Holland)
Walden
July 16th, 1927

Dear Brother:

Of course I am on your side in the matter of *Oil*. It seems to me absurd and even criminal to oppose the publication of a book like *Oil*. Its tendency being the opposition against rotten conditions in the economical life of the United States.

I think you are right in attacking the decay in our society on that very spot, where you can take

277

the strongest position. *Oil* is laying the finger on the most sensitive place, where the parasites must show colour on the most obvious spots. The "Oil swindle" can not be denied, not in America and not in Europe. It is based on falsehood and I believe that it is unjust to call your book communistic or atheistic. It is in its action only honest.

I wish you a good success in a case which is also mine.

Yours with love,

FREDERIK VAN EEDEN

FREDERIK VAN EEDEN

Bussum, (N. Holland)
October 22nd, 1929

Dear Uppy:

I received your letter, in which you told me what Mr. Perdeck had written about our friendship. There is nothing changed between us considering our friendship. And I have received your book *Boston*. Many thanks for that. Wonderful is your book and blessed your work. Forget me not.

Yours,

FREDERIK VAN EEDEN

I have not done so; and I here pass this noble character on to the reader. Our complete correspondence is in the van Eeden museum in Amsterdam and in the Indiana University Library. In 1960 van Eeden's 100th birthday will be celebrated

278

in Amsterdam with complete publication of all his works, including his letters.

I do not know whether I shall meet him in some hereafter. We should both be sad if we were consigned to different regions.

EUGENE O'NEILL [1888-1953]

> Brook Farm
> Ridgefield, Connecticut
> March 26th, 1923

Dear Upton Sinclair:

They have planned the productions pretty well ahead for the Provincetown, but I have asked Kenneth Macgowan to think about *Hell*. Your suggestion is a good one. It would be extremely interesting for us to attempt. The stage there is very tiny, as you know.

If you come east this summer, and are up Boston way, come over the dunes and pay us a visit. At present we are thinking very seriously of coming to California next winter.

> Sincerely,
>
> EUGENE O'NEILL

I have the first act of your new play here and am going to read it the first moment I get away from rehearsing *All God's Chillun*.

America's greatest playwright, in my opinion.

EUGENE O'NEILL

Peaked Hill Bar
Provincetown, Mass.
August 12th, 1923

My dear Upton Sinclair:

Thank you for sending me *Hell*. I'll look forward
to it—but just now I'm "off" reading as all my time
is mortgaged to a new play I'm in the midst of and
which I want to finish before leaving here.

I'm sure glad to know you're a "fan". It's recip-
rocated, believe me! I've been one of yours ever
since way back in *Jungle* days, and I think I've read
everything of yours—except *The Goose-Step*—since
then.

All sincere appreciation and respect to you!

EUGENE O'NEILL

The production never materialized.

EUGENE O'NEILL

Brook Farm
Ridgefield, Connecticut
February 21, 1926

My dear Upton Sinclair:

Not this winter. We're booked for Bermuda. But
almost certainly next winter. And I will surely look
you up right away, and many thanks to you for your

kind offer of lending us a hand. When it comes to information about the real-estate, etc., we shall probably need a lot of same. We think of locating in the vicinity of Santa Barbara or further down the coast in a place called La Jolla which is strongly recommended to us. Do you know it? To be on the water is our first requisite.

I hear they have "pinched" my play *Desire Under the Elms* in your Holy City, Los Angeles. Well, well, and so many of the pioneers are said to have come from New England! Boston has also barred it.

All best to you,

EUGENE O'NEILL

WILLIAM ELLERY LEONARD
[1876-1944]

The University of Wisconsin
Madison
September 30, 1922

Dear Sinclair:

Needless to tell you I was much pleased with the kind thought that prompted the sending of the autographed giftbook [*They Call Me Carpenter*], and much interested in those burning pages of fantastic irony and social criticism. There's nothing to say on the point of view; that the fundamental at-

281

titudes and practices of contemporary society are a hideous mockery of the spirit of that prophet to whom society has built its temples and directed its prayers is, I guess, pretty clear to a number of us. Something of this I felt myself long ago in writing a little book called *The Poet of Galilee,* tho my main interest in those days was in the individual quality of his mind, and less in the social significance of his vision . . . .

As to quoting me by name in your "Goose-Step" book, I can tell better, as you say, when I see what you've found useful to quote. In general unless my name is decidedly useful, I'd just as soon it would be omitted. I'm in an odd and paradoxical situation. I've been befriended in this community against dreadful abuse and slander in my private life by the very people with whom I've become in my social thought so estranged. And tho in my opinion and action I'd as little wish to be bribed by gratitude as by gold, yet I have an instinct to avoid unnecessary unpleasantness, which is human enough, especially when one trails along half-sick. But send the manuscript in due course and I'll let you know. Meantime go to it!

As ever

W. E. Leonard

Poet and professor of literature at the University of Wisconsin, a great mind and heart, Leonard was tormented all his life by a psychological compulsion, which he describes in The Locomotive God.

282

WILLIAM ELLERY LEONARD

New York
November 3, 1922

Dear Sinclair:

Do forgive me. Of course I wasn't the writer of
the unsigned note [I don't remember the note referred to here]. I haven't been well in body or
mind; I've been going from one crisis to another,
compelled, the while, to do the minimum of necessary work with my vitals on fire. Things are almost
at their top-most crisis now. Soon after I wrote you
I met a girl. No "affair." We need each other profoundly and in all ways. To be her husband for ten
years I'd be willing to give up the rest of my life.
And my poor wife is in a state of complete collapse
and—threatens suicide. Send on the O.S.U. stuff.
If I do end by putting a bullet through my fool
head, I want my friends to know that I've tried not
to neglect any of the decent interests, especially of
the spirit of comradeship.

Faithfully yours,

LEONARD

*I must have asked him to read my paragraphs
about Ohio State University in* The Goose-step.

283

The University of Wisconsin
Madison
April 3, 1927

Dear Sinclair:

Oil! is Upton Sinclair at his best, the defusion of
the creative artist with the wise critic of life; it has
vision and power. I'm sure all your friends must be
happy with me. It is great fiction and great thinking
and great knowledge (both of human nature and
social conditions and of a certain industry, the most
sinister of our times). The extraordinary thing is
its objectivity and charity—I mean the most extraordinary for the U. S. of the last decade. The artist
in you seems to have triumphed—which, in my opinion, means you are thus a better propagandist. But
I'm not in shape to write much. I endorse Floyd
Dell's note verbatim . . . .

Faithfully,

W. E. LEONARD

WILLIAM ELLERY LEONARD

The University of Wisconsin
Madison
July 5, 1927

Dear Upton:

The book [*Two Lives*, the story of his marital
tragedy] is now published, and everywhere accepted as essential autobiography, and I've nothing

284

to fear from the enemies who so long hampered my life. There is no reason why you shouldn't speak of the biographic backgrounds as you do—your facts are (unfortunately) correct—except (fortunately) for the mistake "associate"; a year ago (after Frank's coming) I received the inexpressible honor of the title of Full Professor. (Being incidentally last year elected to membership in the good old conservative American Institute of Arts and Letters!)

Tho' as a matter of fact, I seldom make comments on contemporary Non-poets, let me say to you behind the rose-bush that, in spite of admiration for Edgar Arlington Robinson in his short, simple, poignant psychological sketches, I can't but agree with you in substance about these longer poems. I think there is a sort of E. A. R. cult developing—partly, perhaps, in protest (and so far so good) against some tendencies toward crude slapstick in contemporary American verse. But for good or ill, my fault or not, everytime I've begun one of these longer poems I've laid it down unfinished.

I think there is a radical difference between Shakespeare's mixed metaphors and those of most poets; theirs are due to *confusion* of *mind,* his to *compression* of *speech* . . . to take arms against a host of troubles coming on like a sea. In reading his metaphors we so instinctively supply the links that we only note anything peculiar after we've sophisticatedly analyzed. This isn't meant to suggest any change in your statement—but it does emphasize the difference.

I may have told you that my psychological history comes out this fall with the Century Company, entitled (18th C. diction) *The Locomotive God.*

I've been immensely amused at your tilt in Boston. U.S., the pornographist!—Ja, jetzt hört alles auf! [now everything comes to an end!].

Faithfully yours,

W. E. LEONARD

He is referring to the Boston banning of my novel Oil!

BARTOLOMEO VANZETTI
[1888-1927]

Charlestown Prison (Mass.)
May 30, 1922

I am very grateful to you, for your visit.

One must had been prisoner in order to understand what "a good visit" mean. And surely enough, neither you nor the good Dana, can realize what a joy I proved, and I wish to you, to not become able to realized it.

Your book was not gave to me. I do not know what the Warden could have said to you, but if he do not refused the book, I tell you what had happended: After your departure he call on Father Murphy, the boss of the State Prison of Mass. and hashed [*sic*] to him about the book. What it must had followed, you know better than I.

So, I must sorrowfully advise you, to avoid the

286

useless expenditure and work, such as would be the speditions of your book, because they will be barred.

I am sorry of the brevity of your visit, because I would have had time enough to speak of a many interesting things. But I am in jail, and you have your necessity. I hope, nevertheless, that, thanks to the solidarity of the proletariat, and of so many generous hearts, to be able to have a long conversation with you.

Cordially yours,

BARTOLOMEO VANZETTI

Vanzetti was an Italian fishpeddler accused of a payroll murder, and executed in 1927; this world-famous case was the subject of my novel, Boston.

"The good Dana" was Henry Wadsworth Longfellow Dana, grandson of the poet and a tireless friend of civil liberty.

I do not recall the book referred to by Vanzetti.

BARTOLOMEO VANZETTI

Massachusetts State Prison
October 4, 1923

As I realize that you understand the sentiments and thoughts that your solidariety and friendship arise in a man of my conviction and of my principles, I will not try to express them—but I will only testify of them.

I will never forget your visit nor what your golden pen—that so many good battles valiantly fought in

287

behalf of the truth and of the freedom—had wrote in my defense.

What you have said about my innocence is but the truth.

I understand and appreciate the reasons by which you were advised to exalt me far above my little merit. If there is a little of goodness in me—I am glad of it—but really I do not deserve your praisers. (as they are)

I think that there are some prisoners within these very four walls which exile me from society, which are much better than I.

I have finished a short novel which will soon be published—at least—so I was told; and I will send a copy to you. Please do not believe that I am conceited—I know my littleness—Humble I wrote for the humble who must conquer the world to peace and freedom; and I try to make plain humble but ignored truths.

Yours with great heart,

Bartolomeo Vanzetti

The novel, so far as I know, was never published.

JOHN JAY CHAPMAN [1862-1933]

New York City
April 6, 1923

My dear Mr. Upton Sinclair:

I have read a good bit of your book *The Goose-Step* and I must send you a word of thanks for it.

The nature of the American business-mind, and the way this mind looks at education and educational problems of all sorts, has never been so clearly displayed as it is by this book. You expound your thesis in an unforgettable manner and the thesis—as a thesis—is true. One may disagree as to the particular emphasis you place on some illustration or on certain episodes. One may quarrel with your conclusions, or with your remedies; but the picture you draw of our present conditions remains in the mind. The mass of illustrative material which you brought together speaks for you, and will remain as a valuable deposit, a sort of lurid mass of hot smouldering coals, at which historians may warm their hands.

One can hardly expect historians to take one's own hot views on current abuses. The historians will be apt to say that our millionaire barons of today did no worse than other rich men have done in former ages; they attempted to enslave society by bullying and bribing the Education of Society to favor their own interests and prejudices. The historians will say that men like Morgan and Rockefeller and Henry Higginson and Stotesbury were not so malevolent as they looked to their contemporary idealists.

The historians will absolve our business magnates from malice to a greater extent than you or I could do; you and I have been intent on getting dull people to see that the benevolence of our millionaires had a dangerous side to it. This sharpened our pens.

Another idea crosses my mind: though I do not expect you to agree with it,—namely that the support which Socialism receives from any revelations as to the selfishness of the rich is illusory,—or largely illusory. For everyone feels that the weakness lies in human nature itself. The rich will always be selfish; and the poor will always, by comparison, be unselfish.

If the Socialists of today are, on the whole, more unselfish than the plutocrats, it is because they are on the whole more poor and more powerless. Now I am going to say something which will seem to you horribly untrue and almost sacrilegious. Our rich men have been simple-minded, selfish business magnates, crude, materialistic, almost childish in their aims and methods. They have had no dogma, or recondite powerful abstract aim. I fear that if the Socialists once came into power their activities would be governed by some theory which would crush humanity in a manner that Big Business never dared, and indeed never was tempted to dream of.

Yours sincerely,

JOHN JAY CHAPMAN

P.S. If it should cross your mind to publish this, I have no objection; so long as you publish it all. I thought at first of addressing it to you as a public letter.

Chapman, lawyer, biographer, and social critic, possessed of a powerful mind, has recently been the subject of an elaborate biography. I do not expect

290

the Socialists ever to "come into power" in America. I hoped that the Socialists—not the Communists— would fertilize our thinking and bring about a series of "New Deals" and "Fair Deals," with social de- mocracy and social justice as the ultimate goals.

SIR RABINDRANATH TAGORE
[1861-1941]

Bengal, India
1923

Dear Mr. Sinclair:

Enclosed herewith you will find a Postal Order for twenty shillings. Will you kindly send me as many of your books as can be bought with this sum?

With admiration for your personality and your works.

Yours sincerely,

RABINDRANATH TAGORE

Hindu poet, author of Gitanali, *Nobel Prize win- ner, Tagore had come to Pasadena to lecture, a ven- erable, bearded figure in a yellow robe; but as he later told van Eeden, those who had charge of him carefully kept him sheltered from the city's one Socialist author.*

SIR RABINDRANATH TAGORE

Visva-Bharati
Calcutta Office
September 4, 1923

Dear Mr. Sinclair:

The box of books have arrived with the kind messages of your friendship inscribed in each and every one. It was indeed kind in you to respond so generously to my request. I am glad to have this expression of your interest and glad also of the opportunity to give your ideas to the students of my Visva-Bharati.

You asked me my opinion of your books. I have not as yet had the opportunity to read them all, but it was *The Brass Check*, read when it was first published, that made me feel that I should like to know both the man and his works. Your fearless stand for truth, for the things that are right, your viewpoint of the humiliation that worship of money brings, its stifling quality, its empty arrogance, its insidious undermining of self-respect, its valuelessness, all the attributes which are its curse when dollars own the man, these ideas which you inculcated in this particular book immediately made a bond of sympathy. For years I have thought over these things, this especial phase of our modern civilization, and only a few weeks ago I have myself finished a Drama on the same subject. It will be published shortly in English and I shall hope to have the pleasure of sending you a copy.

292

I shall see about the translation of some of your books and let you know.

With the most sincere thanks for your courtesy, and the hope that we may have a personal chat someday concerning men and books and things in general and those in particular which seem to interest us both, I am,

Yours sincerely,

RABINDRANATH TAGORE

EDITH KELLEY [1884-1956]

North San Diego P.O., Calif.
April 6th, 1923

Dear Upton:

It would be trespassing too much on your eyesight and patience to ask you to read the blurred and frowsy carbon copy of my book that I have here. Besides I am afraid that when you read it you will advise me to do what Mr. Harcourt has suggested and which I have already written him that I won't do. However, I have left the way open to a compromise, and I presume that that is how we will settle it. When I hear from him I may have to run to you for advice, which perhaps I should have done before writing him in the first place. Thanks very much for your advice about business arrangements. Those things I know absolutely nothing about, and I may have to come to you for further pointers.

Mr. Alfred Harcourt wrote me that he and three other members of the firm had read my book and that they were all very enthusiastic about it. He also said: "I wonder if you realize what it means to a publisher to find a new novelist with the power to see and write as you do." That looks as if he had a pretty high opinion of the book and encourages me in the idea that perhaps I might be able to drag a five hundred dollar advance out of him after we have settled our differences about the changes he suggests. Lord knows I need it. Then my husband could quit the packing house and we could go into the chicken business in a small way. It is hard for an artist to work in a packing house, even though he is big and husky and used to manual labor. He pulls wool from the half decayed hides of sheep all day long, and the stink gets into his very pores. The hides have to be partly decayed before the wool will loosen. He was home most of this week with an infection in his hand. Every few weeks he is home for several days with such an infection, and of course he runs always the danger of more serious blood poisoning. He is not paid for the days that he is absent. All he gets is free medical treatment. A man is paid no compensation not even his wages for anything contracted on the job unless he is home more than six days, and then he gets sixty percent of ninety percent of his wages. How neatly they have it arranged! They know that all but the very serious things are over in about six days and that when a man is not paid he is anxious to get back on the job whether he is well or not. I imagine that most middle class people who talk about the improved conditions of the working man do not know

294

that the boasted workman's compensation law works out that way. If an artist does not work for the magazines or for some business concern it does not matter how much ability he has if he has not a lot of money to back him and get him before the public.

Of course we were glad to get *The Goose-Step.* My husband and I at once started to read it, quarrelling of course over who should have the book and accusing each other of misplacing the matches we put in for bookmarks when we laid the book down. On account of my household duties I haven't got very far but am already deeply enthralled and looking forward to a rare treat. I was just a few moments ago reading about the professors who had been asked to resign from Columbia. I wonder if you knew Arthur Livingstone? I got to know him rather well during the year before I married for the second time and left New York. He was professor of Italian and made the Italian language and literature live for his students, as he did also for me. But he did not toe the conventional chalk line and was asked to resign some seven or eight years ago.

The educational system seems to be more pernicious here in the West than elsewhere in America. That is one reason why we want to go back East where humanity is less universally warped. One of their ideas here is to have the school building as large and pretentious as possible. This means of course that there are fewer of them. My little girl only eleven has to go to a "Junior High School" which is nearly ten miles away. And we are within the city limits and less than five miles from the centre of the town. The poor kid is exhausted from so much traveling and hates the great big mill through which she is being ground. There are over twelve hundred children in the school. They start at half past eight, have no recesses and only half an hour for lunch, and if I had not interceded and insisted on their letting her out at a quarter past two, she would be there till three o'clock. Everything is reduced to a system. You would be dismayed to hear her tales of how cut and dried everything is. When they express their infantile desire to be given time to play they are told that big girls like them don't need to play. On Saturdays and Sundays she is like a wild thing turned loose. In New Jersey and Imperial Valley she was used to doing as she liked, riding barebacked, rounding up cattle, etc., so she feels all the more acutely the restraints of such a school. Under such conditions a child has no opportunity to make friends or develop at all naturally. The whole thing seems based on western desire to make a display. I never till I came west saw people so smug and complacent and so deft at throwing bouquets at themselves.

Affectionately,

EDITH

Edith had been my secretary, first at Princeton while I was writing The Jungle, *and then at Helicon Hall, 1906-07; see my comments concerning her and Sinclair Lewis in my introduction to these letters.*

296

EDITH KELLEY

North San Diego, Calif.
September 13th, 1923

Dear Upton:

My book *Weeds* was published today. In the course of a week or two you will receive a copy from the publishers. I hope that you and your wife will like it and that you will think it worthy of a few words of commendation.

Congratulations on the measure of success that you have attained in your Los Angeles fight. It takes much courage and strength of purpose to think anything worth fighting for in these dark days. I have spells of sinking of the heart when I think of the condition of the world and the sad outlook of humanity.

Sincerely,

EDITH

Weeds had a critical success but small sales, and has been forgotten—for a while. The "Los Angeles fight" is a reference to my kidnapping, mentioned earlier in this collection, by the police at the harbor of Los Angeles for attempting to read the Bill of Rights of the Constitution while standing on private property with the written consent of the owner.

EDITH KELLEY

October 18, 1923

Dear Upton:

Thanks for the news about your review of *Weeds*.
I shall look for it. I am returning the letter.

Had a very enthusiastic letter about *Weeds* from
Hal Lewis who is at present in France.

EDITH

MAY SINCLAIR [1870-1946]

London,
August 4, 1922

My dear Mr. Sinclair:

Very many and great thanks for the volume on
Love and Society from your *Book of Life*. I read it
with intense interest and admiration and agreement.
You have written the best and sanest thing about
Love and, it seems to me, the best and sanest
thing about Society.

I am not greatly interested in Utopian theories,
but your scheme of reconstruction is a very different thing.

I didn't altogether care for Marie Stopes' book,
Married Love; it had a sort of unctuous sentimental-
ity that to me was a little revolting. I have much
preferred a straight physiological tale. By the way
she is not a physiologist, or a doctor of medicine.

298

She's a palaeontologist. But I think she's courageous and sincere—two great qualities. I congratulate you on your conspicuous possession of them.

If you care for metaphysics I wish you'd look at my book *The New Idealism.* I'd send you it, only I have an idea you DON'T care for metaphysics—not MY sort! I'll send you my new novel when it comes out. I've been appallingly busy finishing it or I'd have written sooner.

Again thanking you, and with kindest regards,

MAY SINCLAIR

This English novelist was not related to me. Her first novel, The Divine Fire, *had a great success in America. It is the story of a young poet, and Jack London wrote me that if he had written that book he would have been able to die happily. I had paid my respects to her in London in 1912.*

WITTER BYNNER [1881-   ]

Chapala, Mexico
July 26th, 1923

Dear Upton Sinclair:

At last a week in a hospital kept me quiet enough to read something even as short and swift-moving as your extraordinary verse-play, *Hell.*

Each time I read something of yours I am amazed first by the vigor and breadth of your conception, and next by its velocity of execution. Here you had a theme worthy of a Dante, and you seem to toss it

299

off between risky readings of the Constitution. As you have more than guessed before from the comments which your work teases out of me, I am always a little saddened, from the point of view of an artist, that you have not taken the years on this or that piece of it which would establish it as a permanently formed work of genius. And then I begin to wonder whether a genius in this generation is not, after all, more vitally concerned in building his art out of substance of men instead of out of the substance of words. The vim and speed which you are putting into these works of yours are probably having more effect in the lives and conduct of men than the same work would have shaped and restrained by years of sensitive application. The trouble with me is that I want you to be both things and am probably asking the impossible. Be it sufficient that I gratefully accept this play from you, often cherishing in it the artist, and more often the man.

Yours always,

WITTER BYNNER

P.S. My Guadalajara friend, Idella Purnell, has suggested to me that she undertake translating the play into Spanish. She was one of my students at Berkeley, is a poet in her own right, is editing the poetry magazine *Palms* and, having lived most of her years in Guadalajara and won the interest lately of several Mexican writers, she would doubtless do a good job in presenting your play to a public astonishingly ready for it. If you think well of this idea you might send her a copy and let her know how you arrange such propositions.

No, I'll give her my copy and you send me another, with your name in it. Meantime, I'll ask Dutton to send you a copy of my translations from Viljrac.

Bynner, American poet and man of all letters; his works include The Way of Life *and* Journey with a Genius.

MONTAGUE GLASS [1877-1934]

Pasadena, California
November 14th, 1923

My dear Upton Sinclair:

Many thanks for the invitation to speak. I should be more delighted than you could possibly believe, to do it, because if I were capable of speaking for forty-five minutes, I could then take advantage of the offers sent by lecture bureaus to provide against what appears to be going to be an indigent old age. This is complicated language, and half reveals the information that I am as incapable of speaking for forty-five minutes as I hope I am of homicide. However, I can and do write a check for five dollars as my first year's dues in the American Civil Liberties Union.

It was a great pleasure to meet you the other evening and to testify to my admiration which is that of thousands for your courageous adventure with the Los Angeles authorities.

We expect to have some good chamber music in about a fortnight and are counting on you and Mrs. Sinclair to be a part of the audience.

Sincerely yours,

MONTAGUE GLASS

Glass is author of the "Potash and Perlmutter" stories.

The "courageous adventure" mentioned here was my arrest at the harbor of Los Angeles, spoken of earlier in this collection.

EDGAR LEE MASTERS [1869-1950]

January 30, 1924

Dear Mr. Sinclair:

Some one sent me the *New York American* containing your article on *The Nuptial Flight;* and I want to tell you the gratification it has given me. It is a happiness not too frequently experienced to find one's book understood as it was intended to be; and to have it favorably appraised on that score is better. But think again and see if I did not weave in what you thought I omitted, namely the influence of seeking money and luxury upon people's lives to their own poisoning. The lives of Nancy C and William set against the others carry that implication.

With all good wishes
Ever

E. L. Masters

Masters, American poet and novelist, is author of Spoon River Anthology.

EDGAR LEE MASTERS

Gramercy Park, New York
December 14, 1927

Dear Mr. Sinclair:

I want to thank you for the introduction to *The Nuptial Flight* [my preface to a new edition of this excellent novel]—a comprehending piece of criticism. I'm glad that in your busy life you could save yourself by using what you said so well at the time the book was published—and just adding what you chose now.

With best wishes to you, my friend, and congratulations upon your continued inspiration to fight all dragons and beasts—

Ever yours,

E. L. Masters

CHARLES FULTON OURSLER
[1893-1952]

MacFadden Publications
New York City
March 26, 1924

Dear Mr. Sinclair:

I am just so excited and happy over your review of *Behold This Dreamer!*, the manuscript of which just reached me, that I am afraid it is going to be difficult to write a coherent letter of appreciation.

It is difficult because it would be hard to convey to you how greatly I appreciate such encouragement from Upton Sinclair.

You ask me if I have read anything of yours. I haven't read anything else much but, as the writers of negro stories insist the negroes say, which I never heard. My introduction to your work came through *The Brass Check*, which I read when I was a reporter on that scarlet, old rag of capitalism, the *Baltimore American*, under the ownership of as bloated and ignorant a capitalist as ever lived, General Felix Agnus! I was one of the so-called star reporters there and was earning $12 a week on which I supported my wife and little girl. You may readily understand how receptive I was to *The Brass Check* and I believe that I have induced more than fifty people to read it. My brother-in-law is deep in the sins of the Associated Press today. It was *The Brass Check* which set me to thinking of social and economic problems.

304

Thereafter, I got to know your other books. I have only recently finished reading *The Profits of Religion,* which has helped me greatly in preparing my new story the principal character of which is a young minister. Having devoured *The Goose-Step,* I now am in the midst of *The Goslings*—just at the point where you tell of the brewer's widow and her activities against the priests of Locust Point. I am glad that there are other books of yours on my shelf to which I can look forward, including *The Metropolis.* Of course, I know *The Jungle.*

You have always been one of my enthusiasms and, during some long and happy conversations with Judge Ben Lindsey on the occasion of his recent visit to New York, we had a great deal to say about your work.

This will give you a little insight into the happy pride that I felt when I read your generous review of my first novel. I don't know just how to thank you, but I am sure the opportunity will come for me to demonstrate practically just how grateful I am. From your letter, I am sure that you did not connect up the supervising editor of Macfadden's with the indecipherable signature and the writer of *Behold This Dreamer!*

You ask for some facts of my life. Here they are:

I am thirty-one years old and was born in Baltimore of the usual poor, but honest parents. I got through the seventh grade in school. Then when I was fourteen years old, I went into a law office for two years. I then became a reporter on the *Baltimore American.* When I was seventeen years old, I got married. When I was twenty-five years old, I came to New York with my wife and two children and, for four years, I was managing editor of a trade paper here. All this time, I was trying to write fiction, selling stories only occasionally. Mr. Macfadden liked my work and two years ago asked me to take my present job. His encouragement was very stimulating and I wrote a number of short stories and serials for these magazines. Then, I decided to try something worthwhile and *Behold This Dreamer!* ran serially in the *Metropolitan Magazine*. I am still living with my wife; I have a boy of ten who wants to be a writer and a beautiful girl of eleven who wants to be an actress and I hope they will both do just that. For my political convictions there is little to say, except that I am occasionally annoyed at you because you are not sufficiently radical.

I am very grateful to you and if there is anything that I can do to help you in your work, always feel ready to call upon me.

Faithfully,

FULTON OURSLER

CHARLES FULTON OURSLER

New York City
November 22, 1926

Dear Upton:

It was darned fine of you to care a hang whether I was hurt or not, though of course I wasn't anything of the kind. In fact your letter is pasted in my scrap-book between Sir Arthur Conan Doyle and the Empress Hermione; I appreciated the letter, and your reading the book and being sufficiently friendly to say honestly what you thought of it. Naturally I would have been happier, if you had liked it all the way; not for the sake of the book alone, but because I feel under a tremendous obligation to you and I want to feel continuingly deserving of the trouble you once took in my behalf, and also because I have always ranked you—before we corresponded as well as now—as one of the few great novelists of our country. Your statement that you would have been willing to read the manuscript and make suggestions for helping it was generous beyond belief for I know how you toil to accomplish all your work, and what a sacrifice of time and energy that would entail. But I have taken the remark in deadly seriousness and intend to send you the manuscript of my next book with a prayer that you will have the time and the good-will to do as much by that. As you say, the book has been variously reviewed; generally better than its predecessors, and its sale is a good deal larger. The only reason for my silence is the fact that I am trying to do a great many things at once, and the people in show business are the slowest moving minds on earth. I cannot make myself interested in plays as art. The whole thing is too artificial for my mind, and, if I did not need money heroically, I do not believe I would write for the theater.

Please, if you do come to New York, give Mrs.

Oursler and myself the pleasure and the honor of having you to dinner. Mrs. Oursler knows your books as well as I—we both hope to have you send us *Love's Pilgrimage*—and we both want to see you, more than any other man in America. Just let us know when . . . .

Cordially,

FULTON OURSLER

P.S. A baby girl, named Grace April, has *just* come to our *house*.

It is this baby girl who, thirty years later, now gives me permission to publish her father's letters. I have forgotten what book occasioned the above letter, but according to the date it must have been Stepchild of the Moon. *I should add that near the end of his life Oursler became a convert to Catholicism, and achieved enormous success with a life of Jesus called* The Greatest Story Ever Told.

SIR HALL CAINE [1853-1931]

Hampstead Heath
London, England
April 28, 1924

My dear Upton Sinclair:

I was glad to receive your letter of April 9th, and I am looking forward, with much interest, to the two books which you have kindly promised to send me.

As to the Moving Picture version of *The Eternal City*, which you have seen, I thank you for writing to me before carrying out your intention of discussing the whole subject in public, and thus giving me an opportunity of saying whether I published any authorized statement on the changes which had been made in the story and theme of my book; what my attitude is to Mussolini and the Fascist Movement, and whether the chief character in the film corresponds to the ideals which I endeavoured to embody in the character of David Rossi.

In the first place, I must say that, owing to ill health, I have not seen the film, and can only judge of it from the reports I have received from persons whose judgment I can trust, and the descriptions of it which have appeared in the press . . . .

As to the practice which is, I am told, only too general on the part of the Cinema Companies of making radical changes not only in the details of the stories they produce from books, but also in the spirit of them, I cannot but question the commercial wisdom whereby a story which has been published in nearly all languages and sold, in our own language, to the extent of more than a million copies, should be so changed as to be unrecognisable to the large public to whom it has already appealed; nor can I quite appreciate the sacrifice (if I may, without immodesty, so describe it) of whatever value attached to the name and work of an accepted writer of forty years standing in favour of the pictorial improvisation of one who, whatever the measure of her technical qualifications, appears, so far as

I know, to be unknown to the general public. But above all, I cannot recognize the wisdom of substituting so great and world-wide a movement as the Christian Socialist movement for one which has been confined to Italy alone, and has, apparently, no appeal for any other country whatever.

I think this policy, if persisted in by Cinema Companies of high standing, is calculated to put the film, notwithstanding its great possibilities, outside the sphere of sincere writers on serious subjects, and thereby to limit its value to the lower part of the public—to make it, in short, as an agent in human progress, as nearly as possible a thing of naught.

A certain reasonable liberty must naturally be allowed to those whose duty it is to transfer a work of art from one medium to another, but where the changes alter, as you say, not only the details of a story, but the spirit of it and its motive, they may properly be described as misrepresentations. Twice, recently, to my deep regret, works of mine, transferred to the screen, in America, have, in varying degrees, been subjected to such and similar misrepresentations, and I cannot but feel that I am thereby a loser in the eyes of that part of the American public whose good-will my books have won for me—to readers who believe that I mean what I say.

With kind regards,
Yours very truly,
HALL CAINE

I agree with this English novelist; "A thing of naught" is an excellent phrase for what the cinema has become. In this case, a pro-Christian novel had been made into a pro-Fascist film.

THEODORE DREISER [1871-1945]

December 18, 1924

My dear Sinclair:

Thanks for *Singing Jailbirds*. But don't forget that the brotherhood of man—(this entirely apart from some of the co-operative phases of socialism) is mere moonshine to me. I see the individual large or small—weak or strong—as predatory and nothing less.

My compliments and regards,

THEODORE DREISER

Singing Jailbirds is a play about I.W.W. strikers in jail. It was produced in Greenwich Village and ran for six weeks or so.

MRS. EDWARD MacDOWELL [1857-1956]

Peterborough, New Hampshire
November 4, 1925

Dear Mr. Sinclair:

Your note of October 26 has just reached me here in Chicago. I am enchanted that Mr. Mencken likes your article so much. Will I be quite honest with you and tell you that it came to me just as I was leaving New York? I went over it very hastily, liked it very much, but didn't realize that it was to be printed, or I would have brought it with me to go over carefully. I don't remember one single point that I didn't like, only I am telling you frankly it was a hurried reading. The moment I start in on my concert work it means deep concentration on what I am doing, as you can easily imagine.

I was so delighted and touched with all you said about Mr. MacDowell. I wish I might go over it again just to be sure there is no small point in the way of data to make sure of; but as I can't I gladly say go ahead and have it printed. Be sure to tell me where it is to appear, so I may get a copy.

It is a wonderful link with the past when I get in touch with his old students who loved him.

Most sincerely yours,

M. MacDowell

Edward MacDowell had been my teacher at Columbia University, 1898-9. His widow promoted his work until her death at the age of ninety-nine. My article appeared in The American Mercury, *January, 1926.*

ISRAEL ZANGWILL

East Preston, Sussex
31st December, 1924

Dear Upton Sinclair:

I don't like to wind up the year without acknowledging the plays you have so kindly sent me. *Singing Jailbirds* almost converts me to expressionistic drama, and though I still fail to see why the audience should join in at the end, when even you are not a member of the I.W.W., I can imagine an artistic reason. And despite some exaggeration, I think it one of your greatest artistic successes, a most vivid and moving piece of work.

Hell I find a more incoherent example of the new drama. Blasphemous, of course, but not so blasphemous as the behaviour of Church, Mosque and Synagogue during the war, and the satire—though the occasional attribution of human motives to Satan and his greater henchmen makes it clumsy—is not a bit too strong. In both these plays there is a big brushwork; but I believe with more moderation and care for style you could achieve something durable.

But better than both of these books I like *The Goose-Step*, which an admirer of yours sent me. Here, you are nailed to the facts—and how wonderful of you to collect them! You must have infinitely more vitality than I, for my tussle with your country a year ago, has left me almost prostrate ever since. But I think there must be more liberty in America after all, for such a book would have landed you in

313

jail in England. I think you overestimate the freedom of speech and thought in other countries; but anyhow, as your facts do not seem to be disputed, you have produced an historic document.

What impressed me most about you was the unfailing optimism, which saw in the underdog none of the canine qualities of the over-dog. Emma Goldman has been writing to me about the "hell" she found in Bolshevik Russia. Still, I suppose if you lost your hope in the world, the world would lose the inspiration of your faith. So I will end by wishing you and the world a happier New Year.

Sincerely yours,

Israel Zangwill

P.S. What I mean about *Hell* is that the allegory does not go on all fours with things terrestrial.

H. L. MENCKEN

The American Mercury
New York
June 18th, 1924

Dear Sinclair:

My apologies for this delay. I went out to Cleveland to see the Coolidge obscenity and then proceeded to Detroit; I got back only yesterday, and fell on your MS. ["Mammonart"] at once.

It is full of excellent stuff, plainly enough, but

God roast me in hell if I believe that it could be used serially—that is, as it stands. Take, for example, this first instalment. It would fill 15 or 16 pages in the magazine, and yet it would leave the book, so to speak, hanging in the air. It does not move directly and briskly, as a serial should, but deliberately and with dispersion, like a book. The digressions, in themselves, are full of interest; for example, the one on trade lies. I'd be delighted to have an article on that subject alone. But I don't believe that the MS. as it stands, is for our great moral periodical. That is my best judgement, reached by prayer.

You missed a capital show. The Coolidge convention was the worst ever heard of.

Sincerely yours,

Mencken

H . L . M E N C K E N

1524 Hollins St.
Baltimore
February 14th, 1927

Dear Sinclair:

The book [*Oil!*] is not yet here. I'll read it with great delight, and send you something for your advertisement.

Scott Nearing dropped in to see me the other day, and in New York, a few days later, I met Roger Baldwin. I begin to move in Bolshevik society! I told both of these fellows that you were a maniac,

315

but very amiable. They agreed as to the second count, but dissented from the first.

Ben Hecht is being comstocked in Chicago, and I may go there to lie for him.

Sincerely yours,

MENCKEN

H . L . M E N C K E N

Baltimore
June 26th, 1927

Dear Sinclair:

Certainly I'll read it. It is scheduled for the train next Monday, when I go to New York. Last week I was swamped with MSS. But if you call me ignorant of revolutionary economics then you libel me most foully. I have read the whole works, from *Das Kapital* to Proudhon and Kropotkin. What is more, I constantly steal and print the ideas of these gents.

It's a pity your visit was so short. Let us go into executive session some time, and bawl each other out at ease. This year I am for Munich and its waters, but next year I hope to come West. When I was in San Francisco two years ago I was too hard worked to see anything save George Sterling's bartenders.

Yours,

MENCKEN

Proudhon was one of the early socialists.

316

H. L. MENCKEN

Baltimore
September 9th, [year unknown]

Dear Sinclair:

Your questions are easy. The government brings my magazine to you only unwillingly. It tried to ruin my business, and failed only by an inch. It charges too much for postal orders, and loses too many of them. A corporation of idiot Chinamen could do the thing better. Its machine for putting out fires is intolerably expensive and inefficient. It seldom, in fact, actually puts out a fire: they burn out. In 1904 two square miles of Baltimore burnt down. I lost a suit of clothes, the works of Richard Harding Davis, and a gross of condoms. The Army had nothing to do with the discovery of the cause of yellow fever. Its bureaucrats persecuted the men who did the work. They could have done it much more quickly if they had been outside the Army. It took several years of effort to induce the government to fight mosquitoes, and it does the work very badly today. There is malaria everywhere in the South. It is mainly responsible for the prevalence of religion down there.

You shock me with your government worship. It is unmanly. Today I got word from a friend who lately had a session with a Department of Justice moron. The moron told him that I was on the official list of Bolshevik agents, and that the *American Mercury* was backed by Russian money.

What do you make of that! I am tempted to confess.

Yours,

H. L. Mencken

Mencken is referring to my citing of post office and fire departments as examples of accepted public ownership.

H . L . M E N C K E N

Baltimore
February 22, 1930

Dear Sinclair:

I find your note on my return from Europe. As always, you are right—save in matters of politics, sociology, religion, finance, economics, literature, and the exact sciences.

I spent three weeks in London, helping to cover the naval conference for the *Baltimore Sun*. It turned out to be the usual witless buffoonery. I am in great hopes that another war will start within five years. If it breaks out, I shall go to work as a Four Minute man.

Yours,

Mencken

He had to wait almost ten years.

318

H . L . M E N C K E N

Baltimore
October 21, 1930

Dear Sinclair:

Your bibliography is really most astonishing. I suspect that you are translated more than any other living American author, and by far. If you have any rival, it is a man recently dead, James Oliver Curwood. The last time I was in Europe I was immensely surprised to observe how widely he was read. Why he should interest Europeans so much I don't know. In your case, it is easier to see the reason. You present a picture of America that fascinates them. I wish I could add that it proves you to be a patriot. Unfortunately, I can't.

Some time soon I hope to print a note about your bibliography in *The American Mercury*.

Yours,

MENCKEN

H . L . M E N C K E N

Hotel Bristol, Vienna
December 13, 1930

The whole town is plastered with your works. The local literati all ask if it is true that you are a teetotaler. I protect you by lying discreetly.

MENCKEN

This note was written on a postcard. I have been a teetotaler for eighty-one years.

H. L. MENCKEN

Dear Sinclair:

I have just finished reading your book on Fox. It seems to me that you have done a magnificent job of editing. Despite the complexity of the material, the story is never obscure, and its interest never drops. I hope to do a review of it for our June issue. I should add, perhaps, that at the end of the book I find myself convinced that Fox is a very slippery fellow, and that putting him out of business was probably a good thing for the movies. He produced, in fact, some of the worst pictures ever heard of.

Yours,

H. L. MENCKEN

My book on Fox, Upton Sinclair Presents William Fox, *was published in 1933; it is an account of the Wall Street banditry by which an immense chain of theaters was taken from Fox, its rightful owner.*

320

H. L. MENCKEN

Baltimore
March 4, 1935

My dear Sinclair:

I greatly fear that you are entertaining yourself with a chimera. The reaction against the New Deal is now in full swing all over the country, and by the end of the Roosevelt administration we'll probably see capitalism in the saddle again and more cocky than ever. The imbecilities of the Brain Trust's Planned Economy will throw the country far in the other direction. This threatened revival of the Hooverism depresses me, but so far as I can see there is nothing to be done about it. I cling to the hope that some day a really civilized government for the United States will be devised. But I don't see the slightest chance that it will ever be devised by hollow politicians of the Roosevelt type.

Is there any chance that you'll be in the East in the near future? I have been toying with the idea of making a westward trip, but if I do so I'll confine myself to the Northwest. I have never been there, and am eager to see it.

Yours,

MENCKEN

F. D. R. was re-elected in 1936, 1940, and 1944. Truman was re-elected in 1948. So the New Deal lasted for seventeen years after this prophecy was written.

H. L. MENCKEN

Dear Sinclair:

I can see nothing unfair or insulting in that somewhat jocose but still quite reasonable speculation.
When you propose to become the savior and boss
of California, and then of the United States, you
invited the opinion of every citizen as to your qualifications, and with them, of your probable course of
action in office. If my own views in that direction
differ from your own it may be only because I am a
better psychologist than you are. It seems to me
that you are a professional messiah like any other,
and would perform precisely like the rest if you got
the chance. Once in power, you would certainly
not be too polite to the money-mad widows and or-
phans whose stocks and bonds now haunt your
dreams.

I admit that you have done more or less hollering
for free speech, but how much of it did you do during the war, when free speech was most in danger?
My recollection is that you actually supported Wilson [In my magazine, *Upton Sinclair's*]. If I am
right, then you also gave aid and comfort to A.
Mitchell Palmer [Wilson's Attorney General who
persecuted liberals and jailed Debs]. Well, so did
every other Socialist in this great Republic—every
one, that is, save a handful. The handful went to
jail—for example, Rose Pastor Stokes and Gene
Debs.

Your frank disapproval of my controversial technic induces me to say with equal frankness that I think your own is much worse. You have spent your life making reckless charges against all sorts of people—some of them, as when you alleged categorically that the *American Mercury* was financed by unnamed "men of wealth," completely false—and yet you set up a horrible clatter every time you are put on the block yourself. It seems to me that a world-saver ought to be more philosophical, not to say more sportsmanlike.

I am against the violation of civil rights by Hitler and Mussolini as much as you are, and well you know it. But I am also against the wholesale murders, confiscations and other outrages that have gone on in Russia. I think it is fair to say that you pseudo-communists are far from consistent here. You protest, and with justice, every time Hitler jails an opponent, but you forget that Stalin and company have jailed and murdered a thousand times as many. It seems to me, and indeed the evidence is plain, that compared to the Moscow brigands and assassins, Hitler is hardly more than a common Ku Kluxer and Mussolini almost a philanthropist.

If you will denounce the orgy of sadistic fury that has gone on in Russia in terms at least as violent as those you have applied to your political opponents for years past, then I'll be glad to print your denunciation, and to hail you with joy as a convert to fair play. And if you will acknowledge publicly that your quack friend, Dr. Albert Abrams, was a fraud, and that your support of his spondylotherapy was idiotic, then I'll engage to cease mentioning it. But you can't ask me to stop discussing you freely, and speculating about your political and other hallucinations so long as you keep on trying to get on the public payroll, trafficking with (and being gulled by) such obvious demagogues as Roosevelt, making whoopee out of the pathetic hopes and illusions of poor and miserable people, and reviling everyone who shows better taste and better sense than you do.

In political controversy there is such a thing as give-and-take. If you want to speak your mind freely, you must let your opponents speak their minds freely, even when what they have to say collides with your vanity and violates your peculiar notions of the true, the good and the beautiful, whether in politics, theology or pathology. It seems to me that you fail here. You are far, far better on the give than on the take. No man in American history has denounced more different people than you have, or in more violent terms, and yet no man that I can recall complains more bitterly when he happens to be hit. Why not stop your caterwauling for a while, and try to play the game according to the rules?

Yours,

H. L. Mencken

Mencken is referring to my EPIC (End Poverty in California) campaign for the governorship of California in 1936; if he had followed my writings he would have known that I protested steadily against Stalin's repressions. And as to my "trying to get on the public payroll," my earnings, after I had paid off my debts from the EPIC campaign, were two or three times as much as my salary would have been if I had been elected governor of California. My wife says that I certainly have the ability occasionally to drive a good friend to fury. Including her!

H . L . M E N C K E N

Baltimore
May 26, 1936

Dear Sinclair:

I observe that Palmer has printed our first exchange of letters in the current *American Mercury,* but that the second pair is missing. Whether he proposes to print them next month I don't know. Readers, I take it, enjoy such debates. In any case, your enemies will be pleased by what I say of you and mine will be pleased by what you say of me.

In a couple of days I shall send you a Maryland madstone, examined and passed by the State Board of Examiners. As an old Marylander, you will know how to use it.

Sincerely yours,

H. L. MENCKEN

My wife packaged this gift intending to return it to him with a note stating "I have now applied the madstone to my husband, who is much improved. Please now apply it to his good friend Mencken." Thus ended a political quarrel.

325

H. L. MENCKEN

Baltimore
October 11, 1939

Dear Sinclair:

My very best thanks for your reply to my inquiry.
Whether I'll make the trip to California remains to
be seen. It depends to some extent on the progress
of the war. If murder begins on a really large scale
there will be no room left in the *Sun* for domestic
politics.

It goes without saying that if I get to California
I'll hope to have the pleasure of seeing you. I note
what you say about the new novel [*World's End*],
and so I'll make our meeting, if there is one, as
short as possible. I trust the manuscript is going
well, and that you are pleased with it. I have just
finished a little book of my own—trivial stuff, but
amusing to write. It consists of reminiscences of
my first twelve years.

Thanks very much for referring my inquiry to
Dr. Taft. I'll certainly be delighted to hear from
him. With best regards,

Yours,

MENCKEN

*I must have told him I was very busy writing.
Dr. Taft is Clinton J. Taft, First Director of the
Southern California Branch, American Civil Lib-
erties Union.*

H. L. MENCKEN

Baltimore
October 27, 1939

Dear Sinclair:

All the information at hand indicates that the Ham and Eggs scheme is bound to be beaten. Thus I'll probably not carry out my plan to come to California for the election. If, however, the referendum carries, I'll certainly be on my way very promptly.

Meanwhile, my best thanks for your friendly reply to my inquiry. Your circular has just come in [a copy of my radio talk attacking the "Ham and Eggs" political campaign program current in California]. It seems to me to be a really first-rate reductio ad absurdum of the whole scheme. How anybody can vote for it after reading what you have to say is hard to imagine.

Maybe I'll get to California anyhow before the end of the year. I certainly hope so.

Sincerely yours,

MENCKEN

In her memoirs, Southern Belle, *my wife tells how we lost an excellent laundress, who was outraged by my radio talk against her "Ham and Eggs" hopes.*

H. L. MENCKEN

Baltimore
September 19th [year uncertain]

Dear Sinclair:

This exposes you to the shame and contumely of all Christian men. Certainly you must be aware that the per capita consumption of alcohol in Western Australia is the largest in the world, and that the Beer Trust is in complete control of the government. Go read the boozy dithyrambs in Dickens, and then meditate upon Jack London's colossal lushing! I expect to hear that you have gone to San Quentin and begged the warden to hang you.

Yours in Xt.,

MENCKEN

Mencken refers here to a clipping from the Western Australian, *which had taken a poll of its readers and reported that I was their favorite among living novelists.*

A fourth installment of Mencken's letters appears later.

WILLIAM E. BORAH [1865-1940]

1927

I read your book and did not find anything in it which shocked me. Now I must read it again as somebody has discovered something. There is one

328

thing for which I am deeply grateful and that is that we did not have these censors in previous periods or we should have been deprived of some of the richest literature in all the world.

WILLIAM E. BORAH

Borah was U.S. senator from Idaho; in this telegram he is referring to my novel, Oil!

NORMAN THOMAS [1884-   ]

League for Industrial Democracy
New York City
June 9, 1927

Dear Upton Sinclair:

I have finished reading *Oil!*

I think it is your greatest novel. If I were writing a literary criticism of it I should follow pretty closely the line of the review in a recent issue of the *Nation.* However, I am not writing a literary criticism. I am instead expressing my astonishment and disgust at the action of the Boston authorities in banning the sale of *Oil!* If they object to the radicalism of the book they are guilty of a very serious infraction of civil liberty. If, as I have heard, the book is condemned on the ground of its obscenity, these censors have no proper justification for their act. Plenty of books circulate even in Boston which are far more objectionable even to a rigorous Puritan than anything you have written. Indeed, there is nothing

329

pornographic about these sections of the book which deal with your hero's sex relations. Your own moral purpose and point of view are evident. Whether you are as conspicuously successful in portraying these relations as in dealing with the relations of father and son, I may doubt. But that is a matter for literary criticism and not at all for official censorship. *Oil!* is a book that ought to be widely read and circulated for the good of the American—including the Boston—soul.

Sincerely yours,

NORMAN THOMAS

Thomas, for several decades a distinguished American Socialist and Presidential candidate, pursues his cause with undiminished devotion.

CLARENCE S. DARROW [1857-1938]

Chicago
June 30th, 1927

My dear Sinclair:

I have just finished reading your last book, *Oil!* Few novels have impressed me as much as this. 1st it is intensely interesting from the beginning. 2nd, it should help the public to see how constant and insidious have been the encroachments upon thought and speech since the war. If it is not already too late your book should be a great help in awakening the people to the imminent danger, 3rd, you know about the production and distribution of Oil, and still more important the production and distribution of "Oil Stock".

I hope the book will be one of the best sellers.

Very truly,

CLARENCE DARROW

It was; and it was translated into twenty-nine languages.

Darrow was a celebrated American lawyer and friend of justice, remembered forever for his defense of evolution in the "Scopes case."

GUTZON BORGLUM [1867-1941]

The Brown Palace Hotel
Denver
July 11, 1927

My dear Sinclair:

Thanks for your letter of the 31st. I received your book—rather new novel—called *Oil!* In a manner I cannot explain, it disappeared almost immediately. I did not think much about that until I found I could not buy it on the bookstand. Send me another and I will be glad to remit. Glad, also, to read it and doubly glad to tell you what I think of it.

I have often thought of you in the past years, and wished that I had been able to have seen something of you. The lives of men in common sympathy curiously rarely flow together and our kind of

331

fighting belongs to the old Knight errantry. It's a lonely job and damn little honor goes with it.

Sincerely yours,

G<small>UTZON</small> B<small>ORGLUM</small>

Sculptor of the colossal, Borglum conceived and carved the great National Monument on the side of Mt. Rushmore in South Dakota.

D. H. LAWRENCE [1885-1930]

Scandicci
Florence, Italy
July 16, 1927

Dear Upton Sinclair:

Many thanks for the copy of *Oil!* I read it with keen interest, and consider it a splendid novel of fact. It is absurd for anyone to call it indecent. It is never indecent, neither in word nor suggestion, but very honest and very decent. If they put a ban on it, it will not be for its indecency.

And why should they put a ban on it? The real hero is "Dad"—J. Arnold Ross—and the thrill of the book is the way he becomes an oil magnate: the old American thrill of a lone hand and a huge success. The book won't make Bolshevists. Whoever reads it will want to be like "Dad," not like Paul or Bunny. And so long as people want to be like J. Arnold Ross, what danger is there! Anyhow he's more of a man than any of the other characters.

332

But the novel seems to me a splendid big picture of actual life: What more do they want?

Anyhow, here's success to you and the book!

Yours sincerely,

D. H. LAWRENCE

Neither Paul nor Bunny were Bolshevists; they were Socialists. The Communists have done their best to confuse the terms.

Lawrence was one of the major English writers of this century, and author of Sons and Lovers, Lady Chatterley's Lover, *and other controversial novels.*

I had read Lawrence's Sons and Lovers *only because Jack London wrote me enthusiastically about it; but I have to report sadly that it and* Lady Chatterley's Lover *were equally uninteresting to me.*

EDITH WHARTON [1862-1927]

St. Brice-Sous-Foret (S&O)
19 August, 1927

Upton Sinclair, Esqre,

I received your novel *Oil!* a few months ago, and read it (from the point of view of your skill as a novelist) with great enjoyment and admiration.

It seems to me an excellent story until the moment, all too soon, when it becomes a political pamphlet. I make this criticism without regard to the views which you teach, and which are detest-

333

able to me. Had you written in favour of those in which I believe, my judgment would have been exactly the same. I have never known a novel that was just good enough to be good in spite of its being adapted to the author's political views.

Having said this, I hasten to add that the charge of obscenity is absurd, and I am glad to join in protesting against it, from the moment that it is clearly understood that my protest applies to that charge only.

I shall be glad if my name is of any use to you in freeing the novel from this unjust and ignorant aspersion.

I should like to add, that while I can understand that the sight of such a life as you describe as being led by your oil millionaires is enough to justify any thoughtful man in the desire to make some radical change in the organization of society, I believe that a wider experience would have shown you that the evils you rightly satirize will be replaced by others more harmful to any sort of civilized living when your hero and his friends have had their way.

Yours sincerely,

EDITH WHARTON

A "great lady" who became a great American novelist in her mature years, Edith Wharton lived in and portrayed the fashionable metropolitan society of her era. Observe her precision and decisiveness.

J. D. BERESFORD [1873-1947]

London
September 7, 1927

My dear Sinclair:

Here are all your letters unanswered and I don't believe I ever thanked you for Floyd Dell's book. But it was not forgetfulness or carelessness. I have been working pretty hard to finish a novel . . . .

My God, your America fills me with despair. I had wrung my hands over your plutocracy often enough before I read your *Oil!* and Floyd Dell's life of you (I feel now as if I knew you so well, and I believe I do) to say nothing of Dreiser's *American Tragedy*—so badly written from a literary point of view, but so extraordinarily impressive. Now, the American abuse of wealth and power seems to me so pitiful and childish that I can fully understand any reaction, however bloody and horrible, coming out of it. On top of it all, too, the Sacco-Vanzetti case! But to me it's pitiful, my dear Sinclair, pitiful. Your masters over there seem to me like great spoilt children. They must have strong intelligence, most of them, but they seem to me of so primitive a kind. But then I have never had any respect for the money-getting, money-spending mind. It never seemed to me worth while. For many years I have been chiefly interested in trying to form some theory of my own concerning the whence and whither of humanity, and if I have not found it yet, I am at least convinced that it is the only search of any value, and by the way one learns many things, in-

cidentally that money-getting beyond one's immediate needs is one of the most fatal methods of wast-
ing one's very short stay down here. We meet
there, anyway. And if we do meet in the flesh, we
shall find many other points of agreement. I have
seen many things in the eyes of that photograph of
you in Floyd Dell's book, not all of them yet confirmed in his story of your life.

Yours,

J. D. BERESFORD

*Beresford was an English novelist and author
of the "Jacob Stahl" series.*

JOHN MASEFIELD [1878-   ]

Boars Hill
1927

Dear Mr. Sinclair:

Many thanks for your letter and for the very
kind thought and gift.

I read *Oil!* with interest and pleasure. It hasn't
done me any harm, but passed some lonely hours
pleasantly, and for this I am grateful to you.

Forgive this scrawl. I have to write with my left
hand.

Good luck and greetings,
Yours sincerely,

JOHN MASEFIELD

Masefield is Britain's poet-laureate.

336

ROBERT HERRICK [1868-1938]

York Village, Maine
June 14th, 1927

Dear Sinclair:

I was reading *Oil!* with much pleasure when your letter came and caused me to finish it in a hurry. Of course there is nothing indecent in it except the indecency of our American manners, and they have been so often faithfully described that moralists should have become used to it by this time. I hardly think, however, that the motive of the Boston censors is "political". A community whose "best citizens" openly advocate the killing of Sacco and Vanzetti whether guilty or innocent could not be expected to accept *Oil!* without a protest . . . . There is such a lot of good stuff in your story that it can't be long suppressed. Indeed, I shouldn't wonder if a Boston prosecution would not prove to be the quickest road to recognition among the intelligent.

Let me congratulate you on your return to fiction. You show that you have not lost the trick, and have gained especially in humor. Too much propaganda still for me,—you are the most credulous of human beings! But it is honest, sincere propaganda, and much of it is new to the novel reader. Congratulations and good wishes for a triumphant vindication, if that is what you want, at the hands of a

Massachusetts court. I'd like vastly to be there and see the farce.

Sincerely yours,

ROBERT HERRICK

The judge said: "We think you have had enough publicity, Mr. Sinclair." And so Oil! *continued to be purchased in New York and carried to Boston on every train.*

Robert Herrick was a professor of literature at the University of Chicago. His novels, such as The Common Lot *and* Together, *deal with modern marital problems and made a deep impression.*

ROBERT HERRICK

Winter Park, Florida
December 18, 1928

Dear Upton Sinclair:

I am very tardy in acknowledging your kind letter and the book on fasting that you were good enough to send me. They went to my Maine home and were forwarded to me here where I am spending the winter. I read the fasting book [my *The Fasting Cure,* published 1911] with much appreciation of what you had to say about the imbecilities of the doctors, of which I have had recently a lot of experience. Indeed, I wrote an article called "Machine Medicine" about my experience at a great Boston hospital last Summer—but doubt if I can get it published. Another sacred cow, our "scientific"

338

medicine! . . . I am tempted by your account of your fasts and have no doubt fasting would benefit a great many people. As it is my diet is a slim one and my weight about thirty pounds below that allotted for my age and height. Besides I am too old and too feeble from heart attacks to venture on any prolonged fast: it would carry me out.

But that is not what I want to write you about. I have just finished your *Boston* which you were so good as to send me and I want very much to get over to you my great admiration and enthusiasm for the book. As you know we have always differed about the mixture of propaganda and art in a novel, I holding that you never let your very real imaginative power have its freedom because determined to overweight it with social beliefs. I confess that I shrank a bit from opening *Boston* in the fear that the same might be true again; also from fear that the spiritual blind spots and stupidity of my people would be caricatured and dealt with roughly. But this time you have triumphed, oh, enormously! Your social reactions, your thesis are fused with your drama magnificently. You had a great theme and you lived up to it, imaginatively, humorously, tenderly. The device of the runaway grandmother was a pure stroke of genius and your presentation of Vanzetti so luminous, so convincing, that I feel it can never die. Indeed, yours will become the real history of the famous case, rather than the voluminous record which few will ever consult and still fewer have the intelligence or the imagination to understand. No matter how many errors you may have made—and it would be inconceivable that you had not made many—how much of your own interpretation you have put on the incidents, yours will be the Sacco-Vanzetti case as known to future generations.

I hope your picture of my people, of their blindness and stupidity, will not become the sole accepted one! Remember that among them are still such souls as Will Thompson, capable of flaming with pure fire for justice. I think by the way you failed to make enough of him, of the sacrifices he made for his sense of right, of the great devotion he showed. Vanzetti and he understood one another. And of course there were many others whose spirits were touched to a greater or lesser degree by the case. New England is not yet dead of dry rot. However, that really is of small importance.

I think also that you failed to get wholly beneath the skin of Lowell and his kind. The exasperating, the perplexing fact about that sort of Brahmin is that he is capable of self-renunciation, devotion, heroism if need be, and that he persuades himself that that is just what he is evincing, at high cost to himself, when he goes out to get the "Wops"! Perhaps it would be impossible to set forth the peculiar mental complex which creates their type of spiritual blindness, the subtle ways in which their minds have been warped. But I am sure you are wrong in laying so much stress on Lowell's great fortune, which I think by the way you have exaggerated. The funny thing about his kind is that they will quite completely ignore their own money interests as few other Americans ever would be able to.

340

However, this was not to be a criticism of your handling of New England! What you have done is beyond such trifling criticism. I am writing Lovett that if he doesn't compel the Pulitzer prize to be given to *Boston* this year he ought in self-respect to get off the Committee and publish his reason. Hitherto there has been an excuse for giving their prize to the piffle they have selected, but with your outstanding, monumental achievement in *Boston,* they would show themselves incapable of literary judgment were they to ignore it. With sincere homage, I am,

> Faithfully yours,
>
> ROBERT HERRICK

Last of all, your book has touched the embers of my own imagination—makes me want once more to draw my sword and go clean out the battlefield.

The Pulitzer Prize was not awarded to Boston, *but it was awarded to* Dragon's Teeth *fifteen years later.*

MAURICE MAETERLINCK
[1862-1949]

> Medan, Par Villennes-sur-Seine
> December 12, 1927

My dear Confrère:

Useless, I think, to tell you that I do not share any of your ideas on the origins and responsibilities of the great war, on communism and socialism; and

341

with the exception of Zane Grey (who is pitiable), of Sherwood Anderson (who is indeed curious) and of Huneker (who is a remarkable erudite although a little too much slave to ephemeral fashions), I do not know any of the authors of whom you speak.

But that does not at all keep me from admiring the virile verve, sane, strong and sincere, with which you criticize them. One senses perfectly that on most of the points, what you say must be the real truth. It is only regrettable that your political and social idea has too often a manifest influence on your literary judgments.

Receive, with my thanks, the expression of my devoted sentiments.

MAETERLINCK

The Belgian poet and dramatist is referring to Money Writes, *my discussion of American literature from an economic point of view; the letter is written in French.*

HALLDÓR K. LAXNESS [1902-   ]

Point Roberts, Washington
April 24th, 1929

My dear Upton Sinclair:

After having sought in vain in all the big towns along the coast, I was at last able to locate my translator in a wood on the boundary of the State of Washington and British Columbia. He had put aside the translation for months, had built a studio in the wood and studied fishing or made sculpture at intervals. I persuaded him to continue with the translation, and we have been working intensely on it the last six weeks. We are soon through, and I will be back in Southern California next month, where I am going to finish the typewriting.

I am sending you the first three books of this horrific novel-tragedy. Although I fear it will be a pest for you to read it through, I feel it as a great privilege to submit it to your consideration, according to your kind permission from last year.

The Great Weaver is my fifth big book, composed in my 23rd - 24th year of age, put down in Taormina, Sicily, in the summer 1925. Since then I have written three books. They are all different from each other. My last book, a collection of revolutionary essays (about four hundred printed pages) was finished in Los Angeles in last February, and is under print in Iceland now, published by the Socialist Party in Reykjavik.

Although the idealogy of *The Weaver* is different from my present mental make-up, my friends and I myself have come to the conclusion that it will make the most successful introduction of my work abroad. The book spans over a vast area of ideas, as you will see. Its main tendency is pointing out the incompatibility of the fundamentals of Christianity to that of life. Previous to it is my two years experience in monastic life. The book is a definite adieu to the religious orgies of my early twenties.

I will not conceal from you the fact that it is an ordeal to me to compare this our English version to the original. The book is in Icelandic considered

343

as one of the best works in prose of our modern literature, as you have seen by extracts of criticisms I sent you last summer. But I stand helpless before the English language, having spent my maturing years mostly outside the English world, and my translator, an Icelandic sculptor and musician, lacks that literary training, which would be necessary to give the translation that brilliancy and fullness of style which has been considered as one of its chief merits in the original. Besides, the Icelandic and English cannot be said to possess a congruity of ideas, so it is almost impossible to render the essence or the flavor of one language to the other. This is especially a hard task for us, who are far from being sufficiently familiar with the affinities of the language into which we are translating.

I have had a hard time defending Upton Sinclair among Western-Icelanders (who turn easily into boosters and hundred percenters here). This controversy has caused both the Icelandic newspapers in Winnipeg to close their columns for me altogether,—which again has caused a good deal of rage. Otherwise in Iceland. *Two* periodicals of highest standing ask me for contribution on this subject (Upton Sinclair, his work and influence in America). I have not yet had the time to finish an elaborate article about you, which I had put down in raw sketch last winter, but I am going to finish it soon. My best thanks for the photos, the one of which must accompany my article about you. The other one I am going to keep for myself as a souvenir.

344

I hope you will find time to grant me a short interview some time, when I am back in Los Angeles in a couple of weeks.

Yours most truly,

HALLDÓR K. LAXNESS

This Icelandic novelist received the Nobel Prize in 1955.

HALLDÓR K. LAXNESS

Reykjavik, Iceland
January 2nd, 1930

My dear Sinclair:

The greatest part of my essay about you is a study of the trends of American civilization as embodied in the commercialism and pointing out your mission of throwing down the standards and creating new ones. The essay is rather good, but as I am terribly busy here (political and literary activities) I regret not to find the time at present to translate more than the final chapter. I am sending you my last book (where you are cited in numerous places), —a collection of political (revolutionary) essays which had already awakened a considerable storm in the country as I arrived here short before Christmas.

I am in receipt of your note about my manuscript being with the Macmillans.—I am sending you the missing chapters of the ms simultaneously to this. They are very badly translated.

345

There has been snowing one day and raining the other since I came here, and if it had not been for my activities, I would already have heimweh for the sunny California, which, by the way, is the most charming country in which I ever lived,—in spite of all.

Best greetings from your sincere friend,

HALLDÓR K. LAXNESS

I do not know whether his essay about me was ever published.

HALLDÓR K. LAXNESS

Reykjavik,
August 26, 1930

My dear Sinclair:

Thanks for your letter of July 9th.

I am sorry to have to tell you that our bookmarket is in a rather hopeless predicament for the time being. They publish mostly translations in newspaper feuilletons, but the limited columns of our labor papers are overstuffed. The bourgeois papers here don't come in question so far as your books are concerned. I have been trying to interest our publishers in *Boston*, but they say it is far too long and would not pay unless abridged; for the time present they complain of hard times. That is the old refrain. Besides, your books are read here to a great extent in English and in Scandinavian transla-

346

tions. It might interest you what an American Icelander told me the other day; he had been trying for years to get your books complete from American libraries, but never succeeded. He had to come to Iceland to find your collected works in a public library. The chief of our public library in Reykjavik tells me, that your books are out most of the time and there are always many people on the waiting list for some of them. I know several workers who practice their English by reading your books. *Boston* has also been read here a great deal in Swedish.

I am getting on well here. The government (they are a left supported by Labor) has increased my subsidy so I am free of care. My wife works in an office. I am just having out a collection of poetry under the title of *Parodies (Hermiljo)*. Hope to finish a new novel, about 500 pages, before Christmas. It is entitled: "Oh, Thou Pure Vine" (pu vinviour hreini-),—refrain of a Salvation Army hymn, deals with proletarian life on a fishing station in East Iceland. I have been living in those places during the summer, collecting material. Next I am going to write another novel dealing once more with the modern struggle for a god,—going to be called "The Great Master Beyond Himalaya". I expect to go to Russia next year.

I'm sending you some views from Iceland if you have never seen any before.

Thanks for your good wishes.

Always your faithful,

HALLDÓR K. LAXNESS

WILLIAM McDOUGALL [1871-1938]

Duke University
Durham, North Carolina
May 14, 1929

Dear Mr. Sinclair:

I shall be very glad to read the account of Mrs. Sinclair's experiments if you are so kind to send me a copy. . . .

One of my pupils at Harvard made a study of telepathy by experiment with apparently positive results and found the passive relaxed attitude very favorable to success.

Sincerely yours,

WM. McDOUGALL

Professor of psychology at Oxford, Harvard, and Duke Universities, McDougall received the unofficial title of "Dean of American psychology." He is referring to the manuscript of Mental Radio, *my book about my wife's experiments with telepathy, published in 1930.*

WILLIAM McDOUGALL

Duke University
Durham, North Carolina
September 24, 1929

Dear Mr. Sinclair:

I have been up North on holiday. Hence my delay in replying. I have written a short introduc-

348

tion [to *Mental Radio*] and will send it to you as soon as it is typed. I hope it may help. I do not ask or receive any fee, since I am merely obeying the behests of my scientific conscience in giving you what support I can.

Sincerely yours,

WM. McDOUGALL

WILLIAM McDOUGALL

Duke University
Durham, North Carolina
October 5, 1929

Dear Mr. Sinclair:

I enclose the few paragraphs which I have written in response to your invitation to introduce your book. I hope they are the sort of thing you desire. As I wrote before, I do not expect a fee for this slight service. If you will send me a copy of your book on Boston with (if not inconvenient) your autograph, I shall feel myself amply rewarded.

Sincerely yours,

WM. McDOUGALL

P.S. I hope to be in Los Angeles in the summer of 1930, and I should esteem it a privilege if I might be an observer of some of your experiments.

In the course of a five-page introduction to the book he states: "The experiments in telepathy, as reported in the pages of this book, were so remark-

ably successful as to rank among the very best hitherto recorded."

WILLIAM McDOUGALL

> Santa Monica, California
> July 9, 1930

Dear Mr. Sinclair:

I am now established here for a few weeks and I should like to give myself the pleasure of calling on you. I don't wish to make myself a nuisance to you and I don't like to risk missing you, as the distance is considerable. Perhaps you will, then, be so kind as to tell me on what day I should find you at home and where I may find you. Mrs. Sinclair can then judge whether I am the sort of person to whom she might feel it possible to demonstrate something of her very interesting powers. I hope your *Mental Radio* is finding a large public. I enclose an English cutting which perhaps you have not seen. I have my car here and Saturday and Sundays are my free days.

> Sincerely yours,
>
> WM. McDOUGALL

He came, and made a number of tests of my wife's telepathic powers. The records of these experiments with M.C.S., successful in a large percentage, were turned over to Dr. Walter Franklin Prince, Research Officer for the Boston Society for Psychic Research, and are reported on in detail in Bulletin XVI of that organization, dated April 1932.

350

WILLIAM McDOUGALL

Duke University
Durham, North Carolina
September 22, 1930

My dear Sinclair:

After a journey of nearly 5,000 miles during
which I saw some lovely scenes, I am established
in a gothic tower on our new and magnificent
campus and find a bunch of letters from you. . . . .

My stay in California was full of interest and enjoyment, thanks largely to the kindness of Mrs. Sinclair and yourself, and if I had done nothing else
during my stay, my contacts with you would have
made it very well worth while. I am disposed to
try to write a new series of Upton letters addressed
to the greatest living American, covering his social
philosophy in a sympathetic but critical spirit. My
youngest son, who is the brainy one of my little
flock, is growing enthusiastic over your books; so
perhaps you have made a convert there of no small
value to your cause.

My very kindest regards and repeated expression
of gratitude for your most friendly response to my
importunities to both of you.

Sincerely yours,

WM. McDOUGALL

P.S. The little book containing my "Island of Eu-
genica" should now be on its way to you.

351

BERTRAND RUSSELL

Harting, Petersfield
England
May 21st, 1929

Dear Upton Sinclair:

I hope you will not think me churlish, but it is
quite impossible for me to express any opinion on
the subject of telepathy. My feeling is that there is
nothing in it, but I do not know enough to support
this opinion, and I am most unwilling to spend time
upon what I believe to be humbug. That being so,
I propose to die without having acquired a right to
pronounce any opinion on the topic. If you had
written a book on a topic about which I either knew
or wished to know something, I would gladly have
done what I could.

Yours sincerely,

BERTRAND RUSSELL

ALBERT EINSTEIN [1879-1955]

Berlin W.
May 16, 1930

Very much honored Upton Sinclair:

I have received the American edition of your
book [*Mental Radio*] and read it in part. I find the

work highly worthy, for there are united in your person various circumstances which rarely occur together: Opportunity to observe that sort of phenomena closely, critical sense, devoted interest in the affair, and great capacity in setting it forth. With me it strikes about as you yourself have reported: "If I say I believe it, even so I do not believe it." But when one of the most independent and character-full men and one of the sharpest observers of our time offers such witness, one has to take it quite earnestly. In this sense I will gladly write an introduction for your book.

With the expression of special respect and honor

Your

A. EINSTEIN

This letter by the discoverer of relativity and friend of all mankind is written in German.

ALBERT EINSTEIN

Caputh b. Potsdam, Germany
May 23, 1930

Much honored Mr. Sinclair:

I thank you heartily for sending of the German translation of *Mental Radio* with the dedication. I have sent the enclosed lines to the Malik Verlag, although I hold myself completely incompetent. I do it, in order to prevent that the German reading world should pass heedlessly by the worthy and careful work of yourself and your wife.

With friendly greeting and all high regard.

Your

A. EINSTEIN

Accompanying the letter, written in German, was the following statement, intended as preface to the German edition. Unfortunately the publisher failed, and the book did not appear.

"I have read the book of Upton Sinclair with great interest, and I am convinced that it deserves the most earnest attention, not only of the laiety, but also of the specialists in psychology. The results of the telepathy experiments which are so carefully and plainly described in this book stand surely far beyond what an investigator of nature considers to be thinkable; but, on the other hand, it not to be thought of that so conscientious an observer and writer as Upton Sinclair should attempt a deliberate deception of the reading world. His good faith and trustworthiness cannot be doubted, and if the facts set forth with great clearness do not rest upon telepathy, but upon some unknown hypnotic influence from person to person, that also would be of high psychological interest. In no case should the psychologically interested pass over this book without heed."

ALBERT EINSTEIN

On board S.S. Belgenland
December 27, 1930

Honored Upton Sinclair:

I thank you heartily for your jolly letter and the telegram of greeting. I rejoice very much, to visit you in your own house, quite without anxiety before the bacillus telepathicus, which there in all corners lurks for the harmless wanderer.

With friendly greetings to you, and to the wife who is bound to you by anxiety even when she is physically separated from you.
Your

A. EINSTEIN

This was mailed upon his arrival in New York.

ALBERT EINSTEIN

Berlin W.
z.Zt. Caputh b. Potsdam
May 26, 1932

Dear Upton Sinclair:

To the most beautiful joys of my life belongs to me your wicked tongue! The sharpness and sureness of aim recalls Voltaire. Hearty thanks for all— and honor me again soon!
Heartily greets you

Your

A. EINSTEIN

This was written in German.

ALBERT EINSTEIN

Wen ficht der schmutzigste Topf nicht an?
Wer klopf die Welt an den hohlen Zahn?
Wer verdachtet das Jetzt und schwoert auf das
   Morgen?
Wen macht kein "undignified" je Sorgen?
     Der Sinclair ist der tapfre Mann.
      Wenn einer, dann ich es bezeugen kann.

In Herzlichkeit

ALBERT EINSTEIN

Translation:

   To whom does the dirtiest pot not matter?
   Who knocks the world on its hollow tooth?
   Who suspects the now and swears by the morrow?
   Who never troubles about "undignified"?
   Sinclair is the valiant man.
   If anyone, then I can attest it.

Handwritten verses on large photograph of Einstein by Odiorne, 1933.
   Someone had told me that my social protest was "undignified," and I told him about it.

ALBERT EINSTEIN

Princeton, N. J.
January 29, 1934

Dear Upton Sinclair:

Your anticipatory report over your activity as Governor of California [my EPIC campaign] has interested me greatly. You know, indeed much better than I, that nothing annoys people more than if one tries honestly to help them. I heartily wish that in your case the matter may come out otherwise.

The attempt at the creation of a quasi isolated economic state within the state would be really worth while to be undertaken.

Joyfully and with best wishes and greeting to you and your wife.

Yours,

A. EINSTEIN

ALBERT EINSTEIN

Princeton, New Jersey
November 23, 1934

Dear Upton Sinclair:

My son, when he was about five years old, attempted to split wood with my razor. You can be sure that it was less bad for the wood than the razor.

I remember that story when I heard from you that you had got yourself into this rude business. As I read that this cup had passed from you, I rejoiced, even though it had not gone exactly according to your wish.

In economic affairs the logic of facts will work itself out somewhat slowly. You have contributed more than any other person. The direct action you can with good conscience turn over to men with tougher hands and nerves.

To you and your wife, the hearty greetings of your

A. Einstein

Einstein is referring to the defeat of my EPIC campaign.

ALBERT EINSTEIN

Princeton, New Jersey
October 23, 1941

My dear Upton Sinclair:

You know how much I admire your original art and the courageous and honest fight you have made during your whole life; and I am deeply grateful to you for having sent me your books. On the other side you must understand that I live in a permanent tension struggling for the solution of my problems and I find very seldom the tranquillity of mind to read literary books. It is not so much the lack of time as the difficulty to concentrate on novels.

I have the feeling that most people in this country don't realize how dangerous our situation is. I must also confess that I feel the whole tragedy of the Russian situation. The senseless destruction of so much precious work accomplished under the most difficult circumstances in only twenty years. It is very difficult indeed to keep up the idea of a deeper meaning in human history.

With kind regards and wishes.   Cordially yours,

A. Einstein

ALBERT EINSTEIN

Princeton, New Jersey
June 10, 1944

Dear Upton Sinclair:

I thank you from all my heart for your last book *Presidential Agent* [volume V of the Lanny Budd series]. I am convinced that you are doing very important and valuable work in giving to the American public a vivid insight into the psychological and economical background of the tragedy evolving in our generation. Only a real artist can accomplish this. For there is only the artistic way to reach a greater public and to impress people effectively. The best objective reasoning can never accomplish that.

I am convinced that you have influenced political thought more effectively than nearly all of the politicians on the stage.—With the expression of my sincere gratitude and with all kind greetings and wishes,

Yours cordially,
A. EINSTEIN

ALBERT EINSTEIN

1953

Dear Upton Sinclair:

I admire very much your book *A Personal Jesus* [published in 1952]. I have not only read it with pleasure and approval but I am also convinced that the book in its honest and understanding critical attitude toward the officially accepted texts is of high educational value.

The attitude of the publishing world towards your beautiful work corresponds somewhat with the attitude of the official world toward the memory of the hero of your book whom you have so lovingly depicted.

With kind regards, sincerely,

A. Einstein

ALBERT EINSTEIN

June 30, 1954

Dear Upton Sinclair:

I thank you much for the gripping book [*What Didymus Did*] which you have sent me . . . It is a beautiful thought to show in a spectacular way how even super-earthly powers must give up the struggle for the improvement of the human fate. The representation of the reaction of the public and of the different organizations is extraordinarily convincing. Also it has rejoiced me that you have sought the cause of evil, not in a particular group or world-outlook, but in the nature of man itself.

One must already be tolerably old, before this becomes clear to one.

With hearty greetings and repeated thanks.

Yours

A. EINSTEIN

What Didymus Did, published originally in 1954, and reissued as It Happened to Didymus, *published in 1958, is my novel about a young man in Los Angeles whom an angel endowed with the power to work miracles.*

This letter is a sad last message from a great mind and noble soul. Einstein died the following year.

M.K. GANDHI [1868-1948]

November 30, 1930

Dear Friend:

I read your *Mammonart* with absorbing interest and *Mental Radio* with curiosity. The former has given me much to think, the latter did not interest me. Nobody in India would, I think, doubt the possibility of telepathy but most would doubt the wisdom of its material use.

I will now avail myself of your kind offer and ask

you to send me your other volumes or such as you
think I should read.

Yours sincerely,

M. K. GANDHI

*The Indian saint and national founder was in
prison at this time.*

M. K. GANDHI

Y.C.P.
March 7, 1932

Dear Friend:

I thank you for thinking of me again. I have
already commenced reading your book. May I tell
you that the consignment you said last year you had
sent me was never received. I inquired then of the
Superintendent and he informed me that nothing
was received after my discharge.

Yours [blotted by postmark]

M. K. GANDHI

*Y.C.P. means Yeravda Central Prison. The book
was probably* The Wet Parade, *my novel of the prohibition era, published in 1931. This note was written on a postcard.*

362

M. K. GANDHI

Yeravda Central Prison
Poona
July 5, 1932

Dear Friend:

I thank you for your letter and *American Outpost,* also the Nobel Prize Pamphlet. This last I do not understand, nor have I ever been able to know its working. Your autobiography I know I shall read with deep interest. I have a recollection that after sending you the post card, I wrote to you saying that I had since learnt that the books you mentioned in your letter had reached the Ashram last year. I hope therefore that you have not sent another consignment. But if you have, I shall see that proper use is made of it. My youngest boy who is also in prison has taken to reading your books. I have sent him my copy of *The Wet Parade* and other books will be sent to him from the Ashram.

Yours sincerely,

M. K. GANDHI

RANGILDAS M. KAPADIA [1893-   ]

Maharaj Mansions
Sandhurst Road
Bombay 4
13th February, 1931

My dear Mr. Sinclair:

I am so obliged to you for your kind letter of felicitations which I received on my release from jail early this month and also the two books. How very kind of you to do so!

I reread in jail *The Jungle, Oil!* and *Boston.* Your works were very popular with the prisoners and even the jail authorities read them, perhaps the latter to lose all their precepts soon. A ruling and capitalist race will have hardly any lessons therefrom.

I saw *Mental Radio* and *Mountain City* [my novel of the Rockies, published 1931] lying there with Mahatmaji [Gandhi] in his prison cell.

Today is the great day for us. If you are following the trend of events, you must have read that the Congress meets today to consider the peace terms and the R.T.C. decisions. It may be truce, it may be war, in case of latter we all shall soon be His Majesty's guests again.

I hope you are doing OK.

With kind regards,
Yours sincerely,
RANGILDAS M. KAPADIA

It was peace, most fortunately.

Kapadia, like Gandhi, was an advocate of freedom for India.

LEWIS BROWNE [1897-1949]

March 19th, 1932

My dear Upton Sinclair,

First of all, our heartiest congratulations on the very dramatic motion picture they have made from

364

your novel [*The Wet Parade*]. Even though the "gentlemen who know what they want but can't spell it" did intensify the violence and the glamour, they managed, we both feel, to preserve the fine spirit of your book. And this side of Paradise—or the U.S.S.R.—that is as much as any honest author can expect.

We were most disappointed that you did not get up to make a speech. The occasion deserved a few words from you. We were glad, however, that some few in the audience had the intelligence to get up and at least call for your appearance . . . .

Myna and I are both grateful for your kindness in inviting us to be present. I am afraid I shall never be able to reciprocate in exactly the same way, for how will they ever be able to dramatize a biography of a Spinoza? However, I am hoping there will be other ways in which we shall be able to give evidence of our appreciation of your thoughtfulness.

With cordial greetings to Mrs. Sinclair, and in the hope that we shall be able to meet soon, I am,

Yours,

LEWIS BROWNE

An amusing circumstance: I was present, but was not called upon by the theater owner because I had failed to honor the occasion by wearing a dress suit. I do not own one, and have always declined to be a ceremonious person.

Lewis Browne was a novelist and scholar; ours was a precious friendship.

LEWIS BROWNE

Colombo, Ceylon
April 2, 1933

Dear Upton,

From the window of this room we can look out on the Sinhalese peasants bathing in the indigo sea— but our thoughts are of you and Craig in Beverly Hills. One reason for that is that we've just received your announcement of the Fox book [*Upton Sinclair Presents William Fox*]. Another is that we've just come down from Sabarmati in the Gujerat country, where we lived for some days in Gandhi's "Ashram" —a Sanskrit word meaning monastery. There his closest followers live in starkest simplicity, practicing celibacy, laboring from before sunrise until dark at spinning and teaching, and subsisting off a diet of curds and black bread precisely like that given their hundreds of colleagues now in prison. We went there to learn what we could of the fight for India's freedom—but stayed to tell about Upton Sinclair. For we at once discovered you were—judging by the books in the small library of the Ashram—the favorite author of those people. Naraindas Gandhi, a nephew of Mahatma, informed us that the great

366

man had read most if not all of your works, and was intensely interested in you as a person.

We travelled 400 miles to Poona in the hope of talking with Gandhi—his followers told us to be sure to tell him what little we knew about you while in his presence—but the prison authorities absolutely refused to let us come near him. (And this despite that he had signified his eagerness to see us, and that he is supposed, as a "State prisoner", to have the right to talk with whomever he pleases. American writers are anathema to the English officials out here.) So we were unable to serve as self-appointed intermediaries between you two. It was our one bitter disappointment on our whole journey thus far.

We are well, but very weary after our five weeks in India. It is a cruel land in which to travel—crueller even than China. And the persecution of all radicals here is indescribable.

We're on our way now to Palestine, where we know we shall feel more at home. And then Europe —especially Germany—for another shot of heartbreak.

We expect to be home early in June—I'm giving a course at U.C.L.A. on the art of writing this summer—and shall try to see you and Craig as soon as is possible, to learn how you survived the quake and the post-Fox tornado.

Until then,

Love,

Lewis Browne

We hope to be able to lay hands on a copy of the

367

new book in Paris or London. We're excited about it, and can't wait till we get home to read it.

EZRA   POUND   [1885-   ]

Rapallo, Italy
September 10, 1934

Dear Upton:

Congrats on nomination. Now beat the bank buzzards and get elected.

"Script" Yr./best item. vide exc. . But you are a bloody *ass* to go on with doles and reliefs etc. *instead* of dividends to ALL. Try to get copy of Vol. 1 No. 1 Social Credit = clearest statement yet.

Land colonies etc. = if you cd. once understand money and banks you cd. get rid of a lot of clutter.

Any how here's luck but try to modernize.

Also get in touch with the Gesellites at S. Antonio, Texas.

Ezra Pound

One vote

Doles a bloody insult—
You don't understand nature of money. Bankers mostly asses who don't know what they do.
"Scrip" Yr. one real sign of awakening,

According to a large wing of "modernists," this is our greatest living poet. He speaks for himself here. I reproduce his letters as well as it can be done in print. They are sprawled on large sheets and most have a large modernist sketch of his head printed in red or blue. His language is his own, not mine. The letters are dated XII, which means the year twelve of Mussolini's reign, or 1934 of Christ's. Take your choice. The reference is to my EPIC campaign. The letters are published here with his consent. At the time the consent was given Pound was confined to a government institution in Washington, D.C., for having broadcast in Italy against the United States during the War.

The "End Poverty in California" movement was to put the unemployed at work to produce for their own use.

Gesellites are the followers of an economic theorist named Gesell.

EZRA POUND

Rapallo
December 12, 1934

Merry Xmas.

Dear Upton S/

John Bankhead is not / god damn it / an author but a SENATOR, about 150 years ahead of that corpse or body, and living in the contemporary world.

The capitalist press has evidently relegated the Congressional record to the status of a secret document, and even you don't KNOW god damn it, that a Stamp Scrip bill was introduced last FEB. (1933). //

If you want to be governor god / damn / it the circulation of my published (and as yet squashed and unprintable) work on economics wd/help you GET IN.

E P

(that's half of yr/ damn EP IC) if you are playin' cross word puzzles.

Your campaign manager better get over a few thousand copies of my ABC/ or have a California edtn//

Your project is ahead of Mark Hanna/ but why shut out ALL the advance guard ?

Mussolini has got a mind a damn sight more open than yours AS EXPRESSED IN YR/ program appears to be.

Of course living in America and getting only doctored news you can't be expected to know that.

I am talking about ECONOMICS / not about the ballot system.

If you try to choke off economic thought, you are no better than any other suppressive system. Can't tie the human mind onto 1880 . Any more than you can insist on mechanical invention stopping with the sewing machine.

If money is certificate of work done / taxes are NOT necessary. The state can pay those certificates direct, without funning round and asking the citizens to return them to the source of issue. Taxes are just one more god damn wheeze to employ a bureaucracy. Habit, me boy; rabbit habit, grabbit and all the ole kyrilie. .

Any state worth a fahrt cd/ pay dividends instead of collecting taxes// then there won't be any needy / and no sons of bitches holding a spinich inquisition as to whether Jim, Jo an Mary had been good noncopulating; presbyterian church goers and VOTED the party ticket in order to qualify for the dole.

HELL in an age of plenty/ WHY dole??

Sure I'll boom you for governor, if you will show some signs of being alive from the neck up.

Yrz

E.P.

Apparently the news of my political defeat had not yet reached Mussolini's realm.

EZRA POUND

Rapallo, Genova, Italy
December 19, 1934

Upton Sinclair, esq.
Station A
Pasadena, California

NUTS/ Upton "How you got licked". You got
licked by being too g:d pig headed to recognize
what has been *thought* during the past 20 years
by HHHHH with clearer heads than your own.

Mop up yr/ tears and start READING modern
economics/ Gesell and Douglas. If ever a man with
enough intelligence to be held responsible for his
acts deserved to be beaten at the polls you are that
man. Even Florida inviting Hollywood, shows
dawn of econ/ sense in black pewky swamps.

Yrs/

E.P.

Buck up and do BETTER

Pound's reference is to my I, Candidate for Governor: And How I Got Licked, *1935.*

EZRA POUND

Rapallo
January 30, 1935

Dear Upton

Thanks for *How you got Licked.*

I wd/ have done anything in my power to get

372

you IN. BUT you are a god damn fool. You got a mind like an old family photograph album.

Any idea you get, stays. You are just as set and incapable of thinking as that tripple shit Villard (who is possibly dishonest).

You are not a monomaniac; but a polymaniac/ with a number of "fixations".

As bad as Perkins or some of those god damn fools in Washington.

Xrtst don't you ever LEARN anything?

All this stuff in yr/ book. OF COURSE, who the hell didn't expect the other side to bribe etc/ IS that news ?

Had you got in, you might have done more harm than good/ heaven knows.

At any rate I hear a MODERN paper is starting in California, admittedly one of the rottenest states in the union. God hellup the nation if you didn't find ANYone in Washington who knew enough to contradict you. That is the GLOOMIEST phase of yr/ book.

All that damn blather about Frank bein' such a sweet suggary man/ what the fkn hell does it matter his being "kindly"/ if he don't know a bung from a barrel, and if he is hypnotized by international banks ? or what the HELL. ??

It is dastardly evasion for F.D.R. NOT to look at MONEY. Gesell floored Marx with one sentence: "Marx found nothing to criticize in money."

Go down and talk to Doc. Fack in San Antonio, Texas, 309 Madison St. and talk to Col/ Mack or some Social Creditor. I hear Steff has at last de-

cided to play in. Hell, thass a ten years delay. However, the Muss. once asked HIM (Steff) hadn't he
LEARNED anything.

R/S/V/P givin me the date yr/ sutures SET/
and the hour in which you finally decided that you
knew EVERY god damn thing there wuz and iz to
be known .

Work is NOT a commodity. You can't eat it.

Young Hen. Morgenthau is reported to have a
brain about the size of a pea. Perkins is a plain
godfahrted fool. About fit to run a district proba-
tion officers job. Mebbe/ but nothing bigger.

Farley/ waaal, even here one knows enough
about Jim/

Have a little fergit/ Forget Upton Sinclair the
Big big noise, and think a little about economics.
Were you more anxious to BE governor, or to govern
and reform California, and bring in a better economic system?

I'm a-askin'

You might still be some use if you got more interested in some Big Man in yourself

E. P.

EZRA POUND

You, Shaw and Wells—3 conceited and braying
asses. who cannot conceive *anything* has been
thought since you were adolescent.

374

what would YOU think of any other man who had been thru what you have been thru in the past 2 years and learned NOTHING.

Ezra Pound

You are too g. d. LAZY to read Douglas & Gesell and too puny to admit the existence of ideas you haven't elaborated in yr own kitchen.

Put yr ego out to grass for a week.

This and the following message were written on postcards.

EZRA POUND

Even as politics. You old O W L . And a man who is man enough to get converted to sane idea instead of trying to hold onto a lot of junk *Because* he has *had* it a long *time*. Such a man has better chance with the only people worth calling friends. You and Townsend ought to forget the earth was flat.

Socialism = Control of Production = 3 inspectors to every workman. To diminish unemployment. Nertz

Yrs

Ez Pound

See Body and git wise   4 July [1936]

EZRA POUND

310 San Gregorio, Venezia
Sept. 26 1936

Dear Upton:

The picture you will present to posterity if they investigate is that of a man who HAD a few ideas in 1890 and absolutely refused to LEARN, or to inspect the facts assembled by my generation. In other words, a damn ass.

You know as little of econ. as the most reactionary republicans. I certainly shall not spend any money on your damn books. Your intellectual cowardice or sloth is such that you DARE not answer my volitionist questions. I shouldn't mind giving you serious criticism IF you were man enough to want it. You now are in class with Masters and Frost, loafers, hiders. Which is a damn pity, as you have been some good at alternating intervals

Ez Pound

If a privvy secretary stops this, I shall learn it.

THOMAS MANN [1875-1955]

z.Z. Arosa
February 2, 1937

Honored Mr. Upton Sinclair:

I thank you heartily for your friendly lines, which I have received here in the Hochgebirge, while your new work [probably *Co-op*, 1936], cordially inscribed to me, awaits me in Zurich. I am extremely pleased by the prospect of making acquaintance with it.

I am especially bound to you for your signing that Appeal. I have immediately passed it on. You have therewith done everything in this matter which anyone could have expected.

With most cordial greetings
Your greatly obliged

THOMAS MANN

This letter from the great German novelist was written in German; I have forgotten what the "appeal" (Aufruf) was. It may have something to do with his desire to bring his family to this country. Later, in Pasadena, he told me that he was having trouble in getting his citizenship papers. I learned by chance that my secretary's brother was employed in the Los Angeles office of the government, and a telephone call brought the magical result in a day or two.

THOMAS MANN

Princeton, N. J.
October 8, 1938

Dear and honored Mr. Upton Sinclair:

Somewhat delayed I learn of your sixtieth birthday and would beg you still today to receive my hearty wishes for good fortune. You may with pride look back upon a powerful lifework, which is deeply impressed in the consciousness of your nation and which surely yet will be increased by many beautiful and significant contributions.

May I permit myself to send you as a gift for your festival day my latest major work, *Joseph in Egypt*. The book has found not a few friends in America, and so I dare to hope that it may entertain you also in occasional idle hours.

Often my wife and I think back upon the happy afternoon and evening we spent with you in Pasadena. May such a meeting here or there right soon be repeated.

With many hearty greetings also to Mrs. Sinclair from us both

Your obliged

THOMAS MANN

This letter was written in German.

THOMAS MANN

Pacific Palisades, California
January 7th, 1942

Dear Mr. Upton Sinclair:

I want to thank you very much for the copy of your strong and truthful new novel which you sent me with your kind inscription [*Dragon's Teeth*]. It is painful reading-matter, especially for a German, but the pain is turned into pleasure by the art of the presentation,—a pleasure, of course, constantly mingled with rage and shame. Whoever knows Nazi-Germany will admit that not a word in your book is exaggerated. While I read it, my principal feeling was one of satisfaction that all this has been written down and preserved for the future.

Naturally, one is inclined to ask whether those to come will believe all these unbelievable things which even our contemporaries never quite could or wanted to believe. Those to come, however, will have less interest in not believing it than our contemporaries, and therefor I count on them.

With sincere congratulations and the expression of my respect as a colleague, I am

Sincerely yours,

THOMAS MANN

Dragon's Teeth, the third of the Lanny Budd novels, received the Pulitzer Prize for 1942.

THOMAS MANN

Pacific Palisades, California
January 18, 1943

Dear Mr. Sinclair:

I was pleased and honored to receive a copy of your latest book, and I did not want to thank you for it before I had read it.

Again I am deeply impressed, as I was after reading the preceding book. The historical portrait is even more comprehensive and colorful than the last time.

Some day the whole cycle will certainly be recognized as the best founded and best informed description of the political life of our epoch.

Please accept my thanks and my congratulations.

Sincerely yours,

THOMAS MANN

The book was Wide Is the Gate, *1943, the fourth Lanny Budd novel.*

THOMAS MANN

Pacific Palisades, California
April 19, 1944

Dear Mr. Upton Sinclair:

Permit me to thank you very sincerely for your article "A Free State". I can imagine that your highly constructive suggestions had a sensational effect at the time of their publication in the widely circulated magazine of the *New York Times,* and rightfully so, as this is undoubtedly one of the best-intentioned and most thoughtful articles that have been written about a future Europe. It was not quite clear to me whether this industrial region has to be understood as an economic one only, or whether it is meant as a political structure. The name "Free State", or Freistaat, would indicate the latter. But beyond this, I ask myself how the American business world which indubitably will have its say in the peace treaty, will react to your suggestion. I have often in these circles met with a

380

distinct and worried antipathy to everything that looks like Pan-Europe or the United States of Europe. The utterance of a fashionable republican lady is still in my ear: If we could use a united Europe, we might just as well have kept Hitler.

With repeated thanks for your kindness and with best wishes for your well-being and your work, I remain,

Very sincerely yours,

Thomas Mann

"A Free State" was my proposal that territories retaken from Hitler should be made an independent state under international guarantee.

THOMAS MANN

Pacific Palisades, California
May 30, 1944

Dear Mr. Upton Sinclair:

It was extremely kind of you to send me the latest fruit of your admirable artistic industry. I read your exciting book in a very short time, and want to express to you my sincere congratulations on the successful completion of this part of your masterful work, which is such a brilliant critique of our time.

With best regards
very sincerely yours,

Thomas Mann

The book was Presidential Agent, *1944, the fifth* Lanny Budd *novel.*

381

THOMAS MANN

Pacific Palisades, California
July 14, 1944

Dear Mr. Sinclair:

I was greatly moved and pleased to learn of the interest your dear wife is taking in my last "Joseph" book. That you wouldn't, at least at present, find the time to read it, was absolutely clear to me from the beginning. I know only too well how it is when one is occupied with one's own, complicated work, and should read other people's books which they have sent. But one day, I think, when you are freer, you will—encouraged by the experience of your wife—be open to the serious jests of my book.

Please accept my best thanks and again my kindest wishes for the progress of your new work.

Very sincerely yours,

THOMAS MANN

THOMAS MANN

Pacific Palisades, California
September 5, 1944

Dear Mr. Upton Sinclair:

It was charming of you to send me the letter from Klaus and your reply. My wife and I were

382

greatly pleased with both of them, and you were quite right to feel that any word from a son so far away is important and interesting to his parents.

With great satisfaction I learned of the progress that *Dragon Harvest* has been making in the meantime. *Joseph the Provider* will not remain on the best-seller list for long, as the reviews in many cases were quite lukewarm and discouraging for the public, describing the book as a terrible mental effort to the reader and as a literary monster overloaded with exacting wisdom. In my opinion, it is an absolutely popular and humorous work—just ask your wife.

With kindest wishes and regards
Very sincerely yours,

THOMAS MANN

Dragon Harvest is volume VII of the Lanny Budd series.

KLAUS MANN [1906-1949]

Beverly Hills
July 14th, 1948

Dear Upton Sinclair,

It was very kind of you to write me the way you did. I am ashamed of my weakness, disgusted with the indiscretion of a "free" but irresponsible press which cruelly publicizes one's most intimate, most painful failures . . . Your good, encouraging words help me in regaining my equilibrium and self-confidence. THANKS.

I am leaving for San Francisco where I expect to stay for some time with one of my brothers. May I drop you a line upon my return to this part of California? I should like to see you again.

Yours,

KLAUS M.

Mann's son is referring to his attempted suicide; a second attempt, alas, succeeded.

VAN WYCK BROOKS [1886-   ]

New York
September 14, 1921

Dear Upton Sinclair,

I have just written for the *Freeman* an article on your last three novels which I am sending you today. I had to say that I didn't like the books and that I didn't believe in them from any point of view. But at least I gave my reasons. I can't at present see those of the opposite side.

If you think it worth while to reply to this article, of course we shall welcome your answer. I know quite well that I haven't got to the bottom of the

384

subject. If you can take me a step deeper down I shall be very grateful to you.

Sincerely yours,

VAN WYCK BROOKS

American critic, Brooks wrote America's Coming of Age, The Ordeal of Mark Twain, The Flowering of New England, *and many other books. Thirty-two years passed between this letter and the next one. I don't know whether it was he or I who changed in the interim.*

VAN WYCK BROOKS

Bridgewater, Connecticut
May 17th, 1953

Dear Upton Sinclair,

I can scarcely believe that five weeks have gone by since you wrote me that extraordinarily interesting letter. But I have had good reasons for not writing. In the first place, I read over at once *The Return of Lanny Budd* [1953] and found that I couldn't put it down. It really won me completely, so I knew that my account of you was all wrong *somehow*, but just how I couldn't at the moment begin to think. I have a single-track mind and it happens to be absorbed in another book that I expect to finish in June, and without getting my wires crossed I have not been able to think out the rightness and the wrongness of my treatment of you. But I have to revise *The Confident Years* this summer for a Japanese translation and for a new edition here in 1954. So I shall have to think this all out soon. Meanwhile you have been in my mind all the time, and I have reread *American Outpost* and at least one of your other books, taking notes about them as I read. I have also talked a lot about you with Lewis Mumford, my very close friend who greatly admires you. (We also have another great friend in common, S. K. Ratcliffe, who often writes to me about you.) If I tried to re-think now what I have written about your work, so long as my mind is full of other matters, I should begin to talk nonsense. All I can say now is that I shall rewrite what I have written and that the result will be quite different.

Now you say that you agree with what I say of other writers, and may I say that what I wrote about you was the only part that left me with a very uncomfortable feeling. You would not gather that I regard you as a great human being, for I do, and, as it happens, I have a deep feeling of friendship with you because of your "basic attitudes", as you describe them. And all the more at present because the literary tide has turned so completely away from all that we have in common.

I see now that what I say about your work must make this very clear, and that I have got hold of you by the wrong handle because I judge you in the usual scale of novelists. When you say that institutions are "higher products of evolution than individuals," the natural answer would have to be: "But novels are about individuals," and when you

386

say in *American Outpost:* "I was impatient of every form of human vanity and stupidity" the natural answer again would be, "Yes, but the business of the novelist is not to be impatient with them but to be *interested* in them." And I think that's right and that great things result from this function of fiction, which you don't achieve at all, *even while* I perceive that if I can't "put down" your Lanny Budd there must be some great virtue in it that is not in the usual fiction.

That's what I've got to think out, and I'll do the best I can with it. You use fiction for ulterior purposes and that is the cause of the great quarrel between you and the critics. But since you do it with immense effect there is obviously something to be said, and some big thing, that these critics have not seen. You are obviously something on a large scale that literature has to include, though you don't fit into any of the usual categories. Would the word Publicist (with marked variations) be right? But I'd better not try now to go in for definitions. I only do want to say again that I'm glad you are alive and that in a time of great talents with small hearts it makes me very happy to think of your big one. I am sure that everything you write does a world of good, for you are a true friend of humankind.

It was kind of you to send me *The Return.* I am sending you one of my earlier histories and my last *Writer in America,* hoping you may find this interesting in parts.

Sincerely yours,

VAN WYCK BROOKS

I did.

VAN WYCK BROOKS

> Huntington Hartford Foundation
> Pacific Palisades, California
> February 1st, 1955

Dear Upton Sinclair:

How good to have a line from you!

Ever since I came here three weeks ago I have been wondering if I could reach and see you. I am only two or three hours away, and I wonder if you would have time to see us if my wife and I drove over some afternoon. We are working here but are free almost any afternoon after an early lunch. Will you send me a line?

Is it true, as Einstein seems to say, that, in the image of Didymus, you have given up hope for improvement in the human fate? That is something I would like to discuss with you.

> Always yours sincerely,
>
> VAN WYCK BROOKS

P.S. I would like to bring you—if it arrives in time—a new revised edition of my book, *The Confident Years*. I added two more pages about you, so at least it is better—but not right yet.

You are a very difficult person to be right about.

They came; and my wife has told about the visit in the last pages of her Southern Belle.

388

VAN WYCK BROOKS

November 1, 1957

Dear Mrs. Sinclair:

A copy of *Southern Belle* came two days ago and I have read it in one gulp. What a history of our time it is, and how well you have done it! No one else could have made such a bridge from the world of your origin to the world of your grown-up years; and how it testifies to your sympathy and imagination that one runs into the other without a break. Then it's all so delightfully lively and vivid in style. It's so full of the people I have known . . . Thank you so much for writing this good book!

VAN WYCK BROOKS

During the year in which my wife wrote Southern Belle, *she was a heart patient, bed-ridden most of the time. Many times every day, and more in the night, I told her that it was a lovely story, and that it would live far into the future. This letter, coming ten days before publication, was like a trumpet call out of the sky. All fears were forgotten.*

CORNELIUS VANDERBILT, JR.
[1898-   ]

Sunday, April 15, 1945
Enroute to San Francisco Conference

Dear Upton,

I want you of all people to have my last three Conferences with Franklin D. Roosevelt while I still remember them. The first of these took place at the White House in Washington on I think January 22. I was then still on crutches after my bad accident in Chicago, December 24th, 1944. The President was in his study. He looked VERY TIRED, THIN and WAN. His hands trembled terribly. His eyes were sunken deep but he was very jolly and gay. He kidded me about 'my old ticker' and my crutches. He said something like this, "Look here boy, I bet I 'go west' long before you do." I asked him *what* he'd bet; and he said "one of those funny little shiney pencils you like so much to carry." I bet him a red nickle I'd go first! He told me at that time that he was leaving "in a day or two" for another "pow-wow with my pals." He said he'd get a rest coming and going. He said "if you weren't on those damned crutches which you acquired from falling out of your upper, I'd ask you to come along."

The next time I saw him was rather dramatically. I was staying with my friend Col. Frank Clarke at the Seaway Apartments in Miami Beach, Florida, recuperating from my accident. The exact date I can't recall, but it was exactly 7 days before the White House announced his return to Washington from Yalta. The body of General Watson had been flown ashore at Miami that morning, and several persons such as Fred Vinson, Jimmy Byrnes, also Admiral Halsey, General Mark Clark, General Kruger and General EISENHOWER were loaded into a plane at the Army Air Base 36 St, Miami, almost in the Everglades and taken out to an aircraft carrier that afternoon. Ed Stettinius arrived a bit later on another plane. I had Iced Tea with Franklin D. Roosevelt in his cabin in the after part of the ship with many distinguished big shots. He looked ever so much better; but was much more serious than he had been before. He said among other things that Stalin wanted to help us in the Pacific as soon as "we declared the war over in Europe, and engaged in mopping up guerrila operations." He said MacArthur didn't want Soviet help, Nimitz did. He said the Hearst papers were going to plug for MacArthur's viewpoint; and he wanted all the Press representation he could get at the Conference he expected to call in San Francisco to STOP HEARST. He said San Francisco would be chosen because "it is the best exponent we have in America today of what the Soviet is trying to do with labor." He said the marvellous Bay Cities, the Peninsular, and the area as far north as Petaluma were more "in fitting with the world labor movement than any other part of America." He pointed out especially how black, yellow and white men *and WOMEN* work hand in hand without trouble doing a supreme war job.

He said if Stalin would give us not only Air

Bases, but also ports at which to land our supplies and from which to start the invasion of the Japanese homeland, we could end the war "years sooner" than in any other fashion.—He said he thought the British could take care of the Indies with SOME HELP from us; and that all the United Nations would have to free China.—He said Stalin had promised to permit us to TRUCK material through Russia to China.

We steamed down the coast of Florida and Stettinius left about 4 hours later by plane for the Conference in Mexico City. I was taken back to Miami that eve in another plane; and Franklin D. Roosevelt left for the North.

The last time I saw him was at the White House about 2 weeks ago—I think it was Tuesday before Good Friday. We had a sort of late supper up in the Lincoln Study. He looked pretty good to me but he seemed to be having trouble with his plates when he spoke. (Some people have suggested he had CANCER of the throat). He talked almost entirely on the need of STOPPING WAR FOREVER. He said he had appointed to the United States Delegation to San Francisco the men he thought Congress would most listen to. He said "the international bankers must not only have their wings shorn, but must have nothing left to fly with save the stump." He said if we didn't prohibit war, outlaw it forever, that all we were doing now would be simply wasted effort. He said he had written to my publisher asking that I be assigned to the Conference and he hoped I'd go, no matter how badly

I felt. He said he needed me there to observe, listen, watch and that few people would think a polite gossip columnist had sense enough to do anything like this. He said we had to make San Francisco work regardless. He said he was going down to Warm Springs for three weeks, then by train through the Southwest to San Francisco. He said he expected to live on a battleship in the Bay there and would address the meeting twice, and attend two banquets. I again advised him as I had often in the past to visit war factories in an OPEN CAR. He said he planned to do this in Dallas, Houston, San Diego, Long Beach and the Los Angeles area too.

Just before this time I had a wire from the *New York Post* telling me they had assigned me to the Conference, but that I HAD to be checked at Walter Reed first. I was in Washington for that checkup when I saw him. After the checkup the Hospital said that because of the condition of my heart I had to FOREGO the Conference if I went on a crowded train with a gang of people unless I could take a male nurse along. They agreed to compromise if I could go by car with my own chauffeur-valet, who has been with me all winter.

The White House made arrangements with the OPA about the car; since it carries Nevada plates there is nothing to worry about anyway, as I have a right to "go home."—I am now on a slow Baltimore and Ohio train enroute to Gary, Indiana, where I shall pick up the car.

When the shocking news of the President's death

393

came in the other evening I wanted to duck the trip to San Francisco and get back to Washington as soon as possible to learn who was the gang about Truman; but as I had a letter in my pocket from Grace Tully which read in part: "We are all so delighted to know you are coming along so well and feeling quite yourself again. The President has sent a little note to Dorothy Backer telling her that he 'thinks it would be a fine thing if you could cover the San Francisco Conference for the Post.' Do take care of yourself and we look forward to seeing you, if not before, at least in San Francisco. The President asks me to send you his very best wishes to which I add mine." I felt I just had to go.

I shall pick up mail at the Riverside Hotel in Reno the end of this week; and at the Palace in San Francisco during the Conference. I'll try to get down to Los Angeles soon; as I want so much to see you.

Yours as always,

NEIL

Cornelius Vanderbilt, Jr., is the prototype of "presidential agent" Lanny Budd, the hero of the eleven Lanny Budd novels; this letter was written three days after President Roosevelt's death.

Index

400

404

409

About UPTON SINCLAIR

Upton Beall Sinclair was born in Baltimore, Maryland, in 1878, of a distinguished but improverished Southern family. After the collapse of his alcoholic father, the family moved to New York where, while still little more than a boy, he began his prolific and controversial literary career. By the age of eighteen, he was publishing more than a million words of "half-dime" novels every year, while working his way through C.C.N.Y. and Columbia. In 1906, his exposé of the Chicago stockyards, *The Jungle*, catapulted him into almost-instant fame; the novel, which was responsible for legislation culminating in the Pure Food and Drug Act, became a best-seller in seventeen languages and virtually made Sinclair's name a household term.

Since that time, Upton Sinclair has been an indefatigable novelist, dramatist, essayist, journalist, pamphleteer, and citizen-of-the-world. He is the

411

author of some eighty full-length books which, in addition to their notoriety among English-speaking peoples, have been translated into approximately sixty languages and published in more than a thousand separate editions in some fifty-five countries. During the Twenties he ran for the U. S. Congress, the U. S. Senate, and the Governorship of California as a Socialist. Since 1915, with frequent interruptions for European travel, he lived in California where in 1934 he was Democratic candidate for Governor.

Still hearty and active at the age of eighty-one, Mr. Sinclair and his wife, Mary Craig Sinclair, now live in the desert town of Buckeye, Arizona.

Among Upton Sinclair's best-known works are *King Coal* (1917), a fictionalized account of a strike in the coal mines of Colorado; *The Brass Check* (1919), a study of American journalism; *Oil!* (1927), a controversial exposé of the California oil monopolies; *Boston* (1928), a fictionalized account of the notorious Sacco-Vanzetti case; and the eleven Lanny Budd novels of high adventure, pressure politics, and international diplomacy, one of which, *Dragon's Teeth,* won the Pulitzer Prize for 1943.